D0915925

INFORMATION ASYMMETRY:
A UNIFYING CONCEPT FOR FINANCIAL AND MANAGERIAL ACCOUNTING THEORIES
(INCLUDING ILLUSTRATIVE CASE STUDIES)

STUDIES IN MANAGERIAL AND FINANCIAL ACCOUNTING

Series Editor: Marc J. Epstein

STUDIES IN MANAGERIAL FINANCIAL ACCOUNTING
VOLUME 13

INFORMATION ASYMMETRY: A UNIFYING CONCEPT FOR FINANCIAL AND MANAGERIAL ACCOUNTING THEORIES
(INCLUDING ILLUSTRATIVE CASE STUDIES)

BY

ANTHONY J. CATALDO II

*Department of Accounting and Finance, Oakland University,
Michigan, USA*

2003

ELSEVIER
JAI

Amsterdam – Boston – Heidelberg – London – New York – Oxford – Paris
San Diego – San Francisco – Singapore – Sydney – Tokyo

ELSEVIER B.V.
Sara Burgerhartstraat 25
P.O. Box 211, 1000 AE
Amsterdam, The Netherlands

ELSEVIER Inc.
525 B Street, Suite 1900
San Diego, CA 92101-4495
USA

ELSEVIER Ltd
The Boulevard, Langford Lane
Kidlington, Oxford OX5 1GB
UK

ELSEVIER Ltd
84 Theobalds Road
London WC1X 8RR
UK

© 2003 Elsevier Ltd. All rights reserved.

This work is protected under copyright by Elsevier Ltd, and the following terms and conditions apply to its use:

Photocopying
Single photocopies of single chapters may be made for personal use as allowed by national copyright laws. Permission of the Publisher and payment of a fee is required for all other photocopying, including multiple or systematic copying, copying for advertising or promotional purposes, resale, and all forms of document delivery. Special rates are available for educational institutions that wish to make photocopies for non-profit educational classroom use.

Permissions may be sought directly from Elsevier's Rights Department in Oxford, UK: phone (+44) 1865 843830, fax (+44) 1865 853333, e-mail: permissions@elsevier.com. Requests may also be completed on-line via the Elsevier homepage (http://www.elsevier.com/locate/permissions).

In the USA, users may clear permissions and make payments through the Copyright Clearance Center, Inc., 222 Rosewood Drive, Danvers, MA 01923, USA; phone: (+1) (978) 7508400, fax: (+1) (978) 7504744, and in the UK through the Copyright Licensing Agency Rapid Clearance Service (CLARCS), 90 Tottenham Court Road, London W1P 0LP, UK; phone: (+44) 20 7631 5555; fax: (+44) 20 7631 5500. Other countries may have a local reprographic rights agency for payments.

Derivative Works
Tables of contents may be reproduced for internal circulation, but permission of the Publisher is required for external resale or distribution of such material. Permission of the Publisher is required for all other derivative works, including compilations and translations.

Electronic Storage or Usage
Permission of the Publisher is required to store or use electronically any material contained in this work, including any chapter or part of a chapter.

Except as outlined above, no part of this work may be reproduced, stored in a retrieval system or transmitted in any form or by any means, electronic, mechanical, photocopying, recording or otherwise, without prior written permission of the Publisher.
Address permissions requests to: Elsevier's Rights Department, at the fax and e-mail addresses noted above.

Notice
No responsibility is assumed by the Publisher for any injury and/or damage to persons or property as a matter of products liability, negligence or otherwise, or from any use or operation of any methods, products, instructions or ideas contained in the material herein. Because of rapid advances in the medical sciences, in particular, independent verification of diagnoses and drug dosages should be made.

First edition 2003

Library of Congress Cataloging in Publication Data
A catalog record is available from the Library of Congress.

British Library Cataloguing in Publication Data
A catalogue record is available from the British Library.

ISBN: 0-7623-0874-5
ISSN: 1479-3512 (Series)

♾ The paper used in this publication meets the requirements of ANSI/NISO Z39.48-1992 (Permanence of Paper).
Printed in The Netherlands.

CONTENTS

SECTION III. THEORY INTEGRATION: INFORMATION ASYMMETRY

APPENDIX CHAPTERS

LIST OF FIGURES, TABLES AND EXHIBITS

PREFACE

The process of *tooling up* for this monograph began and was motivated by conversations with a management accountant. At a local chapter meeting of the Institute of Management Accountants (IMA), discussions relating to misinformation and/or intentional deceit, taking the form of the generation of conditions of *information asymmetry*, arose following a presentation at a regularly scheduled monthly meeting, which immediately followed the April 2000 *crash* of the NASDAQ.

The assistant treasurer and secretary of a publicly traded retailer with a market capitalization of approximately $30 million spent up to 90 minutes, each day, *monitoring* the stock-chat message boards for evidence of unauthorized releases of *insider information* and/or the generation of *mis-information* by disgruntled employees or ex-employees. In fact, based on his personal experience, this monitoring had resulted in the identification of six different persons. However, his firm found it necessary to threaten legal action in only one case. In this single case, the threat was enough, and no legal action was formally taken against the individual.

Additional conversations extended over several months. His assurance that other management accountants spent varying amounts of time *monitoring* the Internet's stock-chat message boards for similar reasons, along with my own unscientific survey, limited to a show of hands at a subsequent monthly IMA meeting, supported his hypothesis. A significant (and, potentially, increasing) percentage of management and management accountants are *monitoring* the Internet and stock-chat message boards for their publicly traded firm. Others are employing outside companies, specializing in providing these *monitoring* services, to do this on their firm's behalf.

These conversations took place as the Nobel Prize in economics, announced on October 10, 2001, highlighted the importance of the role played by *uncertainty* and *information*. George A. Akerlof (University of California at Berkeley), A. Michael Spence (Stanford University), and Joseph E. Stiglitz (Columbia University) received the award for their work on *markets with asymmetric information*. At the foundation of these works, relating to unequal access to information or *information asymmetry*, was the proposition that government intervention or regulation may contribute to market efficiency, which represents a condition desirable for economic growth.

Markets are most efficient when reliable, *public* information is available to assist investors in directing economic resources to their *highest and best use*. Alternatively, markets are less efficient when misinformation, *private* or *hidden* information contributes to the misdirection of these economic resources into less profitable or even unprofitable endeavors.

As the contract for this monograph was being issued, the public was becoming increasingly aware of an audit failure. At issue, in what has been characterized as the "Enron debacle," was the extent and nature of *asymmetric information*. Was the management of Enron aware of alleged financial statement errors and irregularities, and did these same (and other) executives engage in non-GAAP (generally accepted accounting principles) related party transactions and insider sales of Enron stock and stock options, while advising their employees and investors to buy?

The auditors were implicated in the Enron matter. Arthur Andersen was alleged to have shredded many source documents *after* Securities and Exchange Commission (SEC) notification of an impending investigation, complete with specific instructions to retain all documentation. Again, at issue was the extent and nature of *asymmetric information*. Did Andersen possess *private* information that they failed to disclose or was this simply a significant audit failure? Did future auditing/consulting opportunities and conflicts of interest between the relative importance of accounting, auditing and consulting fees contribute to their decision to shred documents and/or to delay timely, *public* information disclosures?

Also related to the Enron/Andersen matter, was the discharge of at least one financial analyst prior to the mass media's coverage of Enron's problems. He alleged that his discharge followed his failure to upgrade/modify his *sell* recommendation for Enron's stock as a preferable investment vehicle. Again, at issue was the extent and nature of *asymmetric information*. To what extent did this brokerage firm's failure to support the analyst's recommendation, in the form of a *public* information disclosure, support and extend an artificially inflated price per share (PPS) for Enron stock? Did the lack of separation or conflict of interest, represented by the underwriter and analyst fees and functions, contribute to delays in the conversion of what represented *private* information to *public* information?

As these events were being publicized, several Enron executives were taking advantage of their Constitutional Fifth Amendment rights, when asked to testify at Congressional hearings. Did these (or other) top executives possess *asymmetric information* that they failed to disclose or act upon?

Among the complaints leveled against Enron was a 401K fund "freeze," via the change in employee deferred compensation fund administrators. Allegedly, selected members of Enron's top management/insiders were suggesting that the PPS of Enron's stock would increase, while they filed Form 144s with the SEC to sell significant portions of their personal holdings. Increasingly, the integrity of the accounting/auditing/consulting profession, the financial analyst/underwriter institutions and profession, and managements of publicly traded companies was being questioned.

Today, Enron represents a contemporary example of the damage that *asymmetric information* can cause to a capitalistic economy. The failure to disclose this information, at inception, may represent the causal factor in what many business newscasters referred to as "Enronitis."

The highly publicized Enron/Andersen case was followed by a barrage of scandalous news releases and allegations, including some cases of completely unsupported rumors, all relating to or involving *information asymmetry*. These matters were reported in the popular and business press. They suggested growing concerns that releases of the *public* information, produced by accounting and financial professionals, as well as the *private* information, possessed and acted upon by insiders and the management of large, publicly traded firms, were dissimilar or *asymmetric*:

- *May 20, 2002*: Computer Associates International, Incorporated (NYSE: CA).
- *May 28, 2002*: Dynegy, Incorporated (NYSE: DYN).
- *May 28, 2002*: Haliburton Company (NYSE: HAL).[i]
- *May 30, 2002*: Microsoft Corporation (NASDAQ NM: MSFT); from 1999.
- *June 1, 2002*: Calpine Corporation (NYSE: CPN).
- *June 1, 2002*: PG&E Corporation (NYSE:P PCG).
- *June 1, 2002*: Reliant Resources, Incorporated (NYSE: RRI).
- *June 5, 2002*: Ex-CEO, ImClone Systems, Incorporated (NASDAQ NM: IMCL).
- *June 6, 2002*: Head of Martha Stewart Living Omnimed (NYSE: MSO).
- *June 7, 2002*: Cendant Corporation (NYSE: CD); from 1998.
- *June 12, 2002*: Omnicom Group, Incorporated (NYSE: OMC).
- *June 13, 2002*: Tyco International, Limited (NYSE: TYC); from 1999.
- *June 21, 2002*: Merck & Company, Incorporated (NYSE: MRK).
- *June 21, 2002*: Rite Aid Corporation (NYSE: RAD); from pre-2000.
- *June 24, 2002*: J. P. Morgan Chase & Company (NYSE: JPM).
- *June 25, 2002*: WorldCom Group (NASDAQ NM: WCOM).

- *June 25, 2002*: Supervalu, Incorporated (NYSE: SVU).
- *June 26, 2002*: Qwest Communication International, Incorporated (NYSE: Q).
- *June 27, 2002*: General Motors Corporation (NYSE: GM).
- *June 28, 2002*: Xerox Corporation (NYSE: XRX).

The above represent only a small sample of news releases, and are only for a five week period. Furthermore, these were not thinly traded or neglected penny stocks. Generally, these firms are (or were) large, well-known, and respected by the investment community and individual investors. However, many of these firms have been involved, directly or indirectly, in behaviors that might be thought to be more characteristic of firms trading in the Over-the-Counter Bulletin Board (OTC BB) or even the PinkSheets or YellowSheets.

To the extent practicable, this monograph contains contemporary references and examples, which will facilitate efforts of researchers to extend investigations of the respective cases and topics introduced.

After providing for the theoretical foundation for information asymmetry in the first three sections of this monograph, emphasis shifts to case studies. Though some overlap or transition is provided for in Sections two and three, section four is almost entirely devoted to case studies and, thus, mostly focused on issues relating to the transmission of information on the Internet. In addition, this section contains examples for discussion in the context of the frameworks and models developed in the earlier sections, devoted to information asymmetry, corporate governance, agency theory and related topics.

ACKNOWLEDGMENTS

This research was partially supported by a 2002 Oakland University School of Business Administration spring/summer research grant. I am grateful for this support.

I am also indebted to those providing reviews of chapters or sections of an earlier draft: Pat Forrest (Western Michigan University) and Petros Panayioto, Jim O'Donnell, and Arline Savage (Oakland University). I am especially indebted to Katja Morgia (Oakland University), for providing an excellent, detailed editorial review of the final draft.

Finally, I am particularly grateful to Marc Epstein for his belief in this project and his continued support through several delays. As always, his editorial comments and insights provided me with the guidance necessary to add value to the final product.

All errors remain my responsibility.

. . . potential investors do not know, and cannot easily verify, the quality of information that a company provides. The Internet cannot do much to reduce information asymmetry costs . . .. On the contrary, the Internet could increase information asymmetry costs by undercutting the effectiveness of the institutions that today provide investors with partial assurance of the quality of the information provided by issuers.

Bernard S. Black

CHAPTER 1. INTRODUCTION

Marketing relationships between buyers and sellers often are characterized by information asymmetry, in the sense that the supplier possesses more information about the object of an exchange (e.g. product or service) than the buyer (Mishra et al., 1998, p. 277).

INTRODUCTION

This monograph, intended to serve multiple purposes, examines *information asymmetry*.

First, it is intended to bridge the gap between financial and managerial accounting. These (presumably) separable sub-disciplines of accountancy often employ different terms, but examine comparable relations between principals and agents. The distinctions between *financial* accounting and *managerial* accounting education have become blurred or less easily defined, as post-Enron (managerial accounting) and post-Andersen (financial accounting) and related issues of corporate governance, agency theory and information asymmetry have experienced widespread popular press coverage. Similarly, the Internet has blurred distinctions between *financial* accounting and *managerial* accounting practice, as the managerial accountant must now be concerned with the broad dissemination of misinformation and, therefore, information asymmetries originating from the stock-chat message boards, their impact on investor sentiment and, ultimately, the firm's stock price and, therefore, their ability to recapitalize for expansion or other purposes.

Financial and managerial accounting research integration may be desirable, but is often difficult, as theoretical component relations may not follow a linear path. This monograph will provide numerous separable and integrated examples in the early chapters, but it can be simply stated, at this stage and in this introductory chapter, that the use of the term *hidden information*, in *managerial*

Studies in Managerial and Financial Accounting, Volume 13, pages 1–300.
Copyright © 2003 by Elsevier Ltd.
All rights of reproduction in any form reserved.
ISBN: 0-7623-0874-5

accounting contexts, is comparable to the term *private information* in *financial* accounting contexts. Therefore, technological improvements in the decomposition of hidden information (managerial accounting) will provide insights into private information (financial accounting) and visa versa.

A preliminary examination of the professional examination requirements of the Certified Management Accountant (CMA) and the Certified Public Accountant (CPA) examinations provide insights into this linkage. These examination requirements, focusing primarily on the CMA, are provided in Fig. 1.1.

This linkage is both theoretical and practical. Many of the complexities surrounding problems requiring solutions to the inefficiencies created by asymmetric information are due to the non-linear relations between financial and managerial accounting theory and practice. In terms used by the information systems analyst, a flat file approach is not suitable; a multi-dimensional

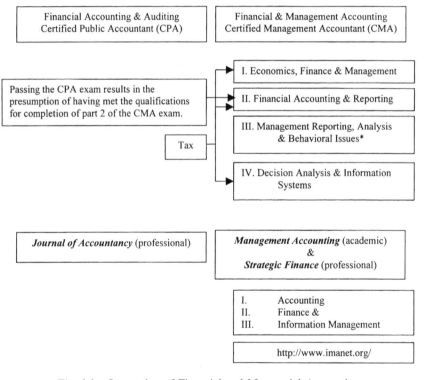

Fig. 1.1. Integration of Financial and Managerial Accounting.

* Traditional component examined by researchers or management accounting topics.

relational data base approach is required. It is, therefore, difficult (if not impossible) to visualize or hypothesize comprehensive models in a two-dimensional figure or exhibit.

Second, given recent contemporary trends and events in U.S. financial markets, it is likely that increasing resources will become available for the study of a wide variety of complex principal-agent problems. At the foundation of these issues will be the elimination or reduction of information asymmetry. Alternatively, the popular press term, "visibility," is used.

Third, two chapters are devoted entirely to case studies (Chapters 7 and 8) for relatively exhaustive practical study and theory application. Managers and managerial accountants and financial professionals associated with both "big cap" (large) and "small cap" (SC; small) public and publicly traded firms will find that these case studies and related appendix chapters provide insights into the potential problems likely to be faced by firms experiencing difficult operating conditions, as well as the decline in investor sentiment that is likely to follow. These cases may provide insights into the strategies necessary to combat mis-information and conditions of information asymmetry (and efforts, by external parties, to manipulate the firm's stock price) likely to originate from Internet-based sources.

In addition, a data base of 126 additional mini-cases are summarized (in tabular form), briefly, in Chapter 9 for hypothesis development and testing. These cases also provide practical insights into the various types (and forms) of information asymmetry. The managerial accountant may find this and the related appendix chapter useful, as the variety of fact patterns presented by these case summaries may mirror those likely to be experienced by their firm. Therefore, review of these case summaries by the managerial accounting professional will enhance his/her ability to anticipate and react to external efforts to influence investor (and creditor) sentiment, stock price manipulation efforts, misinformation, and, therefore, the generation of information asymmetries.

Throughout this monograph, web-based sources of information/data for both researcher and practitioner use and analysis will be provided. In fact, much of the information and many of the sources cited can be easily accessed on the Internet. To the extent practicable, only those sites likely to remain viable for the long-term have been selected.

THE ORGANIZATION OF THIS MONOGRAPH

Section I provides a primer on agency theory and principal-agent problems and solutions. Simply stated, the principal and agent have different incentives. The solution is to establish a structure that minimizes these differences or establish

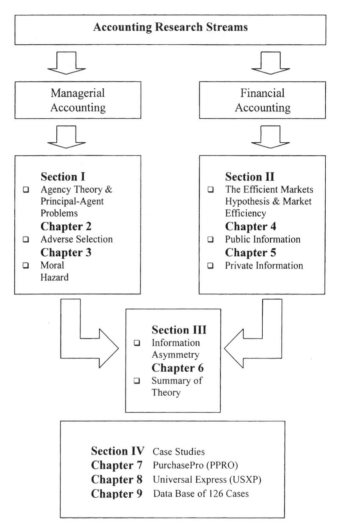

Fig. 1.2. Linking Managerial and Financial Accounting Research Streams.

an over-riding desire for goal congruence. Chapters 2 and 3 introduce and examine information asymmetry and the risks associated with *adverse selection* and *moral hazard*, respectively. Chapter 2 begins with a relatively traditional foundation – the examination of insurance and debt or capital structure applications. Chapter 3 concludes this first section, but proceeds by placing greater emphasis on the risks associated with *moral hazard*. Contemporary issues are more fully introduced in this chapter, which relates asymmetric information to auditor, financial analyst and, therefore, contemporary market and institutional failures.

Section II provides a primer on the efficient markets hypothesis and market efficiency. To the extent practicable, greater levels of market efficiency are presumed to be desirable. In an efficient market, economic resources will be deployed to their highest and best use. Chapters 4 and 5 focus on and examine the constraints applicable for the semi-strong level of market efficiency and the relation of all three levels of market efficiency to *public information* and *private information*, respectively.

Section III narrows the theoretical focus to that of *information asymmetry*. Chapter 6 elaborates on the linkage between *hidden* information (the term more frequently associated with *managerial* accounting research and literature streams) and *private* information (the term more frequently associated with *financial* accounting research and literature streams) (see Fig. 1.2). The presence of asymmetric information is the foundation for later chapters and the case studies that are summarized and examined throughout the remainder of this monograph.

THE CASES

This monograph contains a rich summary of cases, in the form of litigation, filed (primarily) by corporations against those engaged in the distribution of information and misinformation. These cases evolved from Internet stock-chat message board posts.

These cases are likely to be of greatest interest to researchers and graduate students interested in pursuing research into matters not entirely dissimilar from those being addressed in the contemporary press and relating to Enron, Andersen and Merrill. They are, in effect, the small cap (SC) version of what the popular press came to refer to as "Enronitis." The difference, of course, is that investor-speculators in SC stock tend to anticipate higher levels of risk.

Perhaps the clearest cases applicable to agency theory are those involving disgruntled employees (agents). These matters are particularly important to the management and shareholders of the subject firms, management accountants and investor relations (IR) departments, faced with a responsibility and a duty to protect the interests of shareholders (principals) and multiple stakeholder groups.

However, just as the polluter (agent) damages society (principal) in economics-based applications of agency theory, these cases represent those situations where the basher or hyper (agent) damages society (principal) via the distribution of misinformation, by generating additional "noise" in what is an otherwise more efficient information-based market. Therefore, to the extent that Internet stock-chat message board posts take the form of misinformation, they contribute to a less efficient market.

Similarly, the author (agent) and reader (principal) relationship provides for the application of agency theory. In many cases, the author is distributing misinformation in an attempt to deceive the reader. The vehicle or medium, of course, is not that of a book or an article, but is represented by a message posted on the Internet.

Frequently, these cases involve disgruntled employees posting insider information. These matters are not only important to the firm's management and stakeholders, but may warrant regulatory intervention (e.g. the SEC). Some of these cases involved ex-employees working for competing firms and a few even involve ex-employees, disgruntled employees, disgruntled colleagues, some of whom (simultaneously) engaged in short-selling while bashing the firm.

Those who refused employment with subject firms have also taken their frustrations to the public forum of the stock-chat message boards. In these cases, agency theory appears, on the surface, to be inapplicable. Disgruntled creditors, debtors, customers, ex-shareholders and others with business dealings with these firms have also engaged in efforts to seek revenge on the stock-chat message boards.

SUMMARY

The first two sections of this monograph will provide a theoretical foundation for information asymmetry and the integration of financial and managerial accounting education and research. The third section will provide the opportunity to reflect on the contemporary or post-April 2000 NASDAQ "crash" conditions and solutions within this theoretical framework. The fourth and last section of this monograph will be devoted to case studies and exploratory methodologies likely to provide researchers with a foundation for Internet-based research endeavors into topics directly and indirectly related to information asymmetry. Throughout this monograph, the intent is to provide the researcher with a foundation of information necessary to "tool up" for research projects involving the development and analysis of data bases relevant to their discipline-specific applications of Internet-based sources of information.

For the Managerial Accountant or Financial Professional

Chapter 9 summarizes the results of hypotheses and is developed from the data base of 126 mini-cases contained in Appendix Chapter 9.1. The managerial accountant or financial professional will find a review of these cases of interest, to the extent they apply (or may come to apply) to their firm. Generally, the findings from Chapter 9 suggest that regulatory agencies rarely intervene to protect smaller publicly traded firms from cybersmear or the deceitful generation of conditions of information asymmetry. Therefore, the professional may find it useful to scan Chapter 9, and the mini-cases summarized in Appendix Chapter 9.1, before reading this monograph. They will find all of Section IV and related Appendix chapters useful, as they "tool up" to identify stock price reactions to stock-chat message board posts, legitimate news releases, market maker manipulation, and so on. The first three sections will serve to acquaint the professional with applicable theory, terminology, and will, therefore, provide a framework for the organization of thoughts and strategies to protect shareholders and other stakeholders from cybersmear and other forms of information asymmetry.

For the Academic, Researcher or Regulator

The academic, researcher or policy-maker will also find Section IV of interest, but is more likely to find the data base of interest for expansion or academic research, even taking the form of data base extensions. The findings contained in Chapter 9 are supported by theory and are intuitively appealing. Those approaching this topic from a theoretical perspective will find the first three sections useful to "tool up," and as a quick reference for related studies and theory, as they proceed to develop their own research questions and design their own research projects.

SECTION I. AGENCY THEORY AND PRINCIPAL-AGENT PROBLEMS

An agency relationship is present whenever one party (the principal) depends on another party (the agent) to undertake some action on the principal's behalf (Bergen et al., 1992, p. 1).

A theory developed in the 1970s, (*agency theory*) refers to the variety of ways in which *agents*, linked by contractual arrangements with a firm, influence its behavior.

These may include organizational and capital structure, remuneration policies, accounting techniques and attitudes toward risk-taking. *Agency costs* are deemed the total cost of administering and enforcing these arrangements (Bothamley, 1993, p. 15).[2]

INTRODUCTION

Principal-agent relationships exist between stakeholders and management, between layers of management, and between management and employees. All parties are presumed to act in their own best interests. Conflicts arise between these groups in cases where self-interest presides over teamwork and goal congruence.

Management pays wages that (at least partly) depend on employee performance. Management must also establish an internal control structure, which represents monitoring and with the objective of providing assurances and minimizing costs associated with employee performance. The costs minimized by this type of monitoring are referred to as "internal agency costs" and are most frequently associated with *managerial* accounting education and research.

To the extent that investors are able to price-protect themselves, owner-managers are provided with incentives to enter into monitoring arrangements to assure investors that contractual conditions continue to be honored and that management's consumption of perquisites are restricted or minimized (Watts & Zimmerman, 1986, p. 184). The costs that are minimized when the owner-manager agrees to increased monitoring are referred to as "external agency

9

costs." External agency costs are most often associated with *financial* accounting education and research.

Generally, agency costs are a function of conflicts that may arise among employees, managers, creditors, and shareholders of firms. As the potential for these conflicts and, therefore, agency costs, increase, the demand for monitoring increases. Because shareholders and creditors do not have direct access to the firm's accounting or internal controls systems, demand for monitoring includes credible disclosures regarding the firm and the performance of its management. Monitoring consists of operations where the principal observes, measures, and attempts to control the behaviors of agents. In the context of publicly traded firms, both independent auditors and financial analysts represent monitor groups and agency costs are incurred to influence investor (e.g. shareholders and creditors) behavior.

THE PRINCIPAL-AGENT PROBLEM

The principal-agent problem evolves from a lack of goal congruence. First, the principal and agent have different incentives. Second, agents may possess hidden information. Third, agents are (in fact or presumed to be) risk-averse. Finally, it is difficult or costly for the principal to monitor the agent. Figure I.1 summarizes these principal-agent problems.

THE PRINCIPAL-AGENT SOLUTION

The principal-agent solution is to establish a structure for principal-agent goal congruence. Fig. I.1 summarizes these principal-agent solutions.

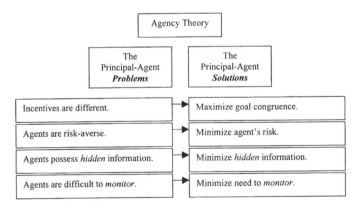

Fig. I.1.   Agency Theory and Principal-Agent Problems and Solutions.

First and foremost, it is important to reduce or eliminate differing principal-agent incentives. Second, as introduced in both Chapters 2 and 3, the exposure of risk to both *adverse selection* and *moral hazard*, respectively, and anticipated by the agent, must be minimized or eliminated. Third, as introduced in Chapter 3, the hidden or private information or these conditions of information asymmetry,[3] possessed by agents, must be rendered impotent, non-beneficial or unprofitable. Finally, if all three of these objectives are achieved, the need for costly monitoring is reduced or eliminated (Chapter 3).

CHAPTER 2. ADVERSE SELECTION

Much of the agency literature refers to precontractual issues as problems of "adverse selection" and to postcontractual issues as problems of "moral hazard" (Bergen et al., 1992, p. 3).

INTRODUCTION

This chapter will introduce theory, models and applications relating to *adverse selection*. Adverse selection problems, as addressed in the corporate governance and agency literature, tend to focus on *pre-contractual* conditions (Bergen et al., 1992, p. 3). The most common applications include insurance and credit markets (Bothamley, 1993, pp. 12–13):

American economist George Arthur Akerlof (1940–) first noted (*adverse selection*, sometimes referred to as the lemon problem), which arises from the inability of traders/buyers to differentiate between the quality of certain products.

The most cited example is the second-hand car industry, in which a trader dealing in, for example, Minis possesses product information that the other buyers/sellers in that market lack. He thus operates at a *comparative advantage* (emphasis added) as the other people in the market cannot tell if he is selling a 'lemon' (poor-quality car). Consequently, there is risk involved in purchasing the good and while the lower price buyers are willing to take this risk, traders selling quality cars are not willing to sell at such a low price. There are three components to this theory: (1) there is a random variation in product quality in the market; (2) an asymmetry of information exists about the product quality; (3) there is a greater willingness for poor-quality car sellers to trade at low prices than high-quality owners. Insurance and credit markets are areas in which adverse selection is important.

Adverse selection and moral hazard are, often, most efficiently addressed in combination. Therefore, while this chapter is primarily focused on the *pre-contractual risk* of *adverse selection*, some discussion of moral hazard is also sometimes necessary. Moral hazard is the primary focus of Chapter 3.

Operational definitions of risk may vary,[4] whether the products are automobiles (Akerlof, 1970), insurance or debt. The first section of this chapter will address insurance applications, including unemployment insurance and employer representatives and/or consultants. A brief, transitional section addresses combined insurance and credit/debt or capital structure, in the form of bank regulatory applications. Finally, a section will follow on debt/equity or capital structure applications. This last section provides to most apparent linkage between risk, information asymmetry, and financial and managerial accounting education and research.

INSURANCE APPLICATIONS

Health, life, auto, home and disability insurance do not represent a comprehensive list, but these categories of insurance may immediately come to mind when a person thinks of "insurance." Both individuals and firms are consumers of insurance. From the firm's perspective, the selection and contracting for insurance represents a *managerial* function, and is more closely associated with *managerial* accounting.

Generally, in the case of an insurance applicant (agent), adverse selection is a process by which the applicant may be uninsurable, or at greater than average risk, but attempts to purchase a policy from an insurance company (principal) at the standard premium rate. Persons who have the greatest probability of obtaining benefits may seek to obtain insurance and conceal information (e.g. information asymmetry) about adverse conditions or additional risks that might result in above standard rate premium adjustments (Hyman, 1999, p. 316). Insurance companies carefully screen applicants for this reason, since their premiums are based on an ideal or average insurance applicant or policyholder (agent).

Figure 2.1 provides a basic model of the agency relationship and classifications of asymmetric information-related outcomes (e.g. adverse selection and moral hazard) applicable to insurance. Adverse selection represents the risk that the insurer will grant a policy at the standard premium rate to an applicant with an above-average risk profile.

Moral hazard, a topic that will be more fully developed in Chapter 3, represents the risk that the insurer, having granted a policy at the standard premium rate to an applicant with an above-average risk profile, will be contractually obligated to pay a claim relating to this higher risk profile. It is the risk of providing insurance at a premium which was inadequate, given the insurance applicant's successful maintenance of a condition of information asymmetry. Therefore, the applicant or insured or claimant may be said to have successfully concealed their true risk profile (e.g. hidden or private information).

The costs associated with adverse selection may be mitigated with premium adjustments, designed to accurately reflect risk. However, if the insurer cannot or does not charge higher premiums that reflect the applicant's higher risk profile, adverse selection may cause high-risk participants to stay with a

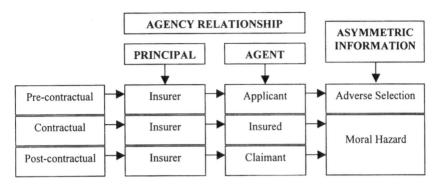

Fig. 2.1. Asymmetric Information, Adverse Selection and Moral Hazard: An Insurance Application.

particular insurance plan. Low-risk participants will, as insurance company experience-related premiums rise, cancel their policies and select another insurance plan with lower premiums, more appropriate for their risk profile.

Life/Health Insurance and Medical Checkup Applications[5]

For those researchers interested in reviewing some of the academic literature on health, medical and life insurance applications of adverse selection, a few studies are summarized below. The section that follows this one focuses on unemployment insurance applications.

Cardon and Hendel (2001) used the National Medical Expenditure Survey (NMES) Health Insurance Plan Survey (HIPS) collected by the Agency of Health Care Policy Research (AHCPR) in 1987 to examine the widely held perception that adverse selection represents the major source of market failure in insurance markets. Their hypothesis was that individuals with higher risk profiles purchase more insurance coverage and, on average, consume more health care. Their examination failed to reveal any evidence of information asymmetry.

Yet, the findings by Cardon and Hendel were consistent with the earlier findings of Phelps (1976), the foundational work upon which their extension was based. Phelps found no systematic relation between predicted illness in individuals and individual choices made for the consumption of insurance. But Marquis and Phelps (1987), in a later extension, found evidence of adverse selection from survey/questionnaire results, dealing with hypothetical supplemental insurance purchases.

Wolfe and Goddeeris (1991) found economically insignificant, but statistically significant, evidence of adverse selection in the Medigap market. Their examination dealt with the purchase of Medicare supplements by individuals more than 65 years of age.

In their game theory-based examination of conflicts between the public health benefits and uninsurability risks, associated with the early detection of illness, Doherty and Posey (1998) formally addressed adverse selection, moral hazard, information symmetry (the benchmark) and asymmetry (where risk profiles were revealed only to the consumer). They found that market mechanisms provided optimal incentives for the acquisition of hidden or private information in those cases where a treatment option is present.

An Unemployment Insurance (UI) Application

Unemployment insurance (UI) is designed to protect individuals against a variety of perils. It partially replaces income for workers experiencing involuntary unemployment, providing for income smoothing through periods of temporary wage interruption. This may provide for the extension of job searches, resulting in re-employment job match optimization.

A private market for unemployment insurance would lack full information and experience risks and the consequence of adverse selection. High-risk individuals would have an incentive to conceal or maintain hidden or private information (e.g. information asymmetry) with respect to the risks of unemployment.

Furthermore, private information might inhibit or thwart the private provision of unemployment insurance. A worker's employment habits and preferences tend to vary over their life-cycle. A review of a worker's employment history, the diversification of his/her assets or skills, or his/her demographic characteristics may not provide for an efficient measure of (future or projected) unemployment risk.

Unemployment presents unique problems with respect to moral hazard. Some will resist unemployment for reasons of reputation, career progress, aversion to idleness, and so on. Alternatively, some would prefer UI, increasingly, as the UI amounts provided approach the equivalent of employment income. Finally, for those indifferent between employment wages and UI benefits, work efforts may decline or, if unemployed, search efforts may only take the form of minimal compliance to retain benefits.

The difficulty associated with the measurement of the risk of unemployment may also contribute to the absence of a private market for UI. These risks, relating to varying demands for differing industries and sectors of the domestic economy, as well as the effects of international agreements or events, include those of economic recession and extend through the potential for insolvency of these private insurance funds. These market risks or imperfections are overcome through the establishment and maintenance of public UI. The mandatory nature of participation is intended to, but does not fully, overcome the problem of adverse selection.

The public UI system does not solve the problem of moral hazard. There is nothing to prevent Government or publicly funded UI from operating in a constant state of subsidy. However, partial indemnification and monitoring may mitigate or reduce public UI systems from loss. For example, workers with below standard workforce participation may be excluded from coverage or benefits, and public UI may provide for the scrutiny of the conditions, leading to separation and the monitoring of job search efforts. Furthermore, the public UI system may provide vehicles to discourage private employers from labor force reductions in the first place.

Employer Representatives and UI Consultants

In the U.S., UI is paid by the employer. Generally, the cost or experience rating, applied to the employer, is based on the frequency and magnitude of claims from ex-employees. Because of this, firms, operating nationwide, provide assistance to employers for the appeal of unemployment insurance claims and the reduction of overall employer UI costs. These firms seek to mitigate the UI costs of adverse selection (in the employment process) and moral hazard (in the separation process).

The rate of UI tax varies by state, as does the taxable wage base or ceiling to which unemployment taxes apply (e.g. $7,000 for Arizona and $15,000 for Connecticut for 2002). Unemployment insurance weekly benefit amounts (WBAs) also vary by state (e.g. $190 for Alabama and $390 for Colorado for 2002), some of which may provide additional UI benefits in the form of a dependent allowance (DA) and based on the number of qualifying dependents (e.g. $6 each for up to 5 dependents for Michigan and up to 56 and two-thirds percent of the average weekly wage (AWW) for New Jersey for 2002).

Generally, each employer has an account and an experience rating (e.g. minimum of 0% to a maximum of 9.75% for Wisconsin for 2001) for unemployment insurance. Once the employer's account balance reaches a predetermined funding level, the firm's experience rating, and the unemployment insurance percentage paid for *all* employees, declines. Alternatively, if a severed employee claims unemployment benefits, these claims are drawn against the (previously fully funded) employer account. As employer UI account balances decline, from the payment of UI benefits to a severed ex-employee, the firm's experience rating, and the unemployment insurance percentage paid for all employees, rises.

Firms providing UI consulting services perform tasks including the following:

- Review of employer accounts for the prior three years for simple errors;
- Identify weaknesses in the firm's hiring practices (adverse selection);
- Train personnel employees to avoid UI claims (adverse selection/moral hazard);
- Identify weaknesses in the firm's separation practices (moral hazard);
- Appeal or protest unfavorable rulings made in claimants favor (moral hazard);
- Coach employer witnesses and/or attend UI hearings (moral hazard); and
- Advise on mergers, acquisitions, voluntary contributions options, and so on.

These consulting firms (agents) advertise their assistance to the firm (principal) in their hiring process, to reduce UI-specific risks associated with hiring applicants (agents), known as adverse selection. These services may include the discovery of employment applicant-related hidden information, reducing the pre-contractual risk preceding the applicant's employment with the firm.

Consulting firms (agents) also provide post-contractual services to the firm (principal), by providing advisory services regarding appropriate separation practices through the UI protest or appeal process. In this case, the ex-employer (principal) and ex-employee (agent) have conflicting positions with respect to the granting of UI benefits. This (and other) effort(s) directed toward UI cost minimization is most closely associated with the *managerial* process; however, to the extent that public accounting firms have developed business in this area

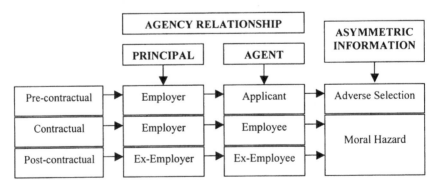

Fig. 2.2.   Asymmetric Information, Adverse Selection and Moral Hazard: An Employment Application.

of consulting, a relationship also exists for public accountants or *financial accounting*.[6]

Figure 2.2 represents a modification of Fig. 2.1, summarizing the relations between the employee/employer and ex-employee/ex-employer in the context of the above discussion. These relations, and agency theory- and asymmetric information-related UI applications, represents a rich area for academic research.

COMBINING INSURANCE AND CREDIT OR CAPITAL STRUCTURE APPLICATIONS

Academic research has combined insurance and credit or capital structure investigations through examinations of regulatory deposit insurance schemes. Consider the case of the regulator, with less information than the management of the bank or financial institution about the inherent risk of the bank's portfolio of assets (adverse selection), and a condition where bank resources are, increasingly, directed toward assets of lower quality (moral hazard).

Much of the academic research in this area employs analytical or experimental designs. For example, Giammarino et al. (1993) examined and developed an optimal design of a risk-adjusted deposit insurance scheme, as described above, where the regulator is unable to monitor the bank. This was an extension of the work of Chan et al. (1992), incorporating the regulator's concern for social welfare into their analytical model. Unlike Campbell et al. (1990), they included bank profits and the explicit costs of bank regulation in their examination, while also presuming conditions of information asymmetry. Bank managers possess and maintain private or hidden information from monitoring loan customers (adverse selection) (Bessler & Nohel, 2000) and may even engage in or be aware of hidden actions to divert economic resources from the bank in order to increase the personal well-being of bank managers and employees (moral hazard).

In a later work, Gorton and Rosen (1995) propose, test and show, analytically, that the bank failures of the 1980s were not a function of fixed rate deposit insurance (moral hazard), but more likely occurred due to management entrenchment.

CAPITAL STRUCTURE AND FINANCIAL/OPERATING LEVERAGE APPLICATIONS

Assets are financed with debt or equity. The greater the level of debt or financial leverage in a firm's capital structure, the greater the (presumed) level of risk.

Financial leverage is a topic introduced in introductory level *financial* accounting and corporate or managerial finance courses. Therefore, this topic is introduced in a fashion comparable to that found in these introductory courses.

Because all assets are presumed to be financed, they are financed with debt or equity, as follows:

$$Assets = Liabilities + Owners'\ Equity \tag{1a}$$

or

$$A = L + OE \tag{1b}$$

and

$$Debits = Credits \tag{2a}$$

or

$$DR = CR \tag{2b}$$

Though increased financial leverage may provide higher returns for equity owners during periods of growth or expansion, higher (lower) debt levels are commonly associated with higher (lower) risk. For example, a lender/creditor may be willing to provide funds, at a lower (higher) rate of interest, to a firm with a lower (higher) debt to equity ratio. For firms with higher levels of debt financing in their capital structure, the increased nominal interest rate charged by the lender/creditor might be referred to as a risk premium.

In the context of corporate governance, agency theory, (pre-contractual) adverse selection and information asymmetry, the supplier, lender, financial institution or bond holder represents the principal, while the firm (both employees and management), loan applicant or corporate bond issuer represents the agent (for debt or L in Eq. (1b), above). The shareholders of preferred or common stock, warrants, or other equity securities are the principal(s) and the firm (again, both employees and management) represent the agent(s). Figure 2.3 summarizes these relations.

Similarly, in the context of introductory level *managerial* accounting and corporate or managerial finance courses, operating leverage is introduced, as follows:

$$Total\ costs = Fixed\ costs + Variable\ costs \tag{3a}$$

or

$$TC = FC + VC \tag{3b}$$

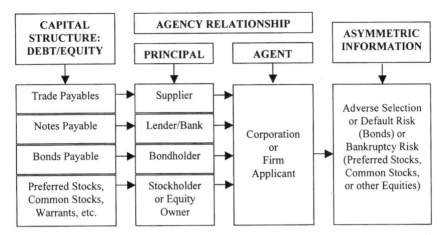

Fig. 2.3. Asymmetric Information, Adverse Selection and Capital Structure: Debt and Equity Components of the Balance Sheet.

Though increased operating leverage may provide higher returns during periods of growth or expansion, higher (lower) fixed costs levels (as a percentage of and relative to total costs) are commonly associated with higher (lower) risk. For example, rent, a fixed cost or expense, continues to require a cash outlay regardless of the firm's level of operating activity. Though it may be possible to eliminate many fixed costs in the long-run, in the short-term, many represent unavoidable or sunk costs.

Figure 2.4 provides a framework for the examination of Eqs (1b) and (3b). Considerable research has been conducted on corporate governance, agency theory, adverse selection and asymmetric information as it relates to the degree of financial leverage in a firm's externally reported capital structure. This, from publicly available information in the form of financial statements and supplemental information, is required and filed with the SEC and required by GAAP, as well as by the Internal Revenue Service (IRS). Public or externally reported financial information for manufacturing firms uses absorption costing, also known as full costing.

Much less research has been conducted on operating leverage because this behavioral information is not publicly available. Cost behavioral information, used for internal decision-making purposes, represents a class of non-public, private or even hidden information, and includes variable or direct costing data, which, if made publicly available, could prove to be strategically useful to competitors. That is to say, requirements for the public release of this

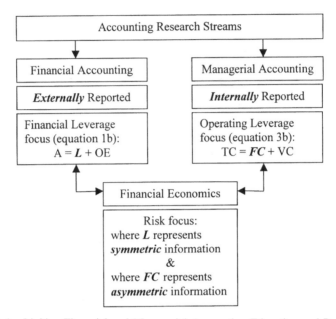

Fig. 2.4. Linking Financial and Managerial Accounting Education and Research: Capital Structure, Financial and Operating Leverage & Symmetric and Asymmetric Information.

information for firm A might prove competitively useful to firm B (e.g. knowledge of a competitor's break even point or contribution margin per unit sold).

As Fig. 2.4 suggests, financial economics (e.g. in the form of an introductory corporate or managerial finance course) bridges the gap between introductory financial and managerial accounting coursework. Similarly, it provides for linkage between financial and managerial accounting research streams.

SOME ACADEMIC RESEARCH ON DEBT AND EQUITY IN THE FIRM'S CAPITAL STRUCTURE

Debt has a low level of sensitivity to private information; equity has a high level of sensitivity to private information (Fulgheire & Lukin, 2001). According to DeMeza and Webb (1987), increased asymmetric information about expected returns will lead investors to increasingly prefer debt to equity. However, as Hellman and Stiglitz (2000, p. 282) emphasize, DeMeza and Webb did not develop their findings under conditions that allowed for both expected returns and risk.

Firms with more growth options or information asymmetries in their investment opportunity sets issue more short-term debt (Barclay & Smith, 1995a). Older firms, with established reputations, are frequently characterized as having lower levels of asymmetric information. Goswami et al. (1995) found that firms financed with short-term debt, where the asymmetry of information was uniformly distributed across dates, used coupon-bearing long-term debt, unrestrictive (restrictive) of dividend payments, in cases where information asymmetry was concentrated around near-term (long-term) cash flows.

Short-term debt financing may be used as a vehicle to mitigate adverse selection (Goswami, 2000), but Scherr and Hulburt (2001) found little evidence that the level of asymmetric information affected debt maturity choices for small firms. Smaller firms with less favorable economies of scale, with respect to the production and distribution of information (about the firm), have higher levels of asymmetry (Pettit & Singer, 1985).

Incentive-signaling theory provides a vehicle to bridge the gap between those who believe that capital structure and debt and equity financing choices have no affect on the value of the firm and those who believe that it does, limiting the actions of managers (Ross, 1977). It suggests that management signals the value of the firm and that these signals affect management compensation.[7] Generally, it is presumed that the moral hazard of false signaling is avoided, as detection would result in penalties that would be imposed on management.

Shareholders find it costly (or impossible) to determine whether or not management is acting in their best interests. High dividend pay outs provide signals and generate certainty with respect to the firm's free cash flow, while providing shareholders with some assurance that management is acting in their best interests (Jensen, 1986).

The information hypothesis, as it relates to dividend announcements and pay outs, has been widely recognized (and even accepted) since the mid-1950s (Lintner, 1956). Watts (1973) examined this hypothesis and found the information content of dividends to be present, but "trivial." A contemporary study of the United Kingdom (Lonie et al., 1996) generated findings, consistent with those of De Angelo et al. (1992), supporting current earnings as the dominant signal, with dividend announcements providing for only a partial and/or inferior substitute signaling mechanism; yet this latter finding was not consistent with contemporary U.S.-based results (Kane et al., 1984; Easton, 1991).

Goetzmann and Jorion (1993) failed to develop strong statistical evidence that dividends were a useful tool in forecasting stock returns. However, Christie and Nanda (1994), examining the effects of the undistributed profits tax of 1936 and 1937, found that the unexpected imposition of a Federal tax on undistributed corporate profits produced a positive revaluation of corporate equity, particularly among lower dividend pay out firms. And Bajaj and Vijh (1995) found that dividend announcements resulted in unconditional positive excess returns, first documented by Kalay and Loewenstein (1985), and that these returns were higher for small-firm and low-priced stocks.

Michaely et al. (1995) found that, consistent with the findings of prior research, reactions were greater for dividend omissions, when compared to dividend initiations. Post-announcement drift from these dividend announcements was more pronounced than those from earnings surprises, and a trading rule using this information generated positive returns for 22 out of 25 years (1964 through 1988).

Alangar et al. (1999), using the proportion of the firm's stock held by institutions as a proxy for pre-announcement levels of information asymmetry, were able to document significant positive relations between the degree of information asymmetry in the stock and the absolute values of announcement-period excess returns. They examined dividend change announcements involving initiations, large increases and decreases, and omissions. Their findings held for all dividend change announcements except for omissions.

Signaling mechanisms for for-profit firms include EPS, cash flow per share and dividends. However, these signals are not available for non-profit organizations. For example, the Board of Trustees (outsiders) for a non-profit hospital may have a risk preference for less risky capital structure. Administrators (insiders), representing all internal claimants on residual cash flows, may want high debt to signal success to outsiders.

Wedig et al. (1996) examined the issuance of tax-exempt debt and capital structures of nonprofit hospitals:

> . . . the issuance of tax-exempt debt is . . . likely to be associated with agency costs of various types. Cash made available (preserved) via the issuance of tax-exempt debt may be invested in risky projects (the asset substitution effect) or consumed by management and employees outright. Actions such as these may increase the risk of bankruptcy, but are undertaken because their cost is borne, in part, by bondholders.

Debt or financial leverage (long-term debt as a percentage of total assets) is a variable relating to external agency costs. Watts and Zimmerman (1986) and Chow (1982) suggest that agency costs increase with financial leverage.

Debt provides managers/shareholders with incentives to adopt investment policies leading to debt reduction and increases in the value of the firm's stock, a potential conflict of interest resulting in the demand for credible financial reporting to debt holders. Debt, therefore, may reduce agency conflicts and increase firm value (Harris & Raviv, 1991b).

In their examination of bank loan agreements, Best and Zhang (1993) found that banks may rely on screening devices other than financial analysts' forecasts and forecast revisions. Additional information is most often developed when initial indicators, representing information available to all, are noisy or unreliable. These findings were inconsistent with those of Boyd and Prescott (1986), but consistent with those by Berlin and Loeys (1988) and supported the position held by Lummer and McConnell (1989) – that is, banks may enter into loan agreements without informational advantages. These findings were inconsistent with financial intermediation theory and the (presumed) alleviation of information asymmetry, based on the production of additional, useful information by banks.

SUMMARY

This chapter focused on the introduction of information asymmetry, as it relates to both *adverse selection* (*pre-contractual*) and *moral hazard* (*post-contractual*). The former was covered in this chapter, while the latter will be more fully developed in Chapter 3.

Information asymmetry was introduced, and a preliminary discussion commenced within the theoretical framework of agency theory and corporate governance. In this chapter, these relations were discussed in the traditional contexts of insurance (see Figs 2.1 and 2.2), including unemployment insurance.

With respect to the study of the firm's capital structure (see Fig. 2.3), discussion began within the traditional contexts most frequently examined by academics. Linkage was provided between a common topical area introduced in *financial* accounting coursework and research (i.e. *financial* leverage) and *managerial* accounting coursework and research (i.e. *operating* leverage). Financial economics provides the linkage between these areas (see Fig. 2.4).

Dividends represent an information signaling or transmission mechanism, where theory implies that the signaling benefits are greater for firms with greater information asymmetry (Alangar et al., 1999). Lower levels of information asymmetry have been associated with higher levels of institutional ownership (Aggarwal & Rao, 1990).

Chapter 3 proceeds to introduce and extend the coverage of information asymmetry, with a primary focus on moral hazard. Contemporary auditor- and financial analyst-related issues will provide the vehicle through which this post-contractual focus will be developed. Limited, applications-based coverage will be provided for tax compliance issues and literature streams, as well.

CHAPTER 3. MORAL HAZARD

Rational ignorance is the lack of information about public issues that results because the marginal cost of obtaining the information exceeds the apparent marginal benefit of doing so (Hyman, 1999, p. 167).[8]

If the opportunity cost of obtaining information about small capitalization stocks were included in the purchase price of the stock, the abnormal return would probably disappear (Lustig & Leinbach, 1983).

INTRODUCTION

In many cases, the market may represent an efficient and effective monitoring mechanism. For example, when in a strange city, you may select a dining establishment based on the number of cars in the parking lot. A full parking lot may suggest high demand for their product, a meal. This may further suggest that the price of this meal is reasonable, given its quality. Alternatively, a national restaurant chain, with a favorable reputation and a standardized product with established quality might prove acceptable (Pratt & Zeckhauser, 1985). In both of these cases, the cost of information asymmetry – those costs associated with the failure to discover hidden or private information - is relatively low (e.g. a poor meal).

The decision-making process is less clear when selecting financial products or investment vehicles. This is particularly true in the case of micro-, small-, or mid-cap stocks that are not followed or regularly investigated and reported on by financial analysts. In these cases, the risks associated with information asymmetry may be quite high – 100% of the amount invested for long positions and unlimited losses for short positions.

The positive branch of agency theory inquiry has been concerned with the design and control mechanisms appropriate for corporate governance. From the intra-organizational perspectives, agency theory represents a *managerial* accounting issue. However, to the extent that internal corporate governance or structural concerns extend to the board of directors (BOD) and audit committees, consultants, underwriters, and public reports of auditors and financial analysts, these issues may be more closely linked to *financial* accounting.

The first section of this chapter will introduce and examine applications of the separable hidden information and hidden action model components of moral hazard. Next, monitoring will be introduced. The sections that follow will provide discussion and representative summaries of the results of the academic literature on auditors, financial analysts, and tax preparation professionals. Auditors (directly, and to a greater degree) and financial analysts (indirectly, and to a lesser degree) have made themselves available to the public, as objective monitors or providers of insurance/assurance services, to mitigate the costs associated with hidden actions or (post-contractual) moral hazard problems. Generally, accounting academics have conducted research to investigate the value that financial accounting and external auditors provide to investors, while finance academics have conducted research to investigate the value that financial analysts provide to investors. Finally, a discussion of the area of tax compliance will be provided, and the chapter will be summarized.

MORAL HAZARD

Moral hazard is a problem most commonly examined as a *post-contractual* issue (Bergen et al., 1992, p. 3). Moral hazard, applied in the theoretical context of adverse selection, consists of separable hidden *action* and hidden *information* components (Arrow, 1985). First, recall the following assumptions:

- Both principal and agent are motivated by self-interest;[9]
- Principals operate under conditions of imperfect or incomplete information; and
- Realized outcomes are determined, in part, by uncertain or unpredictable externalities (e.g. economic and environmental factors).

Hidden *information* relates to the observation (or knowledge) of something, by the agent, not observed (or known) by the principal and is sustained when incentives between principals and agents are incompatible. One example, useful in game theory applications, is the case of an auction where varying conditions of information asymmetry exist. Another is the pre-contractual case of adverse selection, where insurance is provided to heterogeneous applicants, resulting in claims from higher risk applicants (discussed in Chapter 2).

Hidden *action* relates to the efforts of the agent. For example, in the case of the agency relationship between the physician (agent) and the patient (principal), the post-contractual nature of patient error in physician selection (e.g. malpractice) might be characterized as moral hazard. From an internal or *managerial* perspective, an employee may shirk in the performance of his/her duties to management. From an external or *financial* perspective, a manager or

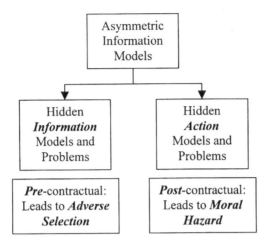

Fig. 3.1.   The Separable Nature of Hidden Information and Hidden Action Models
and Problems.

executive may deceive or shirk in the performance of his/her duties to shareholders. Hidden action is more closely associated with the *post-contractual* stage
of the agency relationship (discussed in Chapter 2).

Figure 3.1 depicts the separable nature of hidden information (pre-contractual)
and hidden action (post-contractual) models and problems, and their association with adverse selection (from Chapter 2) and moral hazard, respectively.

Agency loss is most severe when interests of the principal and agent diverge
substantially and hidden information and hidden action monitoring is costly. It
is for this reason that easily assembled, low cost informational indicators of
output or other hidden actions are so very often used as a monitoring vehicle
(e.g. hours worked). Similarly, low cost alternatives (e.g. on a per share basis)
for the production and assurance of financial information (by auditors) and
financial forecasts (by financial analysts) are desirable.

Long-term relationships are a benefit of good behavior and may lead to
reduced or limited monitoring, as they evolve from short- to long-term. Value,
potentially lost through bad behavior (e.g. loss of reputation or assets subject
to lawsuits), represent a strong incentive for good behavior.[10] Characterized as
relational quality by Arino et al. (2001), these attributes lead to the success of
alliances and:

• allow trust to emerge and complement other governance or control
  mechanisms;

- encourage collaboration beyond the initial agreement;
- promote conflict resolution; and
- accelerate mutually beneficial actions.

Reputation may facilitate initial alliances. For example, Billett et al. (1995) found evidence to compliment earlier findings that an auditor's or investment banker's perceived "quality" or reputation provides a valuable signal about the firm to uninformed investors. They concluded that firms associating with higher credit rating or more reputable lenders achieve higher borrower-firm returns.

Furthermore, Carter et al. (1998) found that the underperformance of initial public offerings (IPOs) was less severe when associated with more prestigious underwriters, and, consistent with prior study findings, when associated with less short-run security under pricing. The benefits, associated with reduced agency loss, are shared by both principal and agent, since both have a common interest to define monitoring and incentive structures that closely approximate one of a costless information *monitoring* structure (Pratt & Zeckhauser, 1985).

Finally, Helou and Park (2001) also examined the effect of underwriter reputation. After controlling for other factors, their procedure for the extraction of a signaling component from the overall measure of underwriter reputation suggested that underwriter reputation significantly and positively affected abnormal returns. They concluded that issuing firms use underwriter reputation to *signal* that their stocks are not overvalued.

MONITORS

Historically, large shareholders, venture capitalists or financial institutions/creditors may have provided for a market-based mechanism to *monitor* public companies. Increasingly, the stock-chat message boards and other information available on the Internet serve as an alternative *monitoring* vehicle or mechanism.

Historically, large shareholders provided the monitoring mechanism and small (or individual) shareholders were able to free-ride on the monitoring efforts and control by these large shareholders (e.g. the Mellons and the Carnegies). As a greater proportion of the population has invested in stocks, often via mutual or pension fund participation, this control and the related monitoring of the management of firms has declined. Generally, mutual or pension funds have not exerted pressures or held public companies accountable for their misdeeds, though contemporary proposals may change this.[11]

Maug (1998) constructed and studied a model of intervention by large investors. He assumed two investment objectives in his study of liquidity and control: (1) the large investor monitors to benefit from capital gains; and (2) trades on private information.

He concluded that (p. 88):

- gains achieved by the large investor monitor are shared with free-riders;
- larger investors profit from volatility, not from increasing mean company returns;
- larger investors profit from capital gains, resulting from monitoring efforts;
- larger investor gains are always insufficient to completely cover monitoring costs;
- less liquid markets will reduce monitoring, large stakes in a single corporation, and greater diversification; and
- when faced with a decision between takeovers and monitoring for underperforming companies, the large investor will select the less costly method in an illiquid market and the more effective method in a liquid market.

Venture capitalists invest relatively heavily in early stage high technology companies where high levels of information asymmetry are present. Monitoring is increased as ratios of tangible to intangible assets increase, market-to-book ratios rise, and R&D efforts rise (Gompers, 1995).

Lerner (1995) found that venture capitalist representation on the BOD increased around the time of CEO turnover.[12] Kirilenko (2001) developed a model showing that separation of the entrepreneur's value of control from the firm's expected payoff, resulting from venture capitalist demands of control, were disproportionately higher than the size that his equity investment might suggest. In return, however, the entrepreneur received better financing terms and continued to benefit from information asymmetry.

In an examination into the structures, likely to enhance the role of delegated monitors (e.g. commercial banks, insurance and finance companies), Rajan and Winton (1995) found that both covenants and collateral represented contractual devices increasing the lenders incentives to monitor.

Increasingly, individual investors are turning to the Internet to monitor for both hidden information and hidden actions. Financial news networks, like CNBC, are, when warranted, providing coverage of stock-chat message board activity. Because this hidden or private information represents asymmetric information, by definition, sources of free information on the Internet may be dated or non-timely and subject to distortion. Greater visibility and the free and timely release of information (e.g. Form 144s of insider trades of securities filed with the SEC) could reduce these information asymmetries.

AUDITORS AS INDEPENDENT PROVIDERS OF ASSURANCE/MONITORING SERVICES

This section will address several topics relating to the independent CPA auditor's attestation services. They include the analysis of the internal controls of the firms audited and two related internal management problem associated with CPA firms – the underreporting of time and premature sign-offs.

Internal Control

Internal control procedures take the form of a priori (prevention or adverse selection) and ex post (detection/correction or moral hazard) controls. Management controls include planning systems. Examples of planning systems include budgeting and forecasting procedures and outputs. Management controls also include monitoring systems such as performance evaluation and exception reports.

Planning systems typify a priori controls; monitoring systems typify ex post controls. A priori controls limit freedom of action by limiting the degree to which decision makers apply personal discretion. Alternatively, ex post controls provide a formal means for the review of decisions already undertaken.

Internal controls are the responsibility of a firm's management and, therefore, a component or function of *managerial* accounting. The review of management's internal control systems represents a significant portion of the independent CPA auditor's examination. Therefore, the internal auditor and external auditor provide for linkage between what might otherwise be viewed as separable *managerial* and *financial* accounting functions, respectively.

CPA firms also face their own internal control problems. As the following section suggests, premature sign-offs – an internal control or managerial issue facing CPA firms - may adversely affect the quality of the audit.

Premature Sign-Off [13]

Premature audit sign-offs and/or the underreporting of time spent on a particular component of an audit represent a typical manager (principal)/employee (agent) problem that continues to face CPA firms making a market in the provision of attestation services or audits. The staff or audit team member may send false signals, cheating with respect to the quality of the audit engagement and program, by underreporting time spent on component tasks. To the extent that the underreporting of time affects future audit engagements, future time expenditure budgets and fees are underestimated, placing time constraints on the subsequent year's audit staff, and so on. Some examples of research findings follow:

- Rhode (1977) found that 55% of auditors would *eat* (the slang term for *under-reporting*) time[14] and Lightner et al. (1983) found the percentage to be as high as 67%.
- Cook and Kelley (1988) found this trend to be increasing.
- Kelley and Seiler (1982) identified past behaviors that lead to reduced audit quality by 7% of audit partners/managers and 21% of senior staff. Their 1988 follow-up study found that these percentages increased to 21% and 22%, respectively.
- Rhode (1977), Alderman and Deitrick (1982), Cook and Kelley (1988), and Kelley and Margheim (1990) found evidence of failures by the auditor to pursue questionable issues.

Researches have identified and used agency cost-related variables to explain demand for external auditing services (Chow, 1982; Simunic & Stein, 1987), examine causal relations to auditor changes (Francis & Wilson, 1988), and study their effect on voluntary audit committee formation (Pincus et al., 1989; Bradbury, 1990). Firm size may be used as a proxy for increased agency costs, and lower levels of management (agents) equity ownership may lead to increased pressures to provide shareholders (principals) with assurance services. Monitoring is more effective for larger firms, as economies of scale are achieved (Anderson et al., 1990, p. 7; ASR 177, 1975, p. 819).

Contemporary Issues

Much research has been conducted on the affects of information on stock prices. From the firm's perspective, the auditor plays the role of attesting to components of the microeconomic news released by the firm. For example, the independent CPA auditor attests to the fair representation of the firm's economic information reporting in the form of earnings per share (EPS).

The auditor provides an independent assurance service. The consultant provides services as an advocate. Generally, consulting services generate higher profits when compared to auditing or assurance services. The incompatibility of these functions is summarized and represented in Fig. 3.2.

The accounting profession came under increased scrutiny following the Enron (NYSE: ENE) bankruptcy and, more recently, the WorldCom (NASDAQ NM: WCOM). As of late June 2002, WorldCom, another firm audited by Andersen, had reported the need to restate their income statements for the prior 5 quarters.

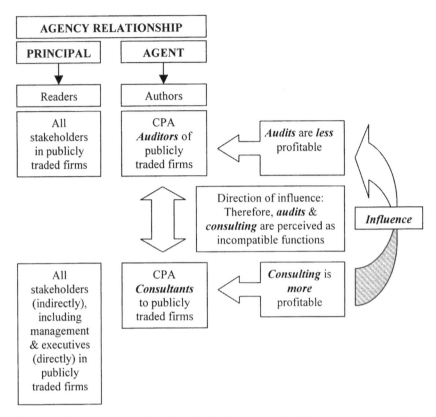

Fig. 3.2.   The Incompatability of Audit (Independence & Objectivity) & Consulting
(Advocacy) Functions.

As the Enron investigations matured, attention was focused on the public
perception of auditor independence or assurance services and consulting
or advocacy services. The "Big 5" accounting/auditing firms included
PricewaterhouseCoopers (PWC), KPMG International, Deloitte Touche
Tohmatsu, Ernst & Young (E&Y), and, of course, Arthur Andersen.

Ernst & Young was the first to separate their accounting/auditing and
consulting services with a sale of the latter to the Cap Gemini computer services
and consulting group on February 28, 2000. With a purchase price of approximately 11 billion Euros, Paris-based Cap Gemini stock trades under the symbol
CAPP on the Paris exchange and in the U.S. Pink sheets (CAPMF).

KPMG International was the second to spin off its consulting practice as
KPMG Consulting, Inc. (NASDAQ NM: KCIN) in a February 13, 2001 IPO.

Arthur Andersen, the accounting/auditing arm of the largest consulting firm in the world, retained the Andersen name in a bitter battle with Accenture, Ltd. (NYSE: ACN). Accenture spent $13 million to popularize its new name. The Accenture IPO occurred on July 19, 2001.

Both PWC and Deloitte Consulting, as of June 2002, intended to separate their accounting/auditing and consulting practices in the immediate future.

Purchasers of insurance (see Chapter 2), as well as those purchasing auditor independence or assurance services, are aware of quality or adverse selection issues. Whether Andersen provides generally high quality audits or not, in the face of the Enron bankruptcy, is not relevant. The brand name, Arthur Andersen, had been irreparably damaged.

Just as insurance companies seek to reduce the risk of adverse selection when approving a customer for the issuance of insurance coverage, consumers of insurance are likely to avoid purchasing policies from firms with a reputation for failing to pay legitimate claims (from Chapter 2). Similarly, publicly traded firms discharged Arthur Andersen as an auditor, en masse, to avoid association with this auditing firm and provider of assurance services. These actions were consistent with the finding of Billett et al. (1995), discussed earlier in this chapter.

Whether the Enron or WorldCom cases represent those characteristics of Arthur Andersen's audit quality, or not, is irrelevant. The highly visible popular press coverage (public information) of the post-SEC order to cease the destruction of documents and the subsequent shredding of Enron documents and/or Andersen's preliminary audit working papers, along with the conviction that resulted from a jury trial, resulted in institutional damage (e.g. the auditing/accounting profession via the public's perception, and the demise, of this very large auditing firm), which lingers and may cause both retail and institutional investors to seek information from alternative sources (e.g. the Internet).

Other aspects of the Enron audit failure include the highly publicized loss of retirement monies by ex-employees, while Enron executives (allegedly) told employees to buy more, only to sell their own shares of Enron stock. Andersen's loss of audit clients suggests that, in the world of auditing, Arthur Andersen's audits (as a provider of assurance services) are perceived as Akerlof's "lemons" (from Chapter 2).

FINANCIAL ANALYSTS AS INDEPENDENT FINANCIAL ADVISORS/MONITORS

Financial analysts generate earnings forecasts and represent a significant, sophisticated user group of financial accounting information. Earnings overestimation by positive-thinking financial analysts has been reported in a variety of studies

(Ajinkya & Gift, 1984; Brown et al., 1985; O'Brien, 1988; Graves et al., 1990; Philbrick & Ricks, 1991; Butler & Lang, 1991; Ali et al., 1992; Stober, 1992).

Independent Investment Advice

The financial analysts, associated with brokerage and underwriting firms, were also negatively implicated in the Enron bankruptcy. At issue was the public perception of objectivity (or lack thereof) associated with secondary disseminations of analyst recommendations of publicly traded firms with which their employers, brokerage/underwriting firms, also maintained more lucrative investment-banking relations.

Furthermore, unlike less lucrative and less direct CPA auditor/consultant compensation schemes, financial analysts were compensated from pools of underwriting fees-related monies. Therefore, compensation for individual financial analysts is directly linked to underwriting fees, providing for a more clearly determinable conflict of interest. As noted by *Reuters*, in an April 25, 2002 news wire:[15]

> Wall Street analysts have been accused of issuing overly bullish recommendations for companies in order to enable investment banking employers to win lucrative financing deals.

Finally, in an article by Shawn Langlois titled, "Stuff your apology in a cybersock: Message boards sound off against Merrill Lynch," investor sentiment with respect to the Merrill Lynch actions, from both YF and Raging Bull (RB) stock chat message boards, were examined.[16]

Window Dressing by Mutual and Pension Fund Managers

Window dressing is, by definition, an overt and frequently openly discussed and (apparently) accepted manifestation of *hidden* or *private* information.[17] Cataldo and Savage (pp. 110–111) concluded that window dressing remains:

> . . . intuitively appealing and very much a part of contemporary Wall Street folklore . . . (and is) consistent with Keynes' *transactions, precautionary,* and *speculative* motivations . . .

As recently as Friday, June 28, 2002, at the end-/turn-of-the-month, end-/turn-of-the-quarter and end-/turn-of-the-semi-annual calendar year, CNBC commentators were attributing the high volume to window dressing by fund managers. Generally, it is widely (anecdotally) held that these efforts are designed to remove "losers" from a portfolio so that quarterly statements, sent to clients, do not include any evidence that the manager of the fund ever invested

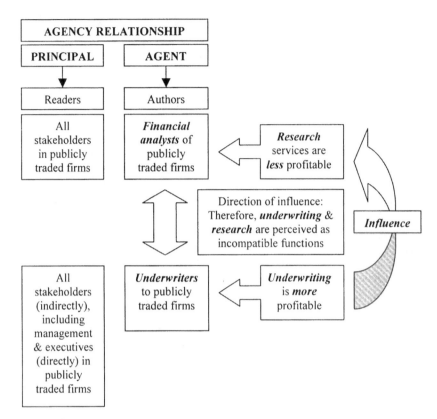

Fig. 3.3. The Incompatability of Analysts (Independence & Objectivity) & Underwriting (Advocacy) Functions.

in these underperforming stocks and is, in fact, now investing fund resources in stocks that show future promise. For example, Grinblatt et al. (1995) found 77% of mutual funds to be "momentum traders," buying past "winners."

This is consistent with the explanation provided by Jansson (1983) – that money managers engage in efforts to manipulate information relating to their performance at the end of the quarter and the end of their fiscal year. Using a variety of techniques, anecdotal evidence suggests that money managers engage in manipulative efforts to *mark up the merchandise, trick the technicians* (i.e. send false signals), *play catch-up, dump their losers, paint the tape,* or otherwise manipulate their month-end holding of specific stocks in the funds that they manage. They may even engage in these transactions to make it easier, even to the extent of lowering their current period performance measures, to achieve favorable comparisons for a subsequent year.[18]

Mutual and pension fund managers tend to sell poorly performing stocks, or 'get rid of mistakes' (p. 231), according to a study conducted by Lakonishok et al. (1991). These findings are consistent with the increase in end-of-quarter trading activity, as observed by Bildersee and Kahn (1987) in their earlier research on this topic, but are not consistent with the 'no evidence of window dressing' findings of Eakins and Sewell (1994), Ligon (1997) or those by Lee et al. (1998). Window dressing, to the extent that it exists, may not only fool hasty individual investors, but may also deceive the board members of pension and mutual funds, who are simply too rushed to adequately monitor the details of stock purchases and sales during the past quarter, concentrating, instead, on the list of current holdings (Dun's, 1983).

Window dressing by pension or money managers of pensions or mutual funds (agents), like the auditor, eating time, represents cheating. To the extent that window dressing behaviors persist, and to the degree for which this false signaling actually succeeds in deceiving the owners or shareholders (principals) of the pension or mutual funds, it represents a market failure that is directly associated with information asymmetry.

If market makers (MMs) window dress, they do so to maximize their own utility. Some academic research suggests that institutional investors tend to stay out of the market when composite indicators give negative signals and buy into the market when composite indicators give positive signals (Athanassakos, 1992).

Bid-Ask Spreads

Increased bid-ask spreads suggest increased uncertainty and/or information asymmetry. Management forecasts are effective in reducing information asymmetry and bid-ask spreads (Coller & Yohn, 1997). Some research results suggest that earnings surprises increase the level of information asymmetry (Harris & Raviv, 1991a; Kim & Verrecchia, 1994). Skinner (1992) explains:

> Under this view, some traders, perhaps because they specialize in following the stock, are especially adept at processing the firm's earnings information. Consequently, if there is a large earnings surprise, these traders are able to ascertain the implications of the surprise more quickly than other traders, providing them with a temporary informational advantage over those other traders and so temporarily increasing information asymmetry in the stock market.

Skinner found an increase in bid-ask spreads, for a large sample of NASDAQ National Market (NM) System firms, at the time of earnings announcements involving large earnings surprises.

Krinsky and Lee (1996) examined three components (i.e. adverse selection cost, inventory holding, and order processing) of the bid-ask spread around earnings announcements, concluding that the adverse selection (inventory holding and order processing) component increased (decreased), significantly, during periods surrounding the earnings announcement. They cautioned that earnings announcements may have an insignificant impact on the bid-ask spread, while simultaneously resulting in increased information asymmetry.

Jang and Lee (1995) found evidence of window dressing in the form of NYSE specialist report closing bid-ask spreads. Like McInish and Wood (1992) and Brock and Kleidon (1992), they found the spread sharply narrowed early in the regular trading session, but widened as closing time approached. However, their findings suggested an additional hypothesis, while referencing the fact that NYSE specialists may be intentionally reducing their closing spreads, solely for the purpose of window dressing, and around the time when quarterly earnings announcements are made.

Al-Suhaibani and Kryzanowski (2000) examined trade orders at the Saudi Stock Market (SSM) for 56 stocks (October 31, 1996, to January 14, 1997). Their results were consistent with asymmetric information models – larger, more aggressive orders were more informative, an observation consistent with the finding that private information was more important for thinly traded stocks.

Contemporary Issues

On May 13, 2002, a series of popular press stories and coverage became focused on the prevalence of "no value," "round-trip" or "wash" trades in the energy sector. Reliant Resources Incorporated (NYSE: RRI) admitted to transactions/trades "intended solely to boost trading volumes and puff up revenues" (Kelly, 2002). These trades involved the two parties, buying and selling electricity to each other at the same price, and comprised approximately 10% of the revenues reported by Reliant for the prior three years.

Reliant claimed that most of these dealings were with CMS Energy Corporation (NYSE: CMS). CMS provided clarification. These trades were with the CMS marketing, services and trading (CMS-MST) unit. CMS denied that any revenues or income were recorded in their own financial statements as a result of these trades with yet another firm, Dynergy (NYSE: DYN),[19] and specifically noted that they stopped engaging in these transactions (CMS Energy Corporation, 2002).

Mirant Corporation (NYSE: MIR) was also included in the March 11, 2002 California Attorney General suit, which related to the alleged sale of emergency energy to California and the probe by the Federal Energy Regulatory

Commission (FERC). Mirant categorically denied any transactions designed to artificially inflate trading volumes or revenue (Dow Jones, 2002).

The popular press coverage of these energy and energy futures trading practices, of course, suggests a design trading strategy to manipulate perceptions relating to their firm's transactions volume and energy prices. If one were to read the stock-chat message boards, they would note that similar allegations are frequently made against MMs, but relating to stock or other securities transactions. Similar behaviors have been exposed in cases of insider (principal) stock trading (BC Securities Commission, 2002):

> A former Vancouver company president . . . admitted that he created the false impression
> of trading activity in his company's stock by trading the stock between brokerage accounts
> that he held . . . admitted to engaging in 105 "wash" trades . . .

These behaviors may also be perpetrated by individual stockholders. For example, an individual with a large position in a stock may, through a review of NASDAQ Level 2 blocks, by market maker, be able to sell shares to him or herself, at an inflated price. The motivation would be to engage in such a transaction at the 4 p.m. close of the regular trading session to defer a margin call.

A preliminary analysis/summary of forty-one 2001 NASD Office or Hearing Officer Disciplinary Decisions is contained in Table 3.1. This summary does not, in and of itself, suggest that market maker manipulation (MMM) is a serious problem.

The topic of MMM is more fully-developed and coverage expanded in Chapter 8, as well as related appendix chapters.

TAX COMPLIANCE AND COMPLEXITY

Generally, academics involved in tax research are interested in the study of tax compliance and complexity issues. Both relate to information and information asymmetry, as the complexity of a tax issue may result in ambiguity, the result of an information deficit, and ambiguity may lead a taxpayer or paid preparer to tolerate higher levels of risk or moral hazard.

Taxpayers possess private information, as may tax preparers, with respect to both quality and quantity of the measures, used to prepare an income tax return, and develop and finalize taxable income and tax liability calculations. Some taxpayers are risk-averse; others are risk-neutral.[20] The IRS has a prior probability distribution they can associate with the taxpayer type and classification, benefiting the IRS as they commit and target their limited resources.

Table 3.1. Summary of 2001 NASD Office or Hearing Officer Disciplinary Decisions (*N* = 41).

Decision Number	NASD & SEC Rule Violations	Pnlty	Profit Comm	Restn	Hrng Costs	Int	Susp [days]
C01000003*	NASD2110,2120,3040,SEC10b	$82.5K			$2.3K	N	180
C10000037*	NASD2110,2120,2210,2230,3110, SEC10b,17a	$240K	$58.6K		$1.8K	N	720
C01000011	NASD2110	$15K			$1.9K	N	–
C10000086	NASD2110			$16K	$1.7K	Y	Perm
C8A000024	NASD2110,8210			$1.7M	$1.8K	N	Perm
C07000033*	NASD2110,3010	$24K			$2.9K	N	Cens
C8B000001	NASD2110					N	Perm
C07000013	NASD2110,8210					N	Perm
C07000003*	NASD2110,8210					N	360
C02000037*	NASD2110,2310	$25K				N	360
C9A000027*	NASD2110,3040		$79.1K		$1.6K	N	90
C07000058	NASD2110,3040	$20K	$4.1K			N	360
C9A990029	NASD2110,8210					N	Perm
CAF000015*	NASD2110	$10K				N	–
C10000139	NASD2110,8210					N	Perm
C10000116	NASD2110,8210					N	Perm
C05000021	NASD2110,8210					N	Perm
C10000140	NASD2110,2120,3040,SEC10b	$40K		$100K		Y	720
C3A990071	NASD2110,2120,2310,SEC10b	$1.1M				Y	–
C8B000013	NASD2110,3040,8210	$30K	$12.9K			N	Perm
C10000006	NASD2110,2120,SEC10b,17a				$8.4K	N	Perm
CAF000040	NASD2110,8210					N	Perm
CAF000033*	NASD2110,8210				$2.4K	N	Perm
C3A000054	NASD2110,3030	$15K				N	10
C8A000059*	NASD2110,3040	$5K	$22K		$1.1K	N	90
C10000029	NASD2110,3010					N	Perm
C07000090	NASD2110,3040	$20K				N	720
C10000046	NASD2110	$10K		$1.7K		Y	90
C8A010014	NASD2110	$5K			$0.8K	N	10
CAF000030*	NASD8210				$2.2K	N	120
C9B000015	NASD2110,8210				$2.1K	N	180
C01000017	NASD2110				$2.0K	N	Perm
C9A000038	NASD2110				$1.8K	N	Perm
CMS000142*	NASD2110,3370,SEC17a	$17K	$145.5K		$3.5K	N	–
C10000122*	NASD2110	$10K			$6.4K	N	10
C05010012*	NASD2110,2310	$40K		$84.4K	$2.2K	I	90
C06010015	NASD2110	$10K			$1.2K	N	30
C3A010009*	NASD2110,3040	$25K			$1.9K	N	90
C01000037*	NASD2110,2210	$10K			$3.6K	N	90
C3A010005	NASD2110,3040	$5K	$130.4K			N	360
CMS000015*	NASD2110,2210	$3K				N	360

Table 3.1.   Continued.

Decision Number	Notes
C01000003*	Engaged in a private security transactions and misrepresented investment banking experience.
C10000037*	316 customer trades through the firm's propriety account; charged undisclosed commissions.
C01000011	Violated prior suspension term; sent private placement offerings to 69 persons.
C10000086	10 unauthorized transactions in 5 customers accounts; failed to appear at the hearing.
C8A000024	Issued false profit & loss statements; unauthorized transactions; failed to respond to NASD inquiries.
C07000033*	Failure to implement supervisory tape recording procedures.
C8B000001	Converted funds of a member firm for personal use.
C07000013	Failure to respond to 2 requests for information from NASD staff (re: unsuitable recommendations).
C07000003*	Failure to respond to a request for information from NASD staff.
C02000037*	Made unsuitable recommendations to a customer.
C9A000027*	Engaged in private security transactions (re: promissory notes).
C07000058	Engaged in 4 private security transactions (re: Medco notes).
C9A990029	Failure to respond to a request for information from NASD staff.
CAF000015*	Failure to respond to a request for documentation from NASD staff.
C10000139	Failure to timely appear for an on-the-record interview with NASD staff.
C10000116	Failure to timely appear for an on-the-record interview with NASD staff.
C05000021	Failure to timely appear for an on-the-record interview with NASD staff.
C10000140	Engaged in a private security transaction; unauthorized transfer; made untrue statements.
C3A990071	Market Maker Manipulation (MMM) issue addressed.
C8B000013	Failure to disclose 3 private security transactions and respond to NASD staff.
C10000006	Engaged in material misrepresentations; unauthorized transactions.
CAF000040	Failure to timely appear for an on-the-record interview with NASD staff.
CAF000033*	Failure to respond to a request for documentation from NASD staff.
C3A000054	Failure to provide notice of outside business activity (re: limited partnership sales for commissions).
C8A000059*	Failure to disclose private security transactions (re: limited partnership sales for commissions).
C10000029	14 alleged causes of action relating to IPO-related MMM (e.g., boiler room-type operation).
C07000090	Failure to disclose private security transactions (re: promissory notes) and forgery.
C10000046	4 unauthorized trades in 2 customer accounts; provided false/misleading information.
C8A010014	Unauthorized transaction.
CAF000030*	Failure to respond to a request for documentation from NASD staff (re: MMM investigation).
C9B000015	Failure to timely appear for an on-the-record interview with NASD staff.
C01000017	Failure to disclose civil action (re: $33K settlement) for fraud and conversion of sister's account.
C9A000038	Wrongful use of converted funds (re: $8,240); prior NYSE actions (re: unsuitable recommendations).
CMS000142*	Shorted 46.7 shares of ENMD; failed to make "affirmative determinations" (re: naked shorted firm account).
C10000122*	1 unauthorized transaction in a customer's account.
C05010012*	Unsuitable recommendations to a customer (re: class B v. class A mutual funds).

Table 3.1. Continued.

Decision Number	Notes
C06010015	Failure to disclose conviction for felony theft.
C3A010009*	Failure to disclose private security transactions (re: non-compensated).
C01000037*	Failure to register web site as advertising; content omitted required material disclosures.
C3A010005	Failure to disclose private security transactions (re: 10% referral fees).
CMS000015*	Unsuitable recommendations and high bids (no MMM, because ineffective); 58K shares short on LOCKC.

*Appealed or called for review.
Legend: where Hrng = Hearing, Susp = Suspension/Suspended, Pnlty = Penalty, Comm = Commission(s), Restn = Restitution, Int = Interest, and Cens = Censored.

Client Advocacy

Preparer advocacy incentives are moderated by both levels of competition and moral hazard (Anderson & Cuccia, 2000). The literature supports the intuitively appealing notion that paid preparers tend to operate in the role of an advocate, and may even be non-compliant, when faced with the decision to enforce or exploit ambiguous areas of tax law (Smith & Kinsey, 1987, Klepper et al., 1988; Klepper & Nagin, 1989; Errand, 1990; Young, 1994; Schisler, 1994). Carnes and Englebrecht (1995, p. 26) found that taxpayer (agent) compliance behavior was very strongly influenced by their detection risk perception.

During April 2002, news that the IRS would resurrect a revised and updated variation of their Taxpayer Compliance Measurement Program (TCMP) audits, under the new name of "national research program" (NRP), was released and covered in the popular and business press. This previously discarded program involved the random selection of a stratified sample of individual federal income tax returns, based on total positive income (TPI). This sample of tax returns was examined in great detail, line item by line item, to identify areas where taxpayer compliance and non-compliance was most likely to exist. The results were used to develop a methodology to assign what the IRS referred to as DIF (discriminant income function) scores. DIF scores were then assigned to tax returns, and used to assist the IRS in the selection of individual income tax returns for audit. In addition, the IRS hired an additional 1,300 new officers and tax agents to assist in this effort, involving the selection of an additional sample of 50,000 tax returns (Martin, 2002).

Taxation involves risks that may lead to IRS challenge, dispute resolution, and even litigation. Cooter and Rubinfeld (1989) describe the four stages of a legal dispute:

(1) Event results in dispute;
(2) Injured party asserts claim;
(3) Pretrial negotiations seek settlement, and, if unsuccessful;
(4) Courts determine the outcome.

Enyon and Stevens (1995) examine taxpayer venue choice from a game theory perspective, since taxpayers are presumed to possess private information. They found that taxpayer venue choice never provides an informative signal in cases where the IRS seeks to maximize revenue, but may result in the transfer of information to the IRS when the IRS' objective function is to minimize incremental social costs (e.g. maintenance of a court system).

Client advocacy interferes with independence in both CPA auditor/consulting and financial analyst/underwriter structures. In taxation, however, independence may be less relevant (Shields et al., 1995).

Seetharaman and Swanson (1998) extended the, presumably, equally efficient agency theory-based trade-offs (e.g. inverse relationship) between debt and management ownership. Citing studies by Jensen and Meckling (1976) and Grossman and Hart (1989), they studied these mechanisms for the mitigation of manager (agent)/stockholder (principal) agency problems in the context of the firm's marginal tax rate (MTR). They found that high MTR firms, when compared to low MTR firms, were less willing to exchange debt for managerial ownership.

Stewart (1995) examined agency theory as applied to the inefficient allocation of resources by management in mutual institutions. Building on the agency problems previously associated with certain ownership structures (e.g. Schleifer & Vishny, 1986), Stewart found that credit unions had higher total personnel and travel expenditures and operating expenditures. These findings suggested that the owners, stockholders, borrowers or members of these mutual institutions (principals) failed to reap the benefits intended for them as these tax subsidies were consumed by the managers and employees of these mutual institutions (agents), seeing to maximize their own personal utility.

Credit unions (generally) followed a one-member, one-vote plan, unlike stock ownership structures where a large stockholder may have significant control over the operation of a company (Verbrugge & Jahera, 1981).[21] The mutual organizational form of the tax exempt credit union, with it's separation of ownership and control, appeared to thwart the original government objectives – that credit unions pass on their tax subsidy to members.

Manzon (1992) found evidence of earnings management, through the use of accruals related to long-lived assets (e.g. depreciation), for the purpose of minimizing (or managing) the corporate alternative minimum tax (AMT; 1986–). He also found some evidence of anticipatory earnings management in the year preceding the imposition of the AMT, consistent with prior findings by Gramlich (1991) and Dhaliwal and Wang (1992).

According to Nichols (1998, p. 2):

> The adoption of the liability method for deferred taxes under either Statement of Financial Accounting Standards (SFAS) 109, Accounting for Income Taxes, or its predecessor SFAS 96 (SFAS 109/96) offered the longest adoption period in the history of the FASB (seven years), providing an excellent opportunity for firms to manage their earnings.

Nichols also found limited evidence of income positioning/smoothing, the big bath hypothesis, and the use of discretionary accounting decisions to manipulate or increase income (p. 4). These practices were more prevalent for firms with debt-to-equity levels exceeding the industry average.

Contemporary Issues

Perhaps the most relevant tax-related topics can be found in the highly-publicized behaviors of the executives and their personal tax problems. These, of course, are the executives of publicly held corporations.

For example, executives of Tyco International, Limited (NYSE: TYC) have resigned and/or become the subject of investigations for failure to report and pay income and sales taxes on bonuses and large purchases, respectively. These, as well as schemes resulting in the establishment of the new IRS NRP, have been associated with large CPA firms – the same firms providing audit-related assurance services and expected to mitigate moral hazard.

SUMMARY

This chapter focused on the introduction of information asymmetry as it relates to *moral hazard* and its separable components, *hidden information* and *hidden action* (Fig. 3.1). It extended the introduction of both *adverse selection* (*pre-contractual*) and *moral hazard* (*post-contractual*). The former was covered in Chapter 2.

The large shareholder, acting as a *monitor*, has played a decreasing role over the past several decades. As the late 1990s experienced growth in the popularity of broad-based, public participation in mutual funds, fund managers and their firms failed to exert large shareholder-like influence on public companies, resulting in increased moral hazard.

Auditors may not be providing the same level of monitoring, through their assurance services. Historically, auditors have played a significant role in the establishment and maintenance of internal controls, an integral part of their audit and a topic relevant to both financial and managerial accounting coursework and disciplines. However, as consulting fees and profits outpaced those generated by auditing, auditors may have failed in their role as an agent and monitor for all stakeholders (Fig. 3.2), again, increasing the risk of moral hazard.

Similarly, financial analysts may have failed to provide unbiased research in developing their "buy," "sell" and "hold" opinions. Though favorable underwriter reputation may have been found to reduce the level of asymmetric information in prior studies (Helou & Park, 2001), contemporary economic incentives, associated with the generation of relatively enormous underwriting fees, may have contributed to their failures to honor their responsibilities as agents and monitors for all stakeholders (Fig. 3.3), increasing moral hazard exposure. Similar issues may warrant investigation and academic research efforts, with respect to SEC and NASD (Table 3.1) investigations of complaints against stock brokers and specialists/market makers (addressed in Chapter 8), some of whom were already under suspension when new complaints warranted further investigation.

Finally, tax compliance and complexity issues may also involve issues of advocacy. Perhaps the most apparent external manifestation and illustration is the IRS restoration of a variation of the TCMP audit, renamed as the National Research Program (NRP). Many highly-paid executives, from publicly traded corporations, have been implicated in Enron-like off-shore schemes or have attempted to reduce their individual taxes through sales tax fraud, and the simple under-reporting of bonus earnings.

SECTION II. THE EFFICIENT MARKETS HYPOTHESIS AND MARKET EFFICIENCY

Stiglitz . . . argues that the costs of maintaining . . . efficiency outweigh the benefits, at least at the margin . . . that financial analysts equate the marginal costs of financial research (which he calls "speculation") with their personal marginal benefit, rather than with aggregate societal benefits (Schwert & Seguin, 1993).

INTRODUCTION

The efficient market hypothesis (EMH) has been examined in the context of three discrete categories of market efficiency. Cataldo and Savage (2000, Table 2.5, p. 22 and Table 6.1, p. 88) provide detailed summaries of all three forms or levels of market efficiency.

LEVELS OF MARKET EFFICIENCY

The market is efficient in the weak form when the price of a security reflects all historical price and volume information. This level of market efficiency is consistent with technical analysis (TA) – the study of historical price and volume charts.

The market is efficient in the semi-strong form when the price of a security reflects all historical information, including the historical price and volume information presumed in the weak form. Therefore, the level of information presumed under the weak form of market efficiency is fully nested in the semi-strong level of market efficiency. Semi-strong efficiency exists where share prices reflect all *public* information, but not *private* information.

The market is efficient in the strong form when the price of a security reflects all information – *public* and *private*. Therefore, the level of information presumed under the semi-strong form of market efficiency is fully nested in the strong level of market efficiency.

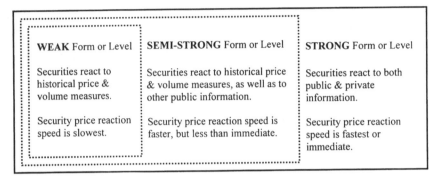

Fig. II.1.   The Three (Nested) Forms or Levels of Market Efficiency.

The strong form of the EMH is an extreme. Few have ever treated it as anything other than a logical completion of the set of possible hypotheses (Jensen, 1978, p. 97).

Figure II.1 illustrates the levels of information in the context of three discrete, but not mutually exclusive, categories of market efficiency. The discrete level of information operationally defined for the weak form of market efficiency is completely nested in the semi-strong form of market efficiency. The discrete level of information operationally defined for the semi-strong form of market efficiency is completely nested in the strong form of market efficiency.

MARKET EFFICIENCY AND LEVELS OF INFORMATION

Both weak and semi-strong forms of market efficiency presume security price reactions to *public* information (Chapter 4).[22] The strong form of market efficiency presumes that security prices will react to both *public* or *symmetric* and *private* or *asymmetric* information (Chapter 5).

Few academics or financial professionals would suggest that stock prices are responsive to *private* or *hidden* information or find support for the strong form of market efficiency. The contemporary case of WorldCom provides an example of a failure for a firm's stock price to represent *private* information, as some *insiders* knew of the capitalization of significant amounts that should have been expensed, leading to overstated earnings per share measures and an inflated stock price for the firm.

Cataldo and Savage (2000, p. 22), in their application of Keynes' theory of individual investor liquidity preferences (1936, pp. 170–171), found the persistence of what have been referred to as "seasonal anomalies" to be consistent only with the *public* information-based weak and semi-strong forms of market efficiency. Generally, knowledge of these seasonals represents *public* information, though this information is seldom useful in generating abnormal economic returns.

Chapters 4 and 5 examine *public* information and *private* information, respectively. Chapter 4 examines challenges to the semi-strong level of market efficiency and contains an illustration of the type of inefficiency that can result from analyst neglect, a condition associated with reduced levels of *public* information or increased levels of *asymmetric* information, but where *hidden* or *private* information is not the cause. Chapter 5 focuses on *hidden* or *private* information, brought into the limelight in the popular press as a concern relating to the broader issue of corporate governance by (1) recent institutional failures (e.g. Enron and WorldCom) and (2) the speed of information dissemination on the Internet.

CHAPTER 4. PUBLIC INFORMATION

The most valuable commodity I know of is information (Michael Douglas, playing the character of Gordon Gekko in the film *Wall Street*).

INTRODUCTION

The operational definitions of both weak and semi-strong forms of market efficiency are consistent with security price reactions to *public* information. The weak form or level suggests that security prices react (slowly) to historical price and volume measures. The semi-strong form or level suggests that security prices react (faster) to historical price and volume measures, as well as to other publicly available information (Figure II.1.).

The "other publicly available information" included in the semi-strong form or level of market efficiency includes both microeconomic or firm-specific news and macroeconomic news. Guidance provided by the publicly traded firm's management, their internally-generated, but externally-reported financial statements and external reports by independent auditors represent publicly available microeconomic news. The same may be said of the opinions provided by financial analysts, covering the publicly traded firm's securities, though their guidance may also include macroeconomic news, as the future of an industry might lead to modifications of their "buy," "sell" or "hold" recommendations.

The depth of available public information is also relevant to any discussion of information symmetry or asymmetry. Therefore, this chapter includes a single case to introduce what some might refer to as market inefficiencies associated with financial analyst *neglect*. This neglect may create a supply/demand imbalance for public information. As demand for public information about a firm's security increases, the investor, speculator or even the day-trader[23] may seek additional information from historically non-existent sources. A variety of Internet web sites, and even the Internet's stock-chat message boards, provide for one new source of additional public information and, whether or not desirable, may enjoy increased use by individual investors as supplemental sources of public information.

Historically, accounting and finance academics, related journals and literature streams have resulted in the production of event studies. These studies

BRAND NAME stocks	GENERIC stocks
• Less information risk • Higher quality of information • Large sample of consensus estimates • Monitoring service or fee • Lower return • Higher price (premium) • Lower uncertainty • More consistency	• More information risk • Lower quality of information • Small sample or no sample of estimates • No monitoring service or fee • Higher return • Lower price (discount) • Higher uncertainty • Less consistency

Fig. 4.1. Brand Name vs. Generic Stocks.

examine the effects of public information releases. As the Internet is a relatively novel medium, the vast majority of these studies pre-date popular access to this new public information transmission vehicle. Therefore, for the researcher willing to invest the time in data base development and analysis, the Internet represents a relatively new medium of information from which to extend traditional research methodologies.

The first sections of this chapter will present illustrative samples of research findings for public releases of information in the form of microeconomic and macroeconomic news. Selected research findings associated with public disclosures by both management and financial analysts will follow and precede the introduction of the topic of neglected firms and related informational deficiencies. Finally, a brief case study and empirical test is provided, covering the market reaction and returns to public information for this neglected firm.

MICROECONOMIC NEWS – QUARTERLY AND ANNUAL REPORTS

Accountants/Auditors seek evidence to support the position that the financial information they produce has value to users of financial information. In much the same way that insurance coverage is sought after by individuals and firms to reduce exposure to risk (Chapter 2), the audited financial statements and auditor's opinion letter for a publicly-traded security provide assurance to the stakeholder (Chapter 3).

Quarterly earnings per share (e.g. EPS) announcements have been found to be useful in predicting annual earnings, and both quarterly and annual earnings information provide useful information (see the seminal work by Ball & Brown,

1968, supplemented and followed by Beaver, 1968; Brown & Niederhoffer, 1968; May, 1971; Brown & Kennelly, 1972; Litzenberger & McEnally, 1977).[24]

Ball (1978) suggested that the abnormal returns, observed after announcements of quarterly earnings, were due to deficiencies in the capital asset pricing model (CAPM). Watts (1978) examined CAPM after taking steps to reduce the effects of CAPM deficiencies. He observed significant abnormal returns, but not economically significant enough to cover transaction costs or friction (e.g. brokerage costs). In a more contemporary analysis, Cataldo and Savage (2000) found CAPM to be deficient, as the equity-based beta measure of risk may fail to capture all risk components (p. 81). CAPM, for example, does not capture or compensate for variations in publicly available information or information deficiencies.

Chen et al. (1997) examined earnings announcements/surprises as they relate to the quantity of information. They hypothesized and concluded that a security, followed by a large number of financial analysts, would result in a higher level of information quality, reflected in relatively low levels of earnings surprises. They also found that the speed of security price reactions increased, suggesting increased market efficiency, as the quality and quantity of information increased.

Because larger firms are followed by more financial analysts, the profits associated with larger transaction sizes supported these higher information costs. This suggests that the "abnormal returns resulting from earnings surprises found in prior studies are more of an information effect than a size effect per se" (502). However, Brauer and Chang (1990), in their examination of closed-end funds and tax-loss selling vs. information as the significant explanation for the January effect, found that information-based reactions could *not* explain the January effect.

Ettredge et al. (1994) investigated firms' motivations for the purchase of timely reviews of quarterly financial information filed with the SEC. They hypothesized that firms, contracting for these timely quarterly reviews, sought higher levels of monitoring to reduce higher internal and external agency costs. Evidence from their logistic regression supported this hypothesis. In addition, they found that the likelihood of these purchases of timely reviews of quarterly financial information was positively associated with firm size, leverage, the issuance of new securities, reviews of quarterly financial information by internal audit staff, and being a utility. They found this likelihood to be "negatively associated with the percentage of common stock owned by managers and directors and with the percentage of foreign-to-total assets" (p. 131).

Penman (1987) examined the presence/absence of seasonal preferences for good/bad news or related informational releases and the extent to which this information was reflected in stock returns. The magnitude of unexpected earnings (i.e. informational content) and trading volume are continuously and positively related (Bamber, 1986). Both price and volume reactions to information must be studied to develop a complete characterization of the information content contained in earnings announcements (Dontah & Ronen, 1993). Greig (1992), Sober (1992), Ou and Penman (1993) and Lev and Thiagarajan (1993) examined market-to-book values and/or analyses of financial information (i.e. fundamental analysis) as predictors that might prove preferable to capital markets research alternatives (e.g. unobservable projections of future cash flows). Holthausen and Larcker (1992) challenged Ou and Penman's (1989) findings. Institutional investors are more likely than individual investors to trade around earnings release (e.g. pre-planned informational releases) dates (Kim et al., 1997).

From an institutional perspective, Hasbrouck (1995) examined homogeneous or closely-linked securities trading in multiple markets. His results suggested that the preponderance of price discovery (e.g. the incorporation of new information), applied to quotes for the thirty Dow stocks, occurred on the NYSE (a median of 92.7%).

MACROECONOMIC NEWS – EVENT STUDIES

Pearce and Roley (1985), in their study of economic news, found that surprise announcements to monetary policy significantly affected stock prices. Jain (1988) found that surprise announcements of economic news (e.g. money supply and Consumer Price Index (CPI)) resulted in stock price-level adjustments of 1 hour or so. Ederington and Lee (1993) found that the release of scheduled macroeconomic news announcements on interest rate and foreign exchange markets resulted in the bulk of the price adjustment within 1 minute, with higher than normal volatility for 15 minutes and slightly elevated volatility for several hours.[25]

Macroeconomic news-related event studies have also been conducted based on day-of-the-week, weekend or Monday effects (see Cataldo & Savage, 2000). Chang et al. (1998) examined and found support for prior findings by Lakonishok and Maberly (1990), Foster and Viswanathan (1990), Froot et al. (1992), and King and Wadhwani (1990). Their study, too, supported the position that weekend, Friday and Monday, and day-of-the-week effects could be partially explained by information asymmetries or asymmetric responses, with respect to the manner in which macroeconomic news was processed on Mondays, as opposed to other days of the week. Generally, the macroeconomic news and news of large firm returns that is quickly processed and impounded into the prices of these large firms, on Fridays, resulted in noise trading or herd behaviors (Froot et al., 1992) and lagging contagion (King & Wadhwani, 1990) for smaller firms, on Mondays.

MANAGEMENT VERSUS ANALYST DISCLOSURES

Williams (1998) examined the incidence of analyst forecasts. In her study of relations between management forecast precision and individual financial analyst forecast error, she found that financial analysts were more likely to revise interim earnings estimates in the presence of imprecise management forecasts. She posited that financial analysts represented information intermediaries between corporations and market participants. Their role was one of translation when management estimates of earnings are imprecise or include uncertainty.

Furthermore, she classified the quantitative management forecast hierarchy as point, range (or closed interval), lower bound, or upper bound:

* Point (the most precise);
* Range (less precise than point, but more precise than upper- or lower-bound); and
* Lower- or upper-bound (least precise).

Some evidence suggests that financial or security analysts respond sluggishly to past news (Chan et al., 1996). Exploitations of errors in analysts' forecasts have been shown to generate superior returns, due to the extreme nature of future earnings growth expectations (La Porta, 1996).

In their examination (1989–1995) of the impact of U.K. Financial Reporting Standard 3 (FRS 3) *"Reporting Financial Performance"* October 1992, Acker et al. (1998) found that this requirement for companies to publish more financial and related information increased the accuracy of analysts' forecasts. Their results confirmed improved analyst-based EPS estimates after FRS 3, especially for smaller companies in the FTSE 100.

NEGLECTED FIRMS – PUBLIC INFORMATION DEFICIENCIES

Arbel (1985) more than adequately explains the applicability of agency theory to information costs, in the context of his paper on generic stocks (e.g. "the small-firm effect," "the neglected-firm effect," "the P/E anomaly," and even the "January effect"):

> Part of the price of these stocks . . . [presumed to be undervalued] . . . is a hidden fee or the monitoring cost, or what financial theory calls 'agency cost.' Somebody serves as the investor's self-appointed agent. Actually, the more popular the stock is, the more numerous

such agents are. These agents are the hundreds of analysts, investment specialists, and port-folio managers who carefully follow the stocks and every relevant aspect of company performance. The result is informational paradise – blue skies, practically clear of any clouds that might cover relevant information.

In this extension to the works of Arbel and Strebel (1983) and Arbel et al. (1983), Arbel (1985) explains that the term 'market anomalies' (p. 4) emerged to describe these phenomena. He concludes that all four are *informational* vari-ables, affecting the investor's perceived risk level. Furthermore, these anomalies do not violate the EMH, but reflect differences in investor risk preferences, where institutional investor constraints prevent self-correction, and that they are likely to continue to persist (pp. 4–5).

Arbel refers to the stocks followed by analysts as "brand name" stocks. Those not followed by analysts are characterized as "generic" stocks. Figure 4.1 summarizes many of the differences between brand name and generic products, along with their comparisons to stock – an equity investment vehicle or product, explicitly stated or alluded to by Arbel.

Brand name (or, generally, big cap) stocks are heavily followed, suggesting that a higher quality of public information is available in the form of a larger sample of financial analyst's or consensus estimates of future earnings per share or revenues measures. Of course, because this information or monitoring service is not costless, this wealth of information affects the price of the stock in what might be viewed as a higher stock price or an information-based premium. Because the cost of the stock is higher, the rate of return for these brand name stocks is lower. The investor in these financial instruments reaps the benefits of greater consistency and lower uncertainty, at the cost of lower returns.

Generic (or, generally, micro- and small cap (SC)) stocks are followed only by a few analysts, if at all. Therefore, the potential for the observation or review of a consensus may not exist. There is little or no financial analyst coverage or monitoring. However, because of this lack of information, there is also no stock price premium. Because of this, these lower priced or generic stocks sell at a relative price discount. Their future returns (and even their future survival) may possess great uncertainty and risk.

Generic stocks are also referred to as *neglected* firms. Arbel (1985) opera-tionally defines and quantifies levels of neglect, as follows:

(1) The number of financial institutions making a market in or holding the stock (e.g. the number of stores carrying the product),
(2) The percentage of the firm's outstanding shares held by institutions, and
(3) 1 multiplied by 2.

According to Arbel (1985, p. 8):

. . . from the investor's point of view, the lower the level of consensus among analysts, the larger is the information deficiency . . .

Returns from Public Information for a Neglected Security

At 9:01 a.m.,[26] on Tuesday, March 18, 2002, a BUSINESS WIRE titled, *Purchase Point Media Corp.: Corporate Update*, was made public. This was a pre-market release by Purchase Point Media Corporation (Purchase Point; PinkSheets: PPMC). It was repeated, almost verbatim, in a COMTEX wire the following day, at 10:13 a.m. The following is an excerpt from the news release:

> Purchase Point Media Corporation had contracted . . . to sell the assets of the Company . . . a Point of Purchase (POP) advertisement program, patents in the United States, Canada, United Kingdom and Germany for a POP advertisement display device for shopping carts and the trademark "The last word(R)" . . . a clear plastic, weatherproof, highly durable, state of the art . . . display device that encloses a glossy color photo insert containing ten, 3 inch by 3 inch POP ads. The panel is 1/4 inch thick, 7 inches high and 16 inches wide. The last word(R) attaches to the back of the child's seat section in grocery carts, so that it is directly in front of the shopper's eyes. Each of the three inch POP advertisement squares, are equal in size to a 21-inch TV 10 feet away . . . Ridgewood Group is currently lining PPMC up with several top executives in both the packaged foods and advertising industry for the sale of PFPMC's assets.

A yellow page directory search, using an Internet search engine, revealed the location of the Ridgewood Group (International), located in New York City. The firm did not appear to have a website, but a telephone number was available for those wishing to investigate the matter further.

Additional relevant information from the news release follows:

> Should the sale of the PPMC's bring in a *mid to high eight figure dollar amount* (emphasis added) as hoped, PPMC intends to declare a dividend and acquire an operating company.

A 'mid-figure dollar amount' would approximate $50 million. Because this was a Vancouver, B.C., firm, the use of Canadian dollars would provide a more conservative measure of the lower range of the proceeds anticipated. Therefore, $50 million (CAN) would approximate $30 million (U.S.) (e.g. a Canadian dollar was worth at least $0.60 (U.S.) at the time of the news release).

Pink Sheets and other financial web sites, including the last filing with the SEC for March 31, 2001, revealed the number of outstanding share of common stock at 11,960,450. $30 million divided by 11,960,450 would provide for a PPS of approximately $2.50 (U.S.). At the time of the news release, the PPS was $0.04.

A review of the stock's trading history from March 31, 2001, through the March 18, 2002, news release date, suggested thin trading. On many trading days, no shares were traded. Therefore, it was not likely that the management of the firm had flooded the market with cheap shares and was now attempting to manipulate the price of Purchase Point's stock. The trading volume following the news release remained very low (see Table 4.1), suggesting that management was not selling into the rally.

This (and more) information would have had to be developed between the 9:01 a.m. news release time and the open of the market at 9:30 a.m. Or did it? The first trade on March 18, 2002, was not executed until 11:38 a.m. This first trade was for 5,000 shares at $0.04 per share.

Table 4.1 summarizes trading activity for March 18, 2002, the day of the 9:01 a.m. news release, as well as the March 19, 2002 trading day. Bid, ask, trade price and volume are provided. Also provided is the total cost of the shares for each trade. Purchase Point represents a neglected stock and the market (in)efficiency associated with neglected firms (i.e. neglected firm effects).

Figure 4.2 provides a graphic example of the impact of the news release on this thinly traded stock. (There were no trades, at all, for thirteen of the trading days from March 7 through June 3, 2002. These trading days have been removed for the purpose of generating this graphic representation).

For all practical purposes, Purchase Point had been a corporate shell for the prior three years. The news release raised the PPS from 2 cents to sixty-three cents (May 3, 2002), prior to the additional news release of a letter of intent (LOI) to purchase a firm for two and one-half million shares of Purchase Point stock. The effect of this May 7, 2002, (dilutive) news release is also presented in Fig. 4.2.

Prior to the May 7, 2002, news release, Purchase Point had provided fourteen positive news releases, relating to the progress of the sale of the firm's intangible assets (some of which were the same news releases, redistributed as many as three times each). These positive progress reports occurred on March 25th, April 18th and May 2nd. For all practical purposes, Purchase Point was "advertising" the upcoming sale of its intangible assets.

As Purchase Point provided these public information updates (i.e. advertising), the PPS increased (i.e. the price discount of this once generic stock declined). Just as advertising moves a product in a grocery store from the generic to the branded product, these news releases had a similar effect. When the news updates included potentially dilutive information, the stock price declined. A simple OLS regression model, using separate dummy variables for "good" news and "bad" news releases, as previously operationally defined, will statistically illustrate this point.

Table 4.1. Purchase Point Media Corporation Trading Activity for March 18–19, 2002.

Time	Bid	Ask	Trade	Volume	Total Cost
18-Mar-02					
7:31:49	$0.025	$0.055			
8:19:19	$0.025	$0.040			
9:01	NEWS				
11:37:58			$0.040	5,000	$200
11:38:23	$0.030	$0.040			
11:38:29	$0.030	$0.055			
11:38:34			$0.040	9,500	$380
12:26:30	$0.040	$0.055			
12:27:10			$0.055	5,000	$275
12:39:33			$0.055	5,000	$275
12:39:35	$0.045	$0.055			
12:39:45			$0.055	6,000	$330
12:39:48	$0.045	$0.080			
12:40:19			$0.080	5,000	$400
Breakin Sequence of rising B/A					
12:50:02	$0.090	$0.100			
12:50:29			$0.100	10,000	$1,000
12:50:33	$0.090	$0.130			
12:51:00			$0.100	5,000	$500
Breakin Sequence of rising B/A					
12:52:29	$0.120	$0.130			
12:52:47			$0.130	5,000	$650
Breakin Sequence of rising B/A					
12:53:31	$0.150	$0.170			
Remaining B/A not provided					
12:53:47			$0.130	5,000	$650
12:55:01			$0.130	5,000	$650
12:55:41			$0.130	5,000	$650
Daily Total				70,500	5,960
19-Mar-02					
7:23:32	$0.120	$0.150			
9:39:28			$0.150	5,000	$750
11:39:30			$0.180	15,000	$2,700
11:39:42			$0.160	10,000	$1,600
12:18:54			$0.130	10,000	$1,300
12:18:57			$0.130	2,000	$260
12:26:24			$0.120	2,600	$312
Daily Total				44,600	$6,922
Two Day Total				115,100	$12,882

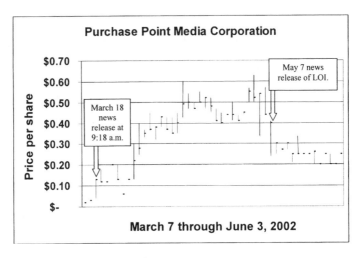

Fig. 4.2. Purchase Point Media Corporation Price per share.

An Empirical Test of Public Information Releases

Using the closing PPS as the dependent variable and dummy variables to separately represent a cumulative measure of good news (GDummy) and a
cumulative measure of bad news (BDummy) releases of information, Eq. (4.1)
and predicted signs of coefficients were developed, as follows:

$$PPS_i = \beta_0 + \beta_1 GDummy_i + \beta_2 BDummy_i + \varepsilon_i \qquad (4.1)$$

$$(+) \qquad\qquad (-)$$

The adjusted R-square was 0.669 (F-statistic = 61.55; p-value < 0.001) for the
60 trading day observations. Both coefficients were in the predicted direction
(GDummy at 11.1 and BDummy at –8.5) and both t-statistics were significant
(p-value < 0.001).

Figure 4.2 illustrates the effect of the initial and subsequent public news
releases of the sale of the firm's intangible assets ("good" news), which led to
significant increases in the PPS of Purchase Point stock. Please note that the
PPS of this security increased from $0.04 to more than $0.60, for a possible
1,400% return in approximately two months, though on relatively thin volume.
Alternatively, the subsequent public news release of the LOI and the dilutive
issuance of additional shares ("bad" news) resulted in a significant decline in
the PPS of Purchase Point common stock.

SUMMARY

This chapter included a simple case study or illustration of the value of public information for a thinly traded or (analyst) neglected security. Neglected firms are, by definition, information deficient. In the case of Purchase Point, the security enjoyed a PPS increase of approximately 1,400% over a two month period. The increase to more than $0.60 per share did not approach the anticipated value of approximately $2.50 per share, but only achieved approximately 25% of the anticipated value of the "advertised" value of the transaction on a PPS basis.

The failure of the security price to continue to increase further is likely to have been inhibited by the anticipated dilutive effects of the LOI news release or may represent a stock price discount more appropriately associated with the adverse selection (Chapter 2) or the neglected nature of this security. In any event, the price of the security has, since, declined to less than $0.04 per share by the end of the 2002 calendar year, as the absence of additional, supportive public information suggested that those responsible for driving the price of this security to 52-week highs may have fallen victim to moral hazard (Chapter 3).

The Purchase Point example was selected for its illustrative simplicity. It is, for all practical purposes, a corporate shell, a generic security (see Fig. 4.1) neglected by analysts (Arbel, 1985), but with a public information release that made it possible for investors or speculators to calculate an approximate return (Williams, 1998). The significant potential returns (Table 4.1 and Fig. 4.2) may explain why many individual or retail investors and day-traders are willing to speculate and accept the risks associated with trading these thinly traded and neglected micro-cap stocks. Chapter 5 will examine *private* information, including coverage of some of the Internet sites and related stock-tip and investment newsletters available for a fee (*private* information).

CHAPTER 5. PRIVATE INFORMATION

Balvers, McDonald, and Miller (1988) note that, with the exception of Merrill Lynch, none of the top five investment bankers had used a non-Big Eight[27] auditor more than once . . . (Mishra et al., 1998).

It is an established fact that inside information is used by the officers and directors in determining what price they are willing to accept or pay for the shares of their own corporations (Finnerty, 1976, p. 213).

Until 1961, trading by insiders in organized markets was almost always lawful (Easterbrook from Pratt & Zeckhauser, 1985, p. 82).

INTRODUCTION

Why do we study varying levels of market efficiency, and seek to reduce or eliminate levels of *hidden* (Chapter 3) or *private* (Chapter 4) information? French and Roll (1986, p. 5) explain the effects of private information on stock price stability:

> . . . private information is the principal factor behind high trading-time variances.

In their examination of how the market processes information, French and Roll (1986) concluded that a significant portion of the volatility in stock prices (1963 through 1982) during regular exchange trading hours was caused by mis-pricing (4–12%), but that the principal factor, as suggested by small return variances over exchange holidays and weekends, was *private* information.

Anecdotally, one might expect that the highly publicized cases of stock price manipulation by Enron and WorldCom, or the roles played by their auditor (Andersen) and underwriters/analysts (Merrill), following the bursting of the NASDAQ stock market bubble in April 2000, have reduced the status of our U.S. institutions, as well as the public's perception of accountants/auditors and financial analysts. We might have concluded that, prior to the broad dissemination of these events, opinions or information, publicly available from stock tip newsletters or from Internet-based stock-tip newsletter, represented a relatively inferior source of public or private information. However, these stock tip newsletters clearly disclose their compensation for news dissemination, usually in the form of free trading shares in the firms they tout. These same levels of disclosure were *not* apparent for many of the financial analysts, where their firms profited through underwriting fees. Therefore, sources of information available for free, via the Internet, may represent a reasonable substitute for the normal good or information previously relied upon and produced by both auditors and financial analysts.

This chapter will introduce some contemporary changes taking place with respect to *private* information, including the SEC's Regulation FD (Fair Disclosure) and the Sarbanes-Oxley Act of 2002. Examples of research, relating to private (and public) information flows, and their value in generating abnormal returns, are also provided. Stock tip newsletters and fee-based services are also introduced. Some of the more-established fee-based sources of information, like *Value Line* and *Moody's*, have previously been studied by academics. A listing of lesser known fee-based sources or stock-tip newsletters is provided for those interested in extending these research methodologies to more contemporary sources of private information. These fee-based sources of information have enjoyed increased favor in the aftermath of Enron, WorldCom, Andersen, and Merrill. This trend may continue, as large Wall Street brokerages are forced to separate their (otherwise unprofitable) research services from their more profitable underwriting and commission-based services (see Chapter 4).

REGULATION FD[28]

Originally proposed in December 1999, the SEC issued Regulation FD in August 2000 (effective October 2000). This was one of three new rules in the SEC release "Selective Disclosure and Insider Trading" Nos 33-7781 and 34-43154, which affected how firms communicate with market professionals and the investing public. The objective of the SEC was to level the informational playing field, preventing firms from releasing market-sensitive information, first, to Wall Street insiders, before public announcements were made.

However, Davies and Canes (1978) examined and provided evidence on the effects of secondary (public) dissemination of information of stock analyst recommendations after primary (private) disseminations had been made to analysts' clients. They found that the secondary dissemination significantly affected stock prices, and there was no reversal in the subsequent 20 trading days.

From a market efficiency perspective, Regulation FD is intended to reduce *private* information and/or to quickly and efficiently transform *private* information into *public* information. As Fig. 5.1 suggests, Regulation FD eliminated

Pre-Regulation FD:

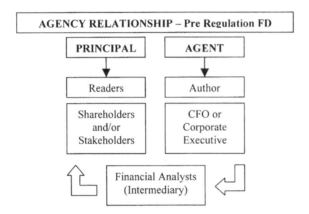

Post-Regulation FD:

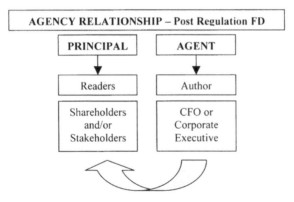

Fig. 5.1. Pre- and Post-Regulation FD.

the securities analyst as an informational intermediary or middleman and shorten the temporary status of *private* information.

Generally, CFOs and other corporate executives are required to disclose information (e.g. press releases and conference calls) in a timely manner. The conference calls are, increasingly, open to small investors and transmitted over the Internet. This method of information dissemination supplements less timely Form 8K filings with the SEC.

THE SARBANES-OXLEY ACT OF 2002

On July 30, 2002, President Bush signed the Sarbanes-Oxley Act of 2002. The Public Company Accounting Reform and Investor Protection Act of 2002 (S.2673) was introduced by Sarbanes, from the Committee on Banking, Housing, and Urban Affairs, on June 25, 2002. The stated objectives were to:

- Improve quality and transparency in financial reporting and independent audits and accounting services for public companies;
- Create a Public Company Accounting Oversight Board (POB);
- Enhance the standard setting process for accounting practices;
- Strengthen the independence of firms that audit public companies;
- Increase corporate responsibility and the usefulness of corporate financial disclosure;
- Protect the objectivity and independence of securities analysts; and
- Improve SEC resources and oversight.

EXAMPLES OF ACADEMIC RESEARCH INTO THE VALUE OF PRIVATE INFORMATION

Huth and Maris (1992) found that *Wall Street Journal* "Heard on the Street" recommendations produced statistically, but not economically, significant stock price movements. Academics have also investigated the information and predictive value of *Value Line*, a fee-based source of information, and *Moody's* ratings.

The "Value Line enigma" is the phrase used to describe the excess returns generated by common stock recommendations made by *Value Line* (Black, 1973; Holloway, 1981; Copeland & Mayers, 1982; Stickel, 1985; Peterson, 1987, 1995). With respect to the speed of adjustment, Stickel found that the price of individual securities adjusted over a multiple-day period. Lewis et al. (1997) found that the performance of *Value Line* in the area of convertible bonds was also good, but only in identifying poor convertible debt performance.

In their examination into "the information value of bond ratings, "Kliger and Sarig (2000) found that *Moody's*[29] bond ratings contained price-relevant information. Their study, using Moody's, concluded that debt value increased (decreased) and equity value fell (rose) when Moody's announced better-

(worse-) than-expected ratings. These rating changes were refinements of the *signals* that *Moody's* had previously sent regarding its assessment of default risk. Previously, Goh and Ederington (1993), also using *Moody's*, had found that downgrades associated with degenerating financial conditions conveyed new negative information, but that downgrades due simply to changes in firms' leverage did not.

Nunn et al. (1983) distinguished between the trades of different insiders. They suggested improved returns could be achieved by focusing on stock purchase decisions by CEOs and directors, along with sell decisions by directors and beneficial owners (p. 22). Lorie and Niederhoffer (1968) had examined insider trades and found them to generate abnormal returns. However, individual investors attempting to trade on this information, which is now available (in a time-delayed format) on the Internet, are not likely to be successful in generating abnormal returns (Rozeff & Zaman, 1988).

In his extension of an earlier work by Penman (1982), Typpo (1996) examined the pre-/post-Insider Trading Sanctions Act (ITSA) period (1982–1987), using the August 10, 1984 breakpoint. The earlier work, by Penman, found evidence of informed insider trading activity prior to earnings forecasts (1967–1974). However, Typpo found evidence of insider buying, at abnormally high levels, prior to good news earnings forecasts. Alternatively, his study did not detect insider selling at abnormally high levels prior to bad news forecasts. Finally, he did not observe the anticipated, post-ITSA reduction in insider trading prior to forecast releases.

Seyhun (1986) also presented evidence that insiders are able to predict abnormal future stock price changes:

> Insiders purchase stock prior to an abnormal rise in stock prices and sell stock prior to an abnormal decline in stock prices (p. 210).

And Hyman (1999) provided linkage between information and market failures:

> Market failures may result from incomplete information (pp. 66–68).

> *Rational ignorance* is the lack of information about public issues that results because the marginal cost of obtaining the information exceeds the apparent marginal benefit of doing so[30] (p. 167).

The Information Content of Private Placements

Private placements of equity, often selling at substantial discounts, are associated with positive abnormal returns (Hertzel & Smith, 1993). Just as the discount associated with neglected firms (see Chapter 4) may result in abnormally high returns, these private placements may signal, publicly, the results of costly gathering of private information to avoid adverse selection and additional monitoring to avoid moral hazard, particularly for smaller firms. These discounts may range from 30% to 50% (SEC, 1971; Arneson, 1981a, b; Johnson & Racette, 1981; Freidlob, 1983).

Hertzel and Smith (1993), in an extension of the works of Myers and Majluf (1984) and Wruck (1989), suggest that the willingness of investors to engage in private placements, combined with management's decision to select this option as an alternative to a public issue, signals to the market management's belief that the firm is undervalued (p. 460). As an illustration, Knobias commonly provides these types of information releases

Hertzel and Smith (1993) make the following additional points, with respect to private placements of securities, the information hypothesis, and the ownership structure hypothesis, from the literature and from their own study:

- Resale restrictions (e.g. collars) provide time for private information to become public, and may be associated with larger discounts and information effects.
- Large blocks, placed with a single investor at a premium, enhance signal credibility, as anticipated future monitoring is not diluted.
- Sales to management/insiders should be associated with lower discounts, since there is little or no information asymmetry.
- Changes in ownership structure, resulting from private placements, may imply increased monitoring.

Voluntary Disclosures of Information

Some firms voluntarily disclose more information to the public than is required to comply with financial and accounting regulations. In an effort to explain this phenomenon, Kim (1993) examined these disparate disclosure policies. Examining a case of continuous cost functions and heterogeneous shareholders, his analytical study concluded that better informed shareholders preferred less disclosure, when compared to relatively uninformed shareholders. This, he concluded, was a function of shareholder differences in adverse selection and risk preferences, as well as shareholder differences in relative monitoring costs and the risk of moral hazard.

Extending the work of Diamond (1985), the foundational and opposing externalities examined by Kim (1993, pp. 747–748), comprised the hypotheses that:

- Disclosure provides for greater information symmetry among investors.
- Disclosure reduces the costs/benefits of private information acquisition.

The Agency Costs of Free Cash Flow

In what he characterized as "the agency costs of free cash flow," an information-based problem, Jensen (1986) recalls that the free flow of economic resources to their highest and best use is required if these resources are to be used efficiently. First, executives may not posses the necessary cost information for their own firm, or that of competitors, to draw conclusions with respect to their firm's placement in the relative high/low cost producer hierarchy. This represents a *managerial* or internal control failure. Second, even when this information is available, they may resist exiting an industry when their firm's large, positive cash flows make it possible to defer exit (Jensen, 1993). This represents a failure of the agency relationship (e.g. moral hazard), as executives fail to act in the best interest of shareholders.

Furthermore, Jensen identified the failure of internal control as originating from the board of directors. The BOD hires, fires, and compensates the CEO, but the CEO may control the flow of information, and the agenda, of items and their examination by the BOD. Furthermore, the contemporary BOD may lack the necessary financial expertise to advise management or take action (Jensen, 1993, pp. 863–864). These problems may be exacerbated when the CEO is also the Chairman of the BOD (p. 866).

Recall that management compensation is most directly associated with problems of moral hazard (Chapter 3), providing incentives (or disincentives) that affect the managerial decision to provide clear signals. If management possesses (and maintains) private information, not publicly made available to the market, the additional problem of adverse selection (Chapter 2) exists. This, in turn, affects the development of optimal compensation contracts (John & John, 1993).

Leveraged Buyouts (LBOs) Going Public

In an examination of a sample of 62 reversals of LBOs (going public between 1983 and 1987) Degeorge and Zeckhauser (1993) found that the market tends to anticipate their observed pattern of superior pre-public offering performance, followed by disappointing post-public offering performance. They posit "inspection period striving" (i.e. pre-public offering) and/or "performance borrowing" (i.e. from post-public offering periods) as possible hidden action- or information asymmetry-based explanations, increasing the risk of adverse selection.

Signaling models assume that managers have better, more timely or private information. Barclay and Smith (1995b, pp. 908–909), in the context of the priority of claims structure of corporate liabilities (i.e. capitalized leases, secured debt, ordinary debt, subordinated debt, preferred stock, and, finally, common stock), operationalize the information asymmetry hypothesis:

> Signaling models generally imply that undervalued firms will issue claims with high priority since they are the least undervalued, and overvalued firms will issue claims with low priority since they are the most overvalued . . .

Using the firm's abnormal earnings as a proxy for firm quality, they assumed that high-quality (under-valued) firms had positive future abnormal earnings and low-quality (over-valued) firms had negative future abnormal earnings. Their findings supported the information asymmetry hypothesis, statically, but the economic impact was modest, at only 2.5% for secured debt. Other results were mixed or failed to support the hypothesis.

The Growth in Mutual Funds

According to Gruber (1996, p. 783):

> Mutual funds represent one of the fastest growing types of financial intermediary in the American economy. The question remains as to why mutual funds and in particular actively managed mutual funds have grown so fast, when their performance on average has been inferior to that of index funds.

This growth occurred despite previously published evidence that the returns for index funds are comparable (Ippolito, 1989).

The growth in mutual funds have contributed to increased conditions of information asymmetry, as the monitoring of corporations by shareholders had been diluted via the increase in the establishment of an intermediary mutual or pension fund manager (agents), acting on behalf of those invested in the mutual or pension fund (principals). Only in the most severe cases, beginning in the late 2001 and early 2002 period when money flows into mutual and pension funds for securities investments became negative, have the larger mutual and pension funds actively engaged regulatory agencies on behalf of their client-investors.

Research & Development (R&D)

Aboody and Lev (2000) found that insider gains, where insiders are operationally defined as "corporate insiders" in the 1934 Securities and Exchange Act to include corporate officers, directors, and owners of 10% or more of any equity class of securities, in R&D-intensive firms were higher than those for firms without R&D (1985 through 1997). They concluded that insiders were taking advantage of information on planned R&D budgets. Therefore, their findings support the hypothesis that R&D expenditure levels represent a major contributor to information asymmetry.

INVESTMENT NEWSLETTERS AND STOCK TIP (PRIVATE) INFORMATION

... two decades ago, Wall Street and academic finance were famously unable to agree on anything. But they did see eye to eye on the worthlessness of investment newsletters (Hulbert, 2002).

According to Mark Hulbert,[31] editor of the *Hulbert Financial Digest*:

... Hulbert Financial Digest has shown conclusively that Wall Street analysts on average perform no better than the typical newsletter.

For researchers interested in pursuing scientific testing and examination of either (or both) pre- and post-Regulation FD results that may have been achieved by varying levels of *private* and *public* information, Table 5.1 provides a listing, as of May 2002, of stock tip newsletters, coverage and subscription costs. This listing was developed from the *CBS MarketWatch* web site and represents the more than 150 newsletters ($N = 152$ for a mean cost of $230 per proprietary newsletter), monitored by Mark Hulbert. Dated or archived subscriptions may be available at significantly reduced costs for longitudinal statistical analyses.

Replacing Historical Beta (β)

In CAPM, Beta (β) represents a measure of *historical* market-related risk. In papers published in 1983 (Strebel) and 1984 (Carvell and Strebel), it was suggested that this *historical* emphasis could be replaced by an anticipated measure, adjusting the historical measure by an estimation risk, using analyst forecasts (Eq. (5.1)), as follows:

$$\beta_n = [\beta_h^2 + \beta_e^2] \tag{5.1}$$

where β_n is the adjusted beta measure, β_h is the historical beta measure, and β_e is the systematic estimation risk measure. Citing the earlier work of Strebel (1983), they explain how the coefficient of variance in the earnings forecasts was used to calculate β_e. Though Carvell and Strebel used *I/B/E/S*, there is no

Table 5.1. A Summary of Selected Stock/Investment Tip Newsletters.[1]

No		Name	S	G	B	F	MF	O	I	Fut	PM	Ut	Cost
1		2 for 1 Stock Split	X										$90
2		Aden Forecast, The	X	X	X	X							$195
3	*	All Star Fund Trader					X						$249
4	*	Bernie Schaeffer's Option Advisor						X					$200
5	*	BI Research	X										$110
6		Big Picture, The	X										$ –
7	*	Blue Chip Investor, The	X										$249
8	*	Bob Carlson's Retirement Watch					X						$72
9	*	Bob J. Brinker's Marketimer					X						$185
10		Bowser Report, The	X										$ 48
11	*	Buy Low, The											UNK
12	*	Buyback Letter, The	X										$125
13		Buyback Premium Portfolio, The	X										$948
14	*	Cabot Market Letter, The	X										$99
15		Cabot's Sector Inspector	X										$97
16	*	California Technology Stock Letter	X										$599
17		C-E Country Fund Report					X						$190
18	*	C-E Fund Digest & Real Estate Securities											UNK
19	*	Charles M. LoLoggia's Superstock Investor	X										$395
20	*	Chartist Mutual Fund Letter, The					X						$100
21	*	Chartist, The	X										$175
22	*	Contrarian's View, The	X										$39
23	*	Coolcat Explosive Small Cap Growth Stock Rpt	X										$139
24		Crawford Perspectives	X	X	X								$250
25		Daily Premium Sound Sector Strategy											$199
26	*	Dennis Slothower's On The Money					X						$119
27		Dennis Slothower's Stealth $tock$	X										$198
28	*	Dines Letter, The	X	X									$195
29		Donoghue's Power Portfolio					X						$999
30	*	Dow Theory Forecasts	X										$259
31	*	Dow Theory Letters	X	X	X								$250

Table 5.1. Continued.

No		Name	S	G	B	F	MF	O	I	Fut	PM	Ut	Cost
32	*	Elliott Wave Financial Forecast, The	X	X	X								$228
33		Equities Special Situations	X										$150
34	*	Equity Fund Outlook					X						$125
35		Eric Dany's Stock Prospector	X										$129
36	*	Eric Kobren's Fidelity Insight					X						$177
37	*	Eric Kobren's FundsNet Insight					X						$177
38	*	F.X.C. Newsletter, The	X		X		X						$139
39	*	Fabian's Sector Investing					X						$399
40		Fidelity Growth Investor	X										$295
41	*	Fidelity Independent Advisor					X						$99
42	*	Fidelity Investor					X						$179
43	*	Fidelity Monitor					X						$116
44		Fidelity Navigator					X						$99
45	*	Fidelity Sector Investor					X						$399
46		Fidelity Sector Trader					X						$480
47		Forbes Special Situations Survey	X										$695
48		Forbes/Andrew Seybold's Wireless Outlook	X										$299
49		Forbes/Lehmann Income Securities Investor	X		X				X				$195
50		Ford Investment Review	X										$144
51	*	fredhager.com	X										$300
52	*	FundAdvice.com					X						$125
53	*	Futures Hotline/MF Timer					X			X			$600
54		Gerald Appel's Systems and Forecasts					X						$225
55	*	Gerald Perrit's MF Letter					X						$89
56	*	Gilder Technology Report, The	X										$295
57		Global Investing	X				X						$99
58	*	Good Fortune					X						$147
59		Granville Market Letter Inc, The	X					X					$250
60		Graphic Fund Forecaster					X						$35
61	*	Growth Fund Guide					X						$99
62	*	Growth Stock Outlook	X										$235
63	*	Ind Advisor for Vanguard Investors, The					X						$199
64	*	Index Rx					X						$149
65	*	Individual Investor Special Situations Rpt											UNK

Table 5.1. Continued.

No	Name	S	G	B	F	MF	O	I	Fut	PM	Ut	Cost
66 *	Insiders, The											UNK
67	International Harry Schultz Letter, The	X	X	X					X			$285
68 *	InvesTech Market Analyst	X										$190
69 *	InvesTech Mutual Fund Advisor					X						$190
70 *	Investment Quality Trends	X										$310
71 *	Investment Reporter, The	X										$279
72 *	Investor's Guide to C-E Funds					X						$475
73 *	Investors Intelligence	X				X	X					$184
74	Jack Adamo's Insiders Plus	X										$300
75 *	John Dessauer's Investor's World	X			X	X						$149
76	John Myers' Outstanding Investments	X										$ 99
77	Kenjol Alpha Timer					X						$399
78	Linde Equity Rpt	X										$185
79 *	Listed Insight	X										$95
80	Livingoffthemarket.com	X										$720
81 *	Louis Navellier's Blue Chip Growth Letter	X										$249
82 *	Louis Rukeyser's Mutual Funds					X						$96
83 *	Louis Rukeyser's Wall Street	X		X		X						$99
84	Lowry's Power & Velocity Ratings	X										$300
85 *	MAIC Investor Adivsory Service											UNK
86 *	Mark Skousen's Forecasts & Strategies	X				X						$187
87 *	Market Logic											UNK
88 *	Market Radar, The	X										$150
89 *	Martin Weiss' Safe Money Report	X				X	X					$189
90 *	Maverick Advisor					X						$349
91 *	Medical Technology Stock Letter	X										$320
92	Merit Advisors					X						$300
93 *	MF Forecaster											UNK
94 *	MF Prospector					X						$129
95 *	MFs Magazine					X						$20
96	Minogue Stock Index Futures Hotline								X			$250
97	Moneyflow					X						$48

Table 5.1. Continued.

No	Name	S	G	B	F	MF	O	I	Fut	PM	Ut	Cost
98	Moneyletter					X						$150
99 *	Morningstar Mutual Funds					X						$425
100 *	Morningstar Stock Investor	X										$89
101 *	Motley Fool	X										$ –
102 *	MPT Review	X										$995
103	mutualfundstrategist.com					X						$95
104	NAIC Investor Adivsory Service	X										$155
105	Nate's Notes	X										$150
106	National Investor, The	X										$95
107 *	National Trendlines	X	X	X		X						$75
108 *	Natural Contrarian	X										$390
109 *	No-Load Fund Analyst					X						$225
110 *	No-Load Fund Investor, The					X						$139
111 *	No-Load Fund*X					X						$149
112 *	No-Load MF Selections & Timing Newsletter					X						$180
113	No-Load Portfolios					X						$ 89
114 *	Oberweis Report, The	X										$169
115 *	OTC Insight	X										$295
116 *	Outlook, The	X										UNK
117 *	Oxford Club, The	X		X				X	X			$125
118	P.Q. Wall Forecast Inc.	X			X							$198
119	PAD System Rpt, The	X				X						$ 69
120 *	Paul Chapman's Hidden Value Stocks											UNK
121 *	Personal Finance	X										$ 97
122 *	Peter Dag Portfolio Strategy & Mgmt, The	X				X						$295
123 *	Peter Eliades' Stockmarket Cycles					X						$252
124 *	Professional Timing Service	X	X	X								$185
125 *	Prudent Speculator, The	X										$295
126 *	Pure Fundamentalist, The	X										$195
127 *	Reminiscences	X										$225
128 *	Richard E. Band's Profitable Investing	X		X		X						$295
129	Richard Geist's Strategic Investing	X										$157
130 *	Richard Schmidt's Stellar Stock Report	X										$199
131 *	Richard Young's Intelligence Report	X				X						$199

Table 5.1. Continued.

No	Name	S	G	B	F	MF	O	I	Fut	PM	Ut	Cost
132 *	Roger Conrad's Utility Forecaster											UNK
133	Ruff Times, The	X		X		X				X		$ 69
134	Sagami's Scientific Investing	X										$198
135 *	Sagami's Stocks on the Move											UNK
136 *	Sector Fund Timer					X						$699
137	Select Investor, The					X						$100
138	Sharon A. Parker's Undiscovered Stocks	X										$189
139	Short On Value	X										$199
140	Sound Advice	X				X						$165
141 *	Sound Mind Investing					X						$ 69
142 *	Spear Report, The	X										$297
143	Standard & Poor's Outlook	X										$298
144 *	Stock Market Leaders	X										$199
145	Stock Trader's Almanac Investor	X										$195
146	Sturza's Medical Investment Letter	X										$360
147	Successful Investor, The	X										$ 72
148	Sy Harding's Street Smart Rpt	X	X	X		X						$225
149	Tech Stock Insights	X										$ 99
150 *	Technology Investing	X										$345
151 *	Timer Digest	X				X						$225
152 *	Todd Market Forecast	X	X	X								$195
153	Top Down Market Forecast	X				X						$100
154 *	Turnaround Letter, The	X										$195
155	U.S. Investment Rpt	X										$269
156 *	Ultimate Timing Service					X						$499
157 *	Undiscovered Tech Stocks											UNK
158	Utility Forecaster										X	$129
159	Vanguard Navigator, The					X						$ 99
160 *	Vickers Weekly Insider Report											UNK
161 *	VL Convertibles Survey, The	X		X								$525
162	VL Inv'mt Survey – Expanded Ed, The	X										$249
163 *	VL Inv'mt Survey, The	X										$598
164 *	VL Inv'nt Survey – Small and Mid-Cap Ed, The											UNK
165 *	VL Mutual Fund Survey, The					X						$295
166 *	VL Special Situations Service, The	X										$495

Table 5.1. Continued.

No	Name	S	G	B	F	MF	O	I	Fut	PM	Ut	Cost
166 *	VL Special Situations Service, The	X										$495
167 *	VP: An Ind Report for Vanguard Investors											UNK
168 *	Wall Street Digest, The											UNK
169 *	Wall Street Winners											UNK
170 *	Zacks Advisor											UNK

[1] *Note:* As of May 2002, the published cost for all of the above newsletters is $34,992. Legend: * = $25 fee for newsletter profile, B = Bonds ($N = 16$), C-E = Closed-End, Ed = Edition, F = Foreign, Fut = Futures ($N = 4$), G = Gold ($N = 10$), I = nterest Rates ($N = 2$), Ind = Independent, Inv'mt = Investment, MF = Mutual Fund ($N = 67$), Mgmt = Management, O = Options ($N = 4$), PM = Precious Metals ($N = 1$), Rpt = Report, S = Stocks ($N = 98$), UNK = Unknown, Ut = Utilities ($N = 1$), VL = Value Line and VP = Vantage Point.

reason why stock tip newsletters could not be used by researchers to develop comparable measures for hypothesis testing.

Knobias

Another source of private information is Knobias.[32] Founded as pennyPI.com, LLC in August 1998, Knobias launched its first website in December 1999. They provide intraday, real-time surveillance and alerting services on all U.S. securities, with special emphasis on NASDAQ NM, NASDAQ SC, OTC BB and PinkSheets securities. Knobias also provides delayed information (e.g. 10 minutes) through COMTEX at no cost, but promote their fee-based subscription or premium services with links to their web site for real-time alerts. A typical Knobias alert might be triggered by a significant increase or decrease in volume or PPS (or block trades, the size of which may suggest institutional buying or selling) for a security and include a summary of recent news, SEC filings and stock chat message board sentiment, speculation/rumor or information.

Thomson Financial

Thomson Financial/First Call, part of The Thompson Corporation (TSE: TOC), is another prominent provider of private or fee-based information.[33] Perhaps best known for their focus on insider trades (e.g. SEC filings of Form 144) and the monitoring of retail vs. institutional trading activity, representatives of Thomson Financial are regularly featured on CNBC.

The Thomson Corporation completed the purchase/merger and integration of First Call and I/B/E/S (1971–) by way of their acquisition of the Primark Corporation (LSE: PMK) in September 2000. Analyst forecasts, available from I/B/E/S, collect consensus earnings estimates, and these analyst forecasts have been used for academic and professional journal articles, published in The *Journal of Finance* (finance – academic), *The Journal of Accounting Research* (accounting – academic), *The Journal of Portfolio Management, The Financial Analysts Journal, The Journal of Investing* and others. As of May 2002, brokers were asked to continue to deliver their analyst estimates to both First Call and I/B/E/S.)

Weiss Ratings

Weiss Ratings News provides a variety of fee-based reports on brokerage firms.[34] In a May 14, 2002 report (Weiss, 2002), their analysis of the largest retail brokerage firms (1997 through 2001) per million customer accounts suggested that the worst records were held by Prudential Securities, Inc., Ameritrade, Inc., and U.S. Bancorp Piper Jaffray, Inc. The best records, or those firms with the lowest measures of abuse per customer account, were Fidelity Brokerage Services, Credit Suisse First Boston, and Edward D. Jones & Co. Weiss provides a brokerage firm safety rating (e.g. A, B, C), much like those provided by Moody's and Standard & Poor's for debt.

SUMMARY

Capitalism is dependent on economic growth, while economic growth is dependent on the free market mechanisms that allow economic resources to rise to their highest and best use. For economic resources to flow, freely, to their highest and best use, *publicly* available information must be available and reliable. If publicly released information is flawed, or varies significantly from information that is hidden or only privately held, the free flow of economic resources to their highest and best use will be perverted. Regulation FD and the Sarbanes-Oxley Act of 2002 are intended to reduce market inefficiencies by reducing recent historical levels of private or hidden information.

As Fig. 5.2 suggests, the speed of security price reaction is the slowest for the weak form of market efficiency. The weak form of market efficiency presumes the existence of private or hidden information, which may not be reflected in a securities' price.

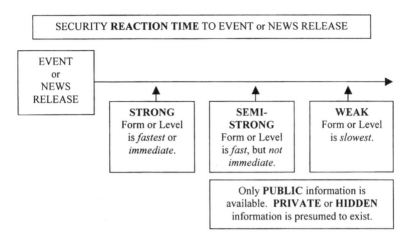

Fig. 5.2. The Speed of Security Price Reaction to the Release of Information Under the Three (Nested) Forms or Levels of Market Efficiency.

The speed of security price reaction is also less than immediate for the semi-strong form of market efficiency, but is faster than that for the weak form of market efficiency. The semi-strong form of market efficiency also presumes the existence of private or hidden information, which may not be reflected in a securities' price.

Finally, the speed of security price reaction is fastest or immediate for the strong form of market efficiency, where private or hidden information is presumed to be immediately reflected in the price of a security. Though few would suggest that this level of market efficiency exists, its' pursuit remains desirable.

The popularity of proprietary newsletters, contained in Table 5.1, has increased in recent years. Just as academic researchers have studied the information value of *Value Line* and *Moody's'*, these relatively recent newsletters represent fee-based sources of private information suitable for hypothesis formation and testing. *Knobias, Thompson Financial* and *Weiss Ratings* represent Internet-based sources of information that have gained increased popularity with both individual and institutional investors in recent years. *Hulbert Financial Digest* may represent one of the most notable sources, as his services monitor and track the performance of many fee-based newsletters.

SECTION III. THEORY INTEGRATION: INFORMATION ASYMMETRY

. . . in the days of the free market . . . there was accountability to the stockholder . . . the Carnegies, the Melons, the men that built this great industrial empire made sure of it because it was their money at stake. Today, management has no stake in the company (Michael Douglas aka Gordon Gekko in the film, Wall Street).

INTRODUCTION

The Chairman of the Federal Reserve, Alan Greenspan, testified before the House on the Economy on February 27, 2002. In response to questions, relating to the Enron case and the general erosion of public confidence in corporate governance issues, Greenspan suggested focus on the structure of relations between parties and alluded to the following:

- The current status of corporate governance is a function of failures to provide for appropriately positioned incentive structures.
- There remains a great need to create incentives for CEOs to function solely in best interest of shareholders. Achieving this objective will lead to the resolution of other, related issues.
- Under the current structure, directors work for shareholders and CEOs work for the Board of Directors (BOD). The CEO no longer works directly for shareholders, but indirectly, through the BOD.
- There has been a shift in the locus of control from the shareholder to the CEO via a shift from the control of the corporation focus to an investment focus, with the stock of the corporation, in the contemporary period, representing only an investment vehicle.
- If the CEO runs the firm in the best interest of the shareholders, corporate governance issues are resolved. Therefore, the critically important issue and solution is to find a structure where the CEO's interest is congruent with those of the long-term shareholders or to identify areas where CEO/-

shareholder divergence has evolved and modify the incentives to reverse or eliminate this incentive divergence.

- In achieving the above objectives, caution should be exercised with respect to presumptions as to the independence of those on the BOD. If everyone on the BOD is independent, competing power factors (e.g. factions) may evolve and corporate governance may suffer. There exists an *asymmetry of information* (emphasis added) between inside and outside directors that will never be fully resolved.
- Those serving on the BOD may not know what to ask the CEO or CFO and, even if they did know what to ask, the CEO and CFO may not be forthcoming to the BOD.

Generally, the academic literature presumes that the agent is risk averse. The principal is typically presumed to be the dominant party and, further, presumed to be risk neutral. Changes in corporate governance, occurring over generations, leave us in a contemporary state where shareholder control is rarely in a limited number of hands, where the directors are appointed and work for the shareholders, and where the CEO is appointed and works for the directors.

THE INFORMATION ASYMMETRY MODEL[35]

The typical information asymmetry model (Copeland & Galai, 1983; Glosten & Milgrom, 1985) assumes that there are liquidity traders and informed (information processing) traders. Informed traders trade based on private informational advantages. Liquidity-motivated trades result from factors other than informational advantages.

Market makers (MMs) generate losses when trading with informed traders, but recover these losses through the bid-ask spread. These models suggest that increased information asymmetry will result in wider bid-ask spreads. A specialist, anticipating increased probability of facing an informed trader in advance of an earnings release, will result in a widened adverse selection component of the bid-ask spread. In these models, information asymmetry risk can increase with increases in either the proportion of informed traders or the precision of their information. During periods of an unusually high number of trades, the spread is widened to protect against informed investors (Easley & O'Hara, 1992).

Furthermore, some informed market participants (e.g. financial analysts or large shareholders) process public information into private information, generating a comparative informational advantage over the specialist, since they are better able to produce superior assessments of the firm's performance on the basis of these earnings announcements (Kim & Verrecchia, 1994).

The inventory holding cost component of the bid-ask spread represents compensation to the specialist for the risks associated with non-diversification. Earnings announcements are typically accompanied by both higher trading activity and higher volatility (Bamber, 1986; Lee, 1992; Lee et al., 1993). This increased exposure to risk leads the specialist or MM to widen the bid-ask spread, though economies of scale may lead them to decrease this spread in percentage terms (Copeland & Galai, 1983).

CHAPTER 6. SUMMARY AND INTEGRATION OF THEORY

Market failures may result from incomplete information (Hyman, 1999, pp. 66–68).

INTRODUCTION

Section I and Fig. I.1 introduced the basic principal-agent problem. Different incentives and the absence of goal congruence, the risk-averse nature of agents and the costly nature of monitoring to identify hidden information are among the problem components.

Chapters 2 and 3 addressed adverse selection (pre-contractual) and moral hazard (post-contractual) (Figs 2.1, 2.2 and 2.3). The risks associated with both are not unlike those introduced in *financial* (financial leverage) and *managerial* (operating leverage) accounting disciplines, where the former represents apparent or public information and the latter represents non-public or private information (Figs 2.4 and 3.1).

As we progress past the post-Enron era, increased monitoring is likely to provide one solution to audit or market failures that may very well be the result of absentee ownership. In recent decades, large shareholders have been replaced by pension and mutual funds, and the monitoring levels that have declined over this period have failed to offset contemporary failures by both auditors and financial analysts to keep separate their roles as providers of assurance services (external or financial) and that of advocacy (internal or managerial) (Figs 3.2 and 3.3).

Information asymmetry: (1) increases transaction costs;[36] which leads to; (2) increases in the required rate of return; and (3) a reduction in the value of equity securities. Buyers and sellers of financial instruments, including equities, want to: (1) reveal information (information *symmetry*) to create value; or (2) conceal information (information *asymmetry*) to capture value. In the case of Enron and WorldCom, auditors and financial analysts facilitated conditions of increased information asymmetry and reduced market efficiency.

Section II and Fig. II.1 provide a basic framework for the examination of three forms or levels of market efficiency. The strong form (or level) represents a theoretically desirable and a practically unachievable target, where security prices reflect both public and private information.

Chapters 4 and 5 addressed public and private information, respectively. Historically, public information releases have included the opinions of independent auditors and financial analysts, though contemporary scandals (e.g. Enron, Andersen and Merrill) have reduced individual investor confidence in these sources of public information. In an effort to restore public confidence, Regulation FD and the Sarbanes-Oxley Act of 2002 represent highly publicized Government actions targeted at reducing the control and manipulation of both public and private information flows.

LINKAGE BETWEEN SIGNALS (AGENCY THEORY) AND HISTORICAL INFORMATION (EMH)

Where hidden or private information is presumed to remain hidden or private, both weak and semi-strong levels of market efficiency apply. Therefore, both weak and semi-strong levels of market efficiency are consistent with the condition of information asymmetry. Alternatively, the strong level of market efficiency is not consistent with conditions of information asymmetry. Still, to the extent practicable, the pursuit of stronger levels of market efficiency is desirable.

The use of signals in research, addressing agency problems and those of information asymmetry, is also consistent with both weak and semi-strong form levels of market efficiency (Cataldo & Savage, 2000, p. 22). The weak form of market efficiency is, perhaps, the most easily associated with signaling. Characterized as technical analysis (TA), a method used by chartists, only historical price and volume information is used. Similarly, the semi-strong level of market efficiency uses this historical information, but includes other publicly available information. Again, the strong level of market efficiency does not apply, since even the insider filing of a form 144 with the SEC comprises a public information release.

In the context of surprises/signals and the EMH, O'Brien (1988) and Ou and Penman (1989) examined surprises in event studies under the weak form of market efficiency, while Stober (1992) examined surprises/signals more closely associated with the semi-strong or strong form of market efficiency; here, the former were based on earnings or fundamental measures, whereas the latter were based on financial analyst forecasts (see Fig. 6.1).

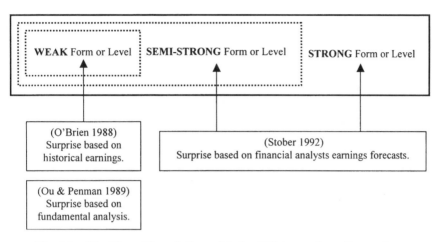

Fig. 6.1.   The Three (Nested) Forms Market Efficiency: Some Research on
Surprises/Signals.

Legal Theory and Literature Applications

Where principals and agents can contract in advance, or where principals can easily monitor the work of agents, regulation is not necessary and may even become a costly hindrance and/or may be potentially harmful. However, where these extreme conditions are not present, conduct regulation may become necessary to control agency costs. Regulatory need is, therefore, a function of the level of information asymmetry, detected in the market in which the relevant principals and agents operate.

In the case of an attorney-client relationship, the client is the principal and the attorney is the agent, where the attorney is hired to perform a function on the client's behalf. Generally, as is the case in all principal-agent relationships, the attorney/agent has some incentive to pursue his/her own interests, which may include shirking or the provision of substandard work.

In addition to the principal-agent relationship, present between the client and the attorney, each may also be involved in principal-agent relationships with other principals and agents. For example, the attorney's relationship with his/her law firm and the client's relationship with his/her corporation represent an agency relationship.

Principals can guard against poor performance by closely monitoring the work of the agent or by doing the work themselves. Of course, this option defeats the original purpose of the agency relationship. Furthermore, higher levels of information asymmetry result in higher costs of monitoring the agent. For example, consider the case where a corporation hires an in-house legal staff to monitor the work of the external law firm. Yet this is precisely what many corporations have done.

Generally, the principal-agent relationship implies (or expressly provides for) a traditional fiduciary relationship, which is present when one party is duty-bound to represent the best interests of the other party, to the extent that relevant matters fall within the scope of the parties' relationship. The fiduciary relationship imposes the highest duty available under the law.

The agent is duty-bound to act with the care and skill standard to his/her locality (or industry) and to exercise any special skills he/she possesses. The agent must also make reasonable efforts to provide the principal with desirable information that is (or may become) relevant to anticipated or existing transactions or relationships. Finally, the agent must obey any reasonable instructions provided by the principal.

Generally, a contributory negligence defense may be ineffective in the case of a principal-agent relationship. The principal is entitled to rely on the agent's care and skill. And, to the extent that the principal relies on the agent's advice with regularity, the agent may be duty-bound to inform the principal of certain facts and other matters, reasonably anticipated to become of importance.

Teams may solve the agency problem, as they may monitor, supervise, and oversee incentives. However, the Internet and the "new economy" present conditions of information asymmetry between principals and agents that is more severe than that experienced in the traditional "brick-and-mortar" world.

Principal-agent theory suggests that it is the agent, and not the principal, who is more influential. The agent has more knowledge or expertise. Therefore, principal-agent theory suggests a hierarchy, which is consistent with both principal-agent theory and network theory.[37]

Principal-agent theory is designed to explain the existence of organizations in a free market economy, where principals control the purse strings, while agents possess superior information, including the opportunity to "shirk" and subject the principal to the moral hazard, associated with reliance on the agents' competence. For the principal to avoid moral hazard, additional costs (of information acquisition) must be borne by the principal.

The principal seeks to achieve equilibrium between: (1) level of control; and (2) level of affordable control. The more disparate the goals of the principal and agent, the greater the need (and cost associated) for information and the related equilibrium.

The principal-agent problems that arise within organizations are more pronounced in cross-organizational relationships. The advantage, associated with having all factors of production in a single entity, includes:

- The establishment of more creative and goal-congruent (between principal-agent) reward structures.
- The conveyance of a single message and a singularity or commonality of purpose.
- The reduction of the losses and inefficiencies associated with breakdowns and delays in bargaining and contracting.

The firm controls all of the above, in the case of the employee/employer relationship.

The more dispersed the authority, the lower the level of achievable goal-congruence between principals and agents. Therefore, where practicable, it is more efficient/less costly for the firm to be responsible for monitoring.

From the Marketing Literature

Mishra et al. (1998) explain that, in customer/supplier relations, customers are faced with both adverse selection and moral hazard problems. Mishra et al. proposed the use of customer bonds/loyalty and price premiums to serve as signals and supplier incentives, respectively. They proceeded to extend their analysis to supplier/employee relations. Again, this extension examines signals and incentives. Their research of this two-level structure was conducted using survey instruments and in the context of firms specializing in providing automotive services (outlets) to customers. These instruments were mailed to the automotive service outlets (illustrated in Fig. 6.2).

An extension of the survey instrument-based examination made by Mishra et al. may be feasible in the context of online security trading. Consider the case of the customer (stock market participant)/on line broker (e.g. Datek or myTrack). As in the case of Mishra et al., both the customer and the on-line broker are faced with both adverse selection and moral hazard problems (Chapters 2 and 3). The two-level structure may be developed by way of the relations between the on line broker/employee, or, in some cases, the broker/market maker relations, where the market maker provides order flow to the online broker. In this case, the two-level structure and the stock trading extension of this two-level structure are illustrated in Figs 6.3 and 6.4, respectively.

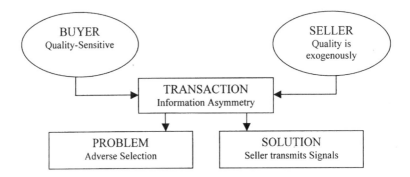

Fig. 6.2. Key Issues in Addressing Information Asymmetry: From the Marketing
Literature.

Note: As adapted from Kirmani and Rao (2000, p. 67).

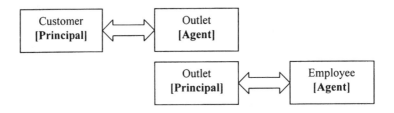

Fig. 6.3. Two-Level Structure Examined by Mishra et al. (1998).

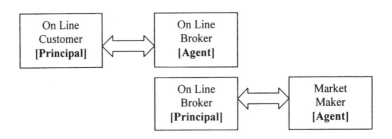

Fig. 6.4. Stock Trading Extension of the Two-Level Structure Examined by Mishra
et al. (1998).

From the Real Estate Finance Literature

Downs and Güner (2000) examined two, potentially conflicting hypotheses in the context of real estate investments. They found that support for these hypotheses was critically dependent on whether investment-analyst attention was measured in an absolute or relative sense (p. 575).

The competition hypothesis suggests that liquidity increases (information asymmetry decreases) with increased investment analysis and the number of informed traders (Admati & Pfleiderer, 1988). This hypothesis is supported when an absolute measure of analyst attention is used (e.g. number of analyst estimates).

The risk-aversion hypothesis suggests that liquidity decreases (information asymmetry increases) with increasing investment analysis (Subrahmanyam 1991), if the number of analysts is small (e.g. neglected firms). This hypothesis is supported when a relative measure of analyst attention is used (e.g. number of analyst estimates divided by the mean number of analyst estimates in the firm's corresponding peer group).

From the Accounting Literature

Two classifications of information, frequently examined in the accounting literature, are: (1) accountability information; and (2) decision relevant information. They are not mutually exclusive.

Accountability information involves reporting on the "control" function. The main characteristics include "objectivity" and "neutrality."

Decision relevant information is operationally defined, in information economics (Bromwich, 1992, p. 122), as that information which may alter existing optimal and/or conduct. In accounting, information is decision relevant if it has predictive and feedback value (FASB, 1978). Predictive value may be direct or indirect, while feedback value may support or refute priors.

INTERNET STOCK-CHAT MESSAGE BOARDS: THE NEW MONITORS?

Has the void created by a contemporary absence of large shareholder monitoring and activism been replaced by Internet stock-chat message board posts? Typically, the bid-ask spread and the information available to trades have been used as proxies for information asymmetry.

InterWAVE Communications

On May 14, 2002, the following YF message board exchange took place:

msg #19215, by *iwavbeliever* at 11:38 a.m.
What gives? Who sold at .92?!

msg #19216, by *tradelogic2001* at 11:43 a.m.
This is how market makers take out the stop losses. About 50,000 shares they picked up this way. But I was waiting for something like this and had 5000 shares at 0.92 which was not filled.

The above, of course, is conjecture. It was an exchange in response to a decline in the bid/ask spread and a flurry of trades occurring within the time span of a single minute, at 11:35 a.m. Though it is quite possible that the market maker (e.g. broker-dealer) may have used the strategy suggested above, it is also quite possible for this strategy to have been employed by another investor, with access to level 2 quotes. (Level 2 allows the market participant to observe the buy and sell orders, as the market maker may also observe this cue, creating opportunities to remove (e.g. buy shares) a relatively high bid to purchase shares at a price significantly below the established market price for a security. Of course, the profitable application of this strategy would be greater for those with access to "stop loss" orders and whether these are "limit" or "market" stop loss orders).

Immediately prior to the above referenced (and very short-lived) trades in InterWAVE (NASDAQ NM: IWAV) stock, the PPS was above $1. Immediately following these trades, where approximately 11,000 shares traded between the price of $0.92 and $0.99 per share, the price and the bid/ask spread for InterWAVE stock recovered to above $1.

InterWAVE opened at $1.08 and closed at $1.05 during the regular trading session on May 14, 2002. This short-lived decline and trades of approximately 11,000 shares was significant, as only 157,300 shares traded during the regular trading session[39] on this date.

Specialists and Market Makers

Specialists and MMs buy when they receive a "good" signal. They sell when they receive a "bad" signal.

Foster and Viswanathan (1996), who examined strategic trading in their analysis of a multi-period model with differentially informed traders, liquidity traders, and a MM, found that informed traders competed with each other for trading profits. They also concluded that traders learn about other traders' signals from their observations of order flow. Using a model based on Kyle (1985), their findings included an initial correlation among informed traders' signals, which had a significant effect on informed traders' profits and the information content of prices.

Huberman and Dominika (2001) point out that neither the market microstructure literature (with its focus on security liquidity), nor the asset pricing literature (with much of its focus on the association between systematic risk and return), explain the systematic, time-varying component of liquidity. However, they were unable to offer a model or a direct proxy for the measurement of liquidity and only offered conjecture on this systematic component of liquidity.

SUMMARY

Asset-specific information deficiencies (*financial*/external) may alter the investment-analysis-liquidity relation, which affects the cost of capital (*managerial*/internal) (Downs & Güner, 2000).

This chapter provides the transition, in focus, from the traditional literature streams on information symmetry to a new medium of information – the Internet. Alternative sources of private information were introduced in Chapter 5. Just as traditional research has examined *Value Line* and *Moody's* ratings, it was suggested, in Chapter 5, that researchers may wish to examine the predictive value of other sources of private information (see Table 5.1). Have the Enron and WorldCom scandals and related auditor and financial analyst opinions found their status reduced from "normal" to "inferior" classification? The remainder of this monograph and appendices will provide a primer for researchers interested in investigating the status of alternative sources of free and public information, available on the Internet.

SECTION IV. CASE STUDIES

INTRODUCTION

In the three chapters that follow, a wide variety of agency relationships are examined. At the foundation of each alleged infringement is the presence of asymmetric information. In the case of the small- or micro-cap stocks, the Internet and the stock-chat message boards provide the means for both information *symmetry* and *asymmetry*.

CASE STUDIES

The first case is that of PurchasePro (Chapter 7). This once big-cap stock was converted to small- or micro-cap status, as were so many since the stock market crash of April 2000. This event is now being compared to the crash of 1929, as so many similarities persist, including discussion of increased regulation by the SEC (compare to the SEC Acts of 1933 and 1934, following the 1929 crash).

PurchasePro has been bashed and touted, the subject of a public information release of inaccurate quarterly EPS measures requiring restatement, open letters by executives to stop short-selling of PurchasePro stock, and attempts by long-term holders of the stock to fill the information void created when the firm's PPS fell below $1 and financial analyst coverage ceased.

PurchasePro, like so many small- and micro-cap stocks and so many post-April 2000 crash stocks, has experienced a paradigm shift of sorts. They no longer operate in the big-cap world, but have become a captive of the information paradigm to which small- and micro-cap stocks have always been subjected. Therefore, the examination of the means of information dissemination, both public and private, in the small- and micro-cap paradigm is relevant.

The second case is that of Universal Express (Chapter 8), which provides an example of a firm destroyed by a convertible debenture, a form of financing of last resort. After winning a judgment, causing an initial increase in the firm's PPS, the firm continues to be bashed and hyped, and public news releases – in the form of firm-issued public relations releases – are extremely frequent. This case is more typical of the small- or micro-cap environment, characterized by the OTC BB and PinkSheets "exchanges."

Chapter 9 follows these two case studies, with summaries of 126 litigation-related and firm-specific cases. This examination classifies what are primarily cases of cybersmear.

INFORMATION AND THE INTERNET

For those who would challenge the importance of the information disseminated on the Internet or on the stock-chat message boards, consider the events following the stock market crash of April 2000. The Enron, WorldCom and (to a lesser extent) Xerox cases, the SEC, financial analysts and independent CPA-auditors have failed to retain the trust of a significant portion of the American public. These institutional failures may have involved *insider*, *hidden*, or *private* information (i.e. information asymmetry) and may have created a mistrust of (formerly) legitimate sources of *public* information. In the aftermath of these failures, and within the theoretical frameworks of corporate governance, prin-cipal-agent relationships, and information symmetry/asymmetry, some very broad research questions follow:

- What is the difference between the financial analyst's "buy" recommenda-tion or the "clean" auditor's opinion letter and the tout, hype or pumping efforts of the sophisticated investor/trader on the stock-chat message boards?
- Similarly, what is the difference between the relationships between the auditor/consultant, financial analyst/underwriter and the investor/trader with a long (short) position in the stock of the firm he/she is touting, hyping, or pumping (bashing) for personal gain?
- Finally, what is the difference between the financial analyst's "sell" recom-mendation, followed by his/her discharge, and the "ignore" feature available on, for example, the RB stock-chat message board?

Given the failure to restore these institutions to their formerly revered status, the answer to all of the above may be "no difference." The similarities should be apparent, and are worthy of examination. The examination of these cases is only the first step in what is likely to become a growing area of interest and academic research, as the Internet greatly accelerates the dissemination of both legitimate and non-legitimate information.

CHAPTER 7: DETAILED CASE STUDY 1: PURCHASEPRO (NASDAQ NM: PPRO)

. . . PurchasePro took an unorthodox step last week to appeal directly to its remaining base of small investors.

"I've never heard of something like this before," says Louis Thompson, president of the National Investor Relations Institute, a Vienna, Va., trade group. "It's an interesting twist" (Aaron Elstein, *The Wall Street Journal Online*, September 3, 2001).

INTRODUCTION

This chapter uses PurchasePro.com, Incorporated (PurchasePro) to examine and classify events in terms of principal-agent relations. PurchasePro is an exciting case for researchers of asymmetric information to select for examination. Like so many technology stocks with post-stock market bubble (April 2000) PPS decreases, financial analysts ceased coverage of PurchasePro, creating an information void, while simultaneously generating the need for increased monitoring for a stock that once traded above $87 per share (December 1999). Opportunities for manipulation and increased volatility, stemming from the dissemination of misinformation (e.g. greater potential for the generation of conditions of hidden or private information and information asymmetry), were also created. Larger firms, in terms of market capitalization, enjoy significant levels of stabilizing institutional ownership and are heavily monitored in the form of *public* information (e.g. popular press news and business news releases), as well as extensive coverage and buy-hold-sell recommendations by financial analysts.

This chapter will provide company background information and details associated with six events selected for examination. The theoretical context of these events follows in a discussion section. Finally, implications developed from this case study are summarized.

COMPANY BACKGROUND

PurchasePro provided Internet business-to-business (B2B) e-commerce products and services, enabling customers to establish and operate online marketplaces to buy and sell products and services in a reverse-auction system, designed to reduce costs for their subscribers. On January 8, 2003, the U.S. Bankruptcy Court for the District of Nevada approved the sale of substantially all of the assets of PurchasePro.com, Inc. to Perfect Commerce, Inc. of Palo Alto, California, for $2.325 million in cash.

Initially, allied with America OnLine, Incorporated (formerly, NASDAQ NM: AOL), PurchasePro enjoyed a stock PPS as high as $87.50 (December 1999). By October 2001, their stock price had fallen to PPS levels as low as $0.37 per share. In early May 2002, shortly after the announcement of a 1-for-5 reverse split, the PPS declined to a level below book value, and to a new low at $0.26.

PurchasePro was the subject of a favorable earnings surprise (February 2001). This information was later found to be inaccurate, and two separate quarterly earnings restatements were necessary (May 2001).

Shortly after this error, and the release of news representing inflated earnings, the chairman and chief executive officer (CEO) of PurchasePro announced his intention to liquidate a portion of his PurchasePro stock holdings (March 2001). This information was provided through Forms 144, properly filed with the SEC. Announcements of the formation of class action lawsuits followed, and the chairman and CEO announced his resignation (May 2001).

PurchasePro appears to have been the subject and target of both a stock price *pump* (August 2001), as well as a subsequent *bashing* campaign (February 2002). These behaviors are more common among penny or micro-cap stocks (e.g. Over-the-Counter Bulletin Board (OTC BB) or stocks traded on the Pink Sheet), where these (often) thinly traded securities possess relatively insignificant levels of market capitalization and, so, receive little or no verifiable financial news or analyst coverage from legitimate sources. Chapter 4 introduced and examined some of the relevant issues surrounding thinly traded or *neglected* stocks.

The new CEO (June 2001) made a direct request to loyal PurchasePro shareholders in an attempt to thwart stock price degeneration, caused by increasing short interest positions (October 2001). A separate open letter from another PurchasePro executive addressed a negative and (presumably) inappropriate comment made by a broadcast news reporter (January 2002). These requests and open comments/letters are very common among thinly traded penny, OTC BB or Pink Sheets stocks.

PurchasePro was selected as a candidate for analysis, in large part, because of the declining PPS, related declining institutional ownership, and related and subsequent reductions in financial and business news and analyst coverage or information. This condition is characteristic of so many of the once expensive pre-stock market bubble (April 2000) stocks. In this respect, PurchasePro was subjected to the types of behaviors more commonly observed and associated with penny stocks. It was this pattern of behavior that provided the motivation for a group of PurchasePro's loyal and long-term investors to develop and publish their own financial analysis on the future and prospects of PurchasePro (March 2002). This latter event was unprecedented.

Figure 7.1 provides a timeline of the following events, in addition to a reference to the new CEO. These events, and their relevance to asymmetric information, are discussed in greater detail in the numbered sections that follow:

(1) PurchasePro had an information failure resulting in two separate restatements of earnings for the fourth quarter of fiscal 2000 (May 2001);
(2) PurchasePro appears to have been the subject of misinformation, an attempted stock price pumping campaign (August 2001);
(3) The new PurchasePro CEO, Richard Clemmer (June 2001–), made a direct plea in an open letter to shareholders (October 2001);
(4) A PurchasePro executive made an open letter response to a negative business news reporter's comments (January 2002);
(5) PurchasePro appears to have been the subject of misinformation, an attempted stock price bashing campaign (February 2002); and
(6) PurchasePro investors provided their own research analysis on PurchasePro (March 2002).

(1) Asymmetric, private information or error?

PurchasePro made an error in a *public* information release – an overstatement of earnings and earnings per share (EPS). This release of inaccurate information, announced by the founder, major shareholder, and previous chairman and CEO of PurchasePro, incorrectly overstated anticipated earnings for the fourth quarter of 2000 (i.e. December 31, 2000).[40] At the foundation of this error, was a failure to apply the *matching* principle of financial accounting.[41] His *public* announcement treated revenues, correctly matched to *future* quarters, as realized in a (then) *current* and fourth quarter. This represented a favorable earnings surprise of quarterly profitability and a short-lived stock price spike in the firm's common stock.

Whether PurchasePro executives were or were not aware of this error is relevant in classifying the original release of the incorrect operating results as *public*

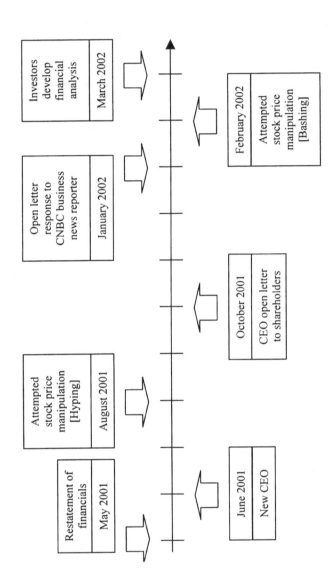

Fig. 7.1. Timeline of Selected PurchasePro Events.

information or *private* information (see Section II and Chapters 4 and 5). The corrected statements of operating results, followed by SEC notifications/filings required to sell a significant portion of his holdings in PurchasePro stock, represent a case of asymmetric information, where Charles E. Johnson, Jr. (CEO) was the agent and shareholders were the principals.

The first news release of favorable (though inaccurate) news/information occurred on February 12, 2001. News of the chairman's intention to liquidate a portion of his holdings was released one month later, on March 12, 2001. April 26, 2001, was a particularly eventful date, with *public* information releases of (negative) earnings revisions, downgrades, and the announcement of the formation of class action lawsuits. News of Johnson's resignation was released on May 21, 2001. This was followed by news of a reduction/restatement of PurchasePro's earnings on May 22, 2001. An additional reduction/restatement was publicized on May 29, 2001.

(Selected headlines (*public* information) for these and other event dates are preserved and contained in Appendix 7.2. Also included are headlines relating to financial analyst's upgrades/downgrades (*public* information), Forms 144 for the sale of securities filed by Johnson with the SEC (*public* information), and the formation of class-action lawsuits against PurchasePro (delayed *public* information), relating to this erroneous earnings-related *public* information release.)

Table 7.1 summarizes the substance of the Form 144 filings made by Charles E. Johnson, Jr. with the SEC (March through July 2001). This information was accessed through the YF web site, where it was available to the public at no cost, but in a delayed *public* information format.

Figure 7.2 graphically represents the number of shares of PurchasePro's common stock, associated with the Form 144 filings contained in Table 7.1. Significance is illustrated by their representation as a percentage of the actual number of shares traded on the filing/anticipated trade dates. Figure 7.3 graphically depicts the decline in the PurchasePro stock PPS over the same five month period (March through July 2001).[42] Many other events were also reported during this period, and the 10.7 million shares sold (or planned for sale) during this five-month period (see Table 7.1) represented only a fraction of the 348.1 million shares (i.e. 10.7 million shares divided by 348.1 million share equals 3.1%) traded during this same period. Alternatively, these 10.7 million shares represented approximately 16.1% of the total number of common shares issued and outstanding (i.e. 10.7 million of the 66.3 million shares issued and outstanding in mid-February 2001).

It is also relevant to note that short interest approximated nearly 17 million shares or 25.6% (i.e. 17 million of the 66.3 million shares issued and outstanding) in mid-February 2001. Many posts on the YF message boards

Table 7.1.   Insider and Form 144 Filings made by Charles E. Johnson, Jr.

Date	Shares	Stock	Estimated Proceeds
30-Jul-01	2,096,296	Form 144	$1,467,388
9-Jul-01	500,000	"	$760,000
30-Apr-01	500,000	"	$1,405,000
27-Apr-01	500,000	"	$1,335,000
17-Apr-01	500,000	Sale @$4.71/sh	$2,355,000
10-Apr-01	330,000	Sale @$3.11/sh	$1,026,300
9-Apr-01	500,000	Sale @$2.65/sh	$1,325,000
6-Apr-01	500,000	Sale @$2.90/sh	$1,450,000
5-Apr-01	500,000	Sale @$3.42/sh	$1,710,000
4-Apr-01	500,000	Sale @$3.02/sh	$1,510,000
3-Apr-01	500,000	Sale @$4.34/sh	$2,170,000
2-Apr-01	300,000	Sale @$6.60/sh	$1,980,000
7-Mar-01	790,000	Sale @$11.70/sh	$9,243,000
6-Mar-01	660,000	Sale @$10.14/sh	$6,692,400
6-Mar-01	2,000,000	Form 144	$20,274,600
Totals	10,676,296		$54,703,688

warned of buying PurchasePro stock during this period and/or associated these Form 144 sales by Charles E. Johnson, Jr. with the decline PPS, however, a preliminary and, admittedly, underspecified statistical test (i.e. regression model) did not support this allegation.

It should also be noted that Richard Clemmer, the new president, filed Forms 144 with the SEC for purchases of 35,000 (August 2001 at an estimated cost of $18,000) and 80,000 (November 2001 at an estimated cost of $58,000) shares. This *public* information, too, was available at no cost on the YF site and was a topic of great interest, discussed on the PurchasePro YF message board.

(2) Information Symmetry in an Overtly Advertised Rally – A Testament to Market Efficiency or a Failure to Assimilate Public Information?

Perhaps because the PPS of PurchasePro common stock declined to less than one dollar per share, PurchasePro stock became a likely target for misinformation and stock price manipulation through the generation of asymmetric information. It was possible to capture the details of one failed attempt at PPS manipulation (e.g. the creation of a false rally) in PurchasePro stock. In this case, it would appear that those engaged in this effort to manipulate the PPS of PurchasePro stock failed to review *public* information, in the form of the Form 144 SEC "proposed sale" filings made by the ex-CEO, Charles E.

C.E. Johnson Form 144 Filings

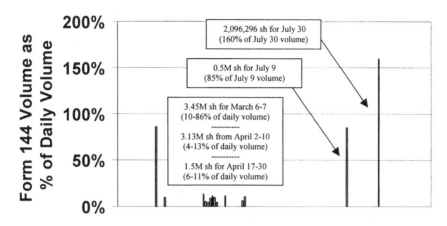

Fig. 7.2. C. E. Johnson Forms 144 Filings.

Purchase Pro (PPRO) Stock

Fig. 7.3. PurchasePro (PPRO) Stock Price per share.

Johnson Jr. This particular event/attempt represents a successful testament to market efficiency and the efficient market hypothesis, as the PPS of PurchasePro stock remained stable throughout this flurry of pre-market (i.e. 8 a.m. through 9:30 a.m.) buying activity.

A summary of the YF message board aliases, date, time, message number, message headline, and notes or references (where applicable) to the PurchasePro target PPS are provided in Table 7.2. These and other posts were clearly intended to broadly and publicly signal and disseminate information and generate anticipation of the upcoming rally in the PPS of PurchasePro common stock.

In early August, a poster with the alias *diggerdawg2001*[43] advertised (*public* information) an upcoming rally in the PPS of PurchasePro stock. This message, directed to another poster's alias (*sledford_98*), follows:

> *Yo sled shed 98 the dawg pound is on the way short sqeeze (sic) is going to sh*t when the pound comes in lol*[44] **watch any 2001 on the board tomorrow night** *(emphasis added) lol we go up*

Only 5 posters used aliases with the 2001 suffix (i.e. *jgfisherman2001*, *diggerdawg2001*, *jjjlongjjj2001*, *bjmagivlry2001dawg*, and *gaapuup2001*). Others, appearing to be associated with these aliases, and engaged in the same manipulative or rallying effort, used 2002 or 2003 suffixes or other aliases. Due to the anonymity of the alias system, used by stock-chat message boards, there is no way of knowing whether these aliases were posted by one (or more) person(s).

One very perceptive poster, known as *rather_amusing*,[45] noticed that some of these aliases were new to the PurchasePro message board and had similar demographic characteristics, as follows:

> *Anyone else notice . . . that all these new posters seem to be 35 and male? lol*

In fact, optional biographical information indicated that *diggerdawg2001*, *jjjlongjjj2001*, *gaapuup2001*, and *holdonupupup2002* were 35-year-old males (see Appendix Chapter 7.1). Other biographical peculiarities were noted for the aliases. For example, *iliveoffpanicselling*, *ifyouwantatripleclickhere*, and *fullblownalcy2002* had voluntarily disclosed their age as 90 years old.

An unanticipated market reaction and/or lack of research may have contributed to the failure of the efforts by the self-described "dawg pound" to generate a rally and upward PPS move in PurchasePro common stock. A message posted by *bigcat_14625*,[46] the morning of the much anticipated PurchasePro stock PPS run-up, reminded readers of *publicly* available

Table 7.2. Selected August 2001 Posts from the Yahoo! Finance Message Boards for PPRO.

Message Board Alias	Date	Time	Msg#	Relevant Portion(s) of Message Header	Notes or Price Target
fly_b2b	8/6/01	8:14P	112012	PPRO will open $1.50 tomorrow and UP!!	$1.50
tnc26	8/7/01	3:04A	112095	PPRO IS WAYS UNDER-VALUE COMPARE . . .	$8.00
cynkev2002	8/7/01	1:43P	112297	GET READY FOR A POP!!!!	N/A
"	"	1:46P	112305	SHORT SQUEEZE COMING SHORTLY	
"	"	2:43P	112380	BUYERS COMING IN SOON . . .	
Jgfisherman2001	8/7/01	3:54P	112482	PPRO gonna bust out AH*	
"	"	11:24P	112014	If Dawgs are in it, Rough ruff Ruff	
"	"	11:35P	113023	Dawgs were 1st in USXP	
"	8/8/01	12:33A	113058	Tomorrow PPRO will avoid going to the	$2.00
Diggerdawg2001	8/7/01	6:38P	112809	DAWG POUND ON THE WAY 2.00	$2.00
"	"	8:14P	112886	GRRRRRRRRRRRRR UP	$2.50
"	"	9:36P	112948	MAJOR SHORT SQUEEZE	Triple PPS
"	"	"	112984	Strong buy strong buy	
"	"	"	112998	we go up	
Jjjlongjjj2001	8/7/01	6:41P	112812	DAWG POUND PUTS THIS OVER 2.00	$2.00
"	"	8:14P	112877	DAWG POUND GOING TO EAT	$3.00
"	"	8:18P	112893	POUND 2001 USXP .04 TO .30	$4.00
"	"	8:28P	112903	60 dawgs coming tomorrow (sic) to	$3.25
"	"	9:19P	112932	CEO SAIS (sic) WE GO UP	
"	"	9:31P	112941	YOU BASHERS AINT (sic) BUYING	8:01AM buys
"	"	9:31P	112944	MY BUDDY DAV SAIS (sic) WE EXPLODE	
"	"	11:11P	113007	no deadcatbouce (sic)	
gaapuup2001	8/7/01	6:44P	112816	we are here and aint (sic) leaving	$3.00
"	"	9:15P	112930	weeeeeeeeeeeee gapup (sic) big	$1.50
holdonupupup 2002	8/7/01	6:40P	112816	the pound put usxp 0.04 to 0.30 800%	$3.50
"	"	8:20P	112897	UP WE GO	

Table 7.2. Continued.

Message Board Alias	Date	Time	Msg#	Relevant Portion(s) of Message Header	Notes or Price Target
"	"	10:59P	112997	strong rumors	
Iliveoffpanic selling	8/7/01	6:59P	112827	KEEP SELLING WEEK (sic) HANDS IM	
"	"	11:49P	113038	CNBC SAID SHORTS WILL	
"	8/8/01	12:19A	113052	WAY OVERSOLD SHORTS COVER	Up 200%/ 1 wk
"	"	12:41A	113062	WAYYYYYOVER SOLDDDDDDD	
Ifyouwanta tripleclickhere	8/7/01	7:03P	112830	ppro is going to hit 2.50	$2.50/ 2 wks
"	"	8:49P	112918	TRIPLE	
"	"	11:41P	113030	BUY PPRO	
"	8/8/01	12:03A	113042	ppro is going to hit 2.50	$2.50/ Christmas
fullblownalcy 2002	8/7/01	7:09P	112833	buy buy buy buy	$5.00
bjmagivlry2001 dawg	8/7/01	8:17P	112892	im in at the open dig	
"	"	9:13P	112929	re strongbuy	Dawgs buy @ AM
justgetin2002	8/7/01	9:12P	112928	STRONGBUY	
Vegasdudesuxdic	8/7/01	11:07P	113003	buy buy buy buy	Short squeeze
thepostman2003	8/7/01	11:39P	113025	TIME TO THREATEN THE SHORTIES	
"	"	11:52P	113040	MY LAST POST IS	$12/12/01
bulls_stock_ referrals	8/7/01	11:43P	113032	Ahoy! So the Dawgs arrived, easy gap up	
fishermn2002	8/7/01	11:46P	113035	CYA Shorts, FYI	
"	8/8/01	12:18A	113051	Pound is coming to Pund Shorts	
Deadcatbouncing	8/8/01	12:32A	113056	IM PUTING (sic) IN 50K SHARES	Buys @ 9:31AM
Pppppppro	8/8/01	12:41P	113388	we purchase 50,000 shares .we add 150,0	

* AH = after-hours trading session from 4 p.m. to 6:30 p.m. or later (e.g. 8 p.m. for Datek brokerage account holders).

information . . . that a significant amount of selling pressure was pending (see Table 7.1 and Figs 7.2 and 7.3):

Charles E. Johnson, Jr., referred to simply as "Junior" on the PurchasePro message board, was the ex-chairman of the board, ex-chief executive officer, and a 10% beneficial owner of PurchasePro common stock. As of July 30, 2001, he continued to hold 7,415,334 shares of PurchasePro as an affiliated person. He had filed a (proposed sale) Form 144 with the SEC to sell 2,096,269 shares of PurchasePro (see Table 7.1). This fact had been reported by Vickers Stock Research via COMTEX on Monday, August 6, 2001 at 5:08 p.m. (public information), but did not show up as a news release on YF news site until shortly after 9 a.m. on the morning (August 8, 2001) of the much anticipated effort to increase the PPS of PurchasePro stock (delayed *public* information). A relatively large number of PurchasePro shares (approximately 60,000) had already traded in the pre-market (8 a.m. to 9:30 a.m.), but the price of the stock appeared to be range-bound between $0.80 and $0.90 per share.

By 10:03 a.m. (on the morning of August, 8, 2001), some posters suggested that the "dawg pound" group might have run out of cash. At 10:03 a.m., *mepusutea*[47] posted the following:

Out of cash soon.

Approximately fifteen minutes later, at 10:19 a.m., *wilybbunch*[48] suggested the same plight for the group:

So out of cash. Hypsters influence

The much publicized (public information) rally effort failed to achieve the desired objective of a significant increase in the PPS of PurchasePro stock. However, this failure to raise the stock price may have inadvertently supported the $0.80 to $0.90 PPS range in the pre-market trading session, preventing further declines in the PPS.

To place the size of "Junior's" 2.1 million share sell order in context, during regular market hours (9:30 a.m. to 4 p.m.), 4.3 million, 1.5 million, and 0.7 million shares traded on August 7, 8, and 9, 2001, respectively. The relatively large volume on August 7, 2001, might reasonably be attributed to the normal investor rebalancing and anticipation, preceding the 4:45 p.m. PurchasePro quarterly earnings announcement and conference call. In contrast, less than 1 million shares traded, per day and during regular trading hours, for the 5 trading days following the quarterly earnings announcement and conference call . . . from August 9 through 15, 2001.

Having failed at the effort to increase the PPS of PurchasePro stock, *jimtheclam*[49] made an attempt to lead PurchasePro investors to the IBIZ boards, as follows:

IBIZ GOING UP BIG TOMORROW. JOEY BUY IBIZ

The body of this post suggested the potential for a 500% gain.

IBIZ/nice volume/nice action. STUCK IN THE MUD

The body of this second post also suggested the potential for a 500% gain.

Another poster, *ifyouwantatripleclickhere*[50] assisted in the hype for IBIZ with a message that was identical to the first IBIZ post by *jimtheclam*.[51]

The redirection of those from one stock chat message board to another (or from one pump and dump to another) is a common tactic employed by those attempting to generate a rally from one stock to another to another. The uncommon ingredient, in the case of PurchasePro, was the dismal failure of this highly publicized rally effort.

A sophisticated short-term investor (or speculator) might be inclined to follow a pump and dump from one stock to another, if successful. But the PurchasePro effort did not achieve success.

Finally, the poster alias *cynkev2002*,[52] one of the first to post hype on the PurchasePro board for the failed August 8, 2001 rally effort, took a very different tactic. On August 9, 2001, the day following the failed attempt to increase the price of PurchasePro stock, he posted the following:

AOL and PPRO BUYOUT. AOL AND PPRO

America On-Line (AOL) provided 80% of the revenues for PurchasePro for the prior quarter, owned about 5% of PurchasePro stock, and had provided $100,000 to Amazon.com (AMZN). It was reasonable for PurchasePro shareholders to anticipate that AOL might assist PurchasePro, in the event that their cash needs increased. Therefore, the AOL/PurchasePro association was a favorable factor in maintaining buy and/or hold interest in PurchasePro stock.

Generally, these efforts are also associated with rumors of a short squeeze. In this case, the "dawg pound" posted messages, taking credit/responsibility for the recent increase in PPS for another stock, Universal Express, which is featured as the case study for Chapter 8.

It is reasonable to conclude that the failed August 8, 2001, pump of PurchasePro's stock price left those, spearheading the hype, with large positions in the stock. If a long position was developed in PurchasePro stock, resulting in "dead money," follow-up posts and monitoring for an appropriate opportunity to profitably liquidate would follow.

This section illustrates a failed effort to rally the PPS of PurchasePro when this effort was publicly disclosed. Appendix 7.2 contains a series of illustrations of non-publicly disclosed, successful efforts, occurring where these rallies were the result of private or asymmetric information. The informational content of these stock-chat message board posts relate to an overtly signaled effort to generate excitement and buying pressures for a pre-planned PPS increase for PurchasePro common stock. These posts are characteristics of the type of hyping, pumping and/or touting that is seen, from time to time, by those who are very familiar with the stock-chat message boards. They are, however, difficult for the intermittent visitor to locate, and are provided as an illustration for those interested in conducting research in this area.

Several points warrant mention:

First, researchers and graduate students, interested in case study and content analysis research techniques, are likely to find these types of stock-chat message board postings of greatest interest. Regulators will also find this sample of interest, to the extent that it may contribute to their refinement of monitoring efforts.

Second, this summary does not contain all posts, but a representative sample of the breadth of the posts relating to what appears to have been a planned effort to increase the PPS of PurchasePro stock.

The failure of this effort is likely due to several factors:

First, the posts were confined to the YF stock-chat message board for the target stock, PurchasePro.

Second, the quantity of posts, suggesting the increase in PurchasePro PPS, were relatively small, when compared to successful efforts (see Appendix Chapter 7.2), which may require several hundreds of messages. This might be compared to the case of a neglected stock (Chapter 4) or the financial analyst recommendation, where only one or two analysts follow and/or recommend a stock.

Third, some of the examples contained reference to the excessive use of alcohol (e.g. msg #'s 110300, 113058 and 113061 made by *iliveoffpanicselling*, *jgfisherman2001* and *fullblownalcy2002*, respectively). The reference to being drunk or drinking was likely to have resulted in the reduced credibility of the posts.

Fourth, there were not enough different aliases. Successful efforts, like those more briefly summarized in Appendix Chapter 7.2, involved at least tens of aliases. Whether these are the same persons posting under multiple aliases or not does not appear to be relevant, unless extremely apparent. Just as the academic literature suggests that larger numbers of financial analysts, recommending a stock as a "buy" ("sell"), are more likely to lead to a PPS increase (decrease), the same is true of the stock-chat message boards.

Finally, the group appears to have failed to adequately prepare by researching the public information available in the form of SEC Forms 144 filed by the ex-CEO (see Table 7.1). Therefore, it is likely that many shares were sold into this pre-market rally by sophisticated investors.

(3) Information Symmetry in the Form of a Public Plea from the New CEO

The new CEO of PurchasePro, Richard Clemmer, directly enlisted the assistance of shareholders (and potential shareholders) in a release of *public* information. These direct communications to shareholders appear to be representative of a growing trend to combat misinformation or asymmetric information disseminated on the Internet.

In his open letter to shareholders, he suggests that shareholders take measures to prevent the borrowing of their PurchasePro shares by those wishing to take short positions in PurchasePro stock. These measures included: (1) removing long position PurchasePro shares from the broker's or street name; and/or (2) removing long position PurchasePro shares from the shareholder's margin account and placing them into a separate cash account, as follows:

Dear PurchasePro Stockholder:

Let me begin by thanking you . . .
Management believes that the current [low] stock price is attributable, in part, to heavy pressure from "short selling" in the market . . . we are asking all of our shareholders to . . . call your brokers and have your PurchasePro stock taken out of street name or place your holdings into a cash account . . . (b)y registering your shares in your name or holding them in a cash account, a short seller would not be able to borrow your stock without your permission . . . (i)f you have any questions . . . please call Steve Stern, PurchasePro's vice president, corporate communications and investor relations . . .

Regards,
Richard Clemmer
President and CEO

(4) Information Symmetry – A Public Challenge to a Violation of the Principal-Agent Relationship

PurchasePro's vice president for corporate communications and investor relations (IR)[53] directly addressed what PurchasePro perceived to represent a failure of the agency relationship between a financial journalist and the public. He did this in an open letter to Ted David of CNBC:

We are appalled that you would make the statement on your broadcast yesterday that 'PurchasePro is not even worth talking about . . . they'll probably be delisted.' . . . we believe that the statement you made yesterday was journalistically irresponsible.

Thank you in advance for your consideration.
Cordially,
Steven D. Stern
Vice President, Corporate Communications & Investor Relations

(5) Information Symmetry *in a Publicized Leakage of an Overtly Advertised Bashing Campaign – A Testament to Market Efficiency?*

On February 17, 2002, a warning of an incoming team of paid bashers was leaked on the PurchasePro YF message board. The message was copied and also linked to the point of origin, the RB message boards:

> *. . . from the heart, you guys have been the best bunch of jokers I've ever had the opportunity to irritate. I will miss bashing this stock . . . (t)hings will be red for awhile, but don't worry . . . (f)rom what I've heard . . . you'll be dancing the Irish jig. They've set the stage well...(I) hope my name will be one admitted to the Basher Hall of Fame . . . (I) want to thank (name withheld), (name withheld) and (name withheld) . . . also like to thank (name withheld) for allowing me to put food on my family's table . . . (I've) been called to another mission . . . XOXO, IFTA and **PPRO** (emphasis added).[54]*

Though the YF message board for PurchasePro (PPRO) was monitored, no significant, organized effort to depress the stock price of PurchasePro was observed on this date. This may or may not have been the direct result of a large number of messages posted to warn of the forthcoming effort.

Furthermore, this message was posted on February 13, 2002. As of the end of June 2002 – more than four months later, the stock from the RB message board of origin had only continued to decline, without even a hint of the recovery alluded to in the message.

Finally, a review of the posting history for this alias, on the RB message boards where the message originated, indicated that approximately 30 additional messages had been posted through June 2002.

Though this evidence is inconclusive, it is also not consistent with the "paid basher" hypothesis and fact pattern. It does, however, provide: (1) an illustration of the sequential steps that researchers may use to investigate stock-chat message board claims, in this case a testable hypothesis; and (2) provide some explanation for the "paid basher" claims so often made on the stock-chat message boards.

(6) An Illustration of a Public *Information Disclosure in an Environment of a Perceived Need for* Public *Information – Dissatisfaction and Increased Mistrust of Institutional Public Information*

The Enron case, where financial analysts testified that they were deceived by Enron management into believing that the future for Enron was bright, resulted in the culmination of growing public attention on brokerage and underwriting firms. As an example of the sentiment, a WorldCom downgrade by Goldman Sachs will illustrate.

On May 10, 2002, during the early morning, pre-market hours of CNBC programming, Goldman Sachs was criticized for their 7:46 a.m. downgrade of WorldCom Group (NASDAQ NM: WCOM) and their tracking stock, MCI Group (NASDAQ NM: MCIT) from *market perform* to *market under perform*. The downgrade was reported to be based on analyst's beliefs that the telecommunications environment was unlikely to improve and followed WorldCom's debt downgrade to *junk* status from the prior day. Table 7.3 summarizes a small sample of financial analyst recommendations and ratings, including Goldman Sachs, for WorldCom from the YF web site as of May 10, 2002.

Figure 7.4 graphically presents the closing PPS of WorldCom Group common stock from June 1, 2000 through May 11, 2002. At the time of the Goldman Sachs downgrade from their *recommended list* to *market outperform* (July 11, 2001 from Table 7.3), WorldCom stock closed at $14.16 per share. At the time of the Goldman Sachs downgrade from *market outperform* to *market perform* (April 22, 2002 from Table 7.3), WorldCom stock closed at $4.01 per share. Finally, following the downgrade from *market perform* to *market under perform* (May 19, 2002 at 7:46 a.m.), WorldCom stock had a regular session (9:30 a.m. to 4 p.m.) opening price of $1.86 per share.

Table 7.3.   A Sample of Analyst Recommendations for WorldCom Group as of May 10, 2002.

Date	Analyst	Action	From	To
6-Feb-02	AG Edwards	upgrade	Hold	Buy
7-Mar-02	AG Edwards	downgrade	Buy	Hold
22-Apr-02	AG Edwards	downgrade	Hold	Sell
15-Nov-01	Credit Lyonnais	initiated	–	Buy
8-Feb-02	Credit Lyonnais	downgrade	Buy	Add
4-Apr-02	Credit Lyonnais	downgrade	Add	Hold
27-Jun-00	CSFB	downgrade	Strong Buy	Buy
1-Nov-00	CSFB	downgrade	Buy	Hold
22-Apr-02	CSFB	downgrade	Hold	Sell
11-Jul-01	Goldman Sachs	downgrade	Recommended List	Market Outperform
22-Apr-02	Goldman Sachs	downgrade	Market Outperform	Market Perform
16-Oct-01	Jefferies & Co	initiated	–	Hold
26-Apr-02	Jefferies & Co	downgrade	Hold	Sell

WorldCom Group

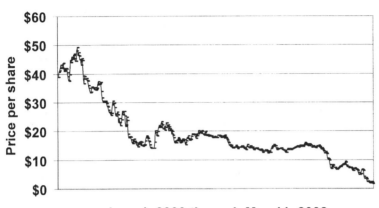

June 1, 2000 through May 11, 2002

Fig. 7.4. WorldCom Group Price per share.

The ridicule of financial analyst's recommendations were (and remain) commonplace on CNBC. This negative sentiment toward financial analysts has also appeared on the stock chat message boards, where these analysts are commonly criticized, as their records are examined and discussed among stock chat message board participants.

An early afternoon *Reuter's* article, written by Brian Kelleher and released on March 11, 2002, summarized an unprecedented, PurchasePro-related event:[55]

> . . . *a group of do-it-yourself researchers are trying to take the place of Wall Street pros, at least for one company. More than a dozen PurchasePro.com Inc. shareholders, frustrated that big investment banks no longer provide research on the business-to-business software maker, put out their own report on Monday to rally support for the Las Vegas-based company. The investors expect PurchasePro shares to soar more than 480% over the next 12 months . . . (n)ot surprisingly, they believe their PurchasePro shares are undervalued . . . (s)keptics could argue that their conclusion is biased, as they own shares of the company . . . (t)he group's position is no different from the money managers who appear on TV and in print every day, talking up shares of companies they own.*

This unprecedented case, where shareholders play the role of the financial analyst on a stock-chat message board, suggests that researchers of (previously thought to be) legitimate sources of public information (i.e. financial analysts) may wish to apply comparable research methodologies to information releases originating on the stock-chat message boards.

CASE DISCUSSION

This chapter has examined both legitimate and non-legitimate *public* information releases relating to PurchasePro. PurchasePro was a former big cap stock.
Like so many formerly big cap stocks, the post-April 2000 stock market crash
has converted many of these high PPS stocks to penny or micro-cap stock
status. Along with this new status, financial analyst coverage decreases or disap-
pears. Therefore, this sophisticated agent has been eliminated by market forces
(e.g. the decision by brokerage houses to avoid coverage of low PPS stocks).
In the case of PurchasePro, the stock once traded above $87 per share (December
1999).

Detailed discussion and examination were provided for six events. Seven
events, including that of the installation of a new CEO, are presented in Fig.
7.1. These events are summarized in Fig. 7.5. Four of these six events are represented in the headlines summarized in Appendix Chapter 7.1, provided to give
the researchers some sense of the sequence of events facing PurchasePro during
the period summarized in this chapter.

In the framework of agency theory, and, perhaps, at its most fundamental
level, *consumers* or *readers* of public information releases represent principals,
while the *authors* represent agents. The detailed events discussed in this chapter
are summarized in a variation of the numerical sequence and framework,
presented in the body of this chapter, but consistent with the relations presented
in Fig. 7.5.

PurchasePro Executives (Agents)

The former CEO of PurchasePro announced higher than anticipated earnings
per share (EPS), also known as a favorable earnings surprise (February 2001).
This public information provided a positive signal, resulting in an increase in
the PPS of PurchasePro stock. However, this public information was in error,
requiring two separate and downward restatements of EPS (May 2001).
Announcements of class action lawsuits quickly followed (May 2001). Errors
of this type are associated with increased uncertainty and risk, as they generate
concerns that additional future restatements may be required. Therefore,
the decision to buy, sell or hold PurchasePro stock resulted in the introduction
of or in increased levels of adverse selection (Chapter 2) or moral hazard
(Chapter 3).

The ex-CEO (agent) of PurchasePro filed Form 144s with the SEC (March
2001), signaling his intention to sell portions of his holdings in the firm's stock.
The academic literature suggests that insider or CEO purchases (sales) are

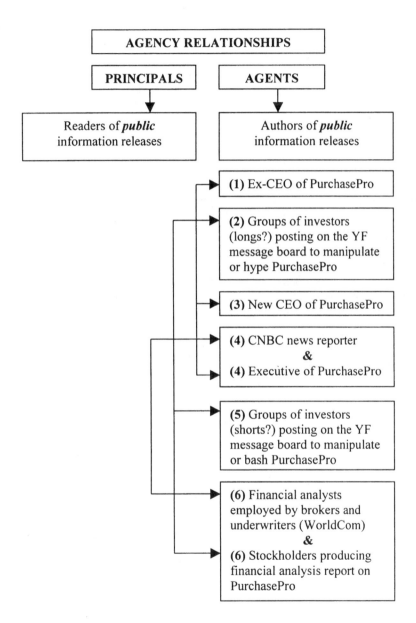

Fig. 7.5. Summary of Public Information Releases Examined in Chapter 7.

associated with future abnormal and positive (negative) returns, as they relate to the future PPS for a firm's stock (Chapter 3). The information provided by these SEC filings remains private, in the short-term, representing both hidden information and hidden action (Chapter 3).

The release and/or conversion of SEC Form 144 filings to public information may be delayed by as long as 30 to 45 days, after which it is available, free of charge, to the public. Premium services are available to permit accelerated Internet access to information related to these otherwise hidden actions. In this application, these fees for premium, accelerated SEC filing services represent one additional cost of monitoring (Chapter 3).

The announcement of a new CEO of PurchasePro (June 2001) was followed, several months later, by an open letter to shareholder principals (October 2001). In this public release, the new CEO suggests actions that shareholders may take to reduce the number of shares available for short selling, an action publicly known and associated, by both sophisticated and many unsophisticated investors, to reduce the PPS of a firm's stock. This public release signals, to shareholder principals, reasons other than PurchasePro financial statement-based fundamentals (or future prospects) for the decline in the firm's PPS. This decline in PPS is relevant, as PurchasePro requires recapitalization for survival (December 2001 and February 2002 news headlines, from Appendix chapter 7.1) and a lower PPS results in increased dilution, which may (and, in fact, does) require a reverse split to correct (May 2002 news headlines, from Appendix Chapter 7.1) in an effort to avoid exchange de-listing.

In an open letter, directed to a well-known CNBC reporter (agent), the PurchasePro executive in charge of Investor Relations (agent) takes exception to the negative, forward-looking and conjectural statements made about the firm (January 2002).[56] These statements possessed the potential for signaling a further decline in the PPS for PurchasePro stock and/or the failure of the PPS to recover, post-dated the first PurchasePro recapitalization effort (December 2001, from Appendix Chapter 7.1), but pre-dated the second PurchasePro recapitalization effort (February 2002 news headlines, from Appendix Chapter 7.1). Did these comments possess the potential to disrupt PurchasePro's recapitalization efforts?

Shareholders or Traders (Principals or Agents)

A failed pump or hype effort takes place, after those reading the YF stock-chat message boards are publicly informed, in advance, of the anticipated increase in the PPS for PurchasePro stock (August 2001). It is reasonable to conclude that those involved in this effort were principals, already holding long positions in PurchasePro. They may have failed to adequately consider publicly available information relating to SEC Form 144 filings, made by the ex-CEO of PurchasePro, suggesting some level of unsophisticated investor involvement in the effort.

A cancelled or failed bashing campaign, perhaps due to public disclosure on the YF PurchasePro stock-chat message board, may have been thwarted (February 2002). Alternatively, this may merely represent a flippant or non-serious threat. If a serious threat, it is reasonable to conclude that those involved would represent those principals with an existing short position in PurchasePro stock or seeking to take a long position (or become principals) in the stock after the anticipated PPS decline.

Principal investors, holding disclosed long positions in PurchasePro stock, produced and publicized their own informative analysis of the firm's future prospects (March 2002). This public information release was designed to fill the void left when financial analysts ceased coverage of the firm, after its PPS declined, and was unprecedented.

Broadcast Reporters and Financial Analysts (Agents)

A CNBC news reporter (agent) made some comments, viewed by the management of PurchasePro (agents) and shareholders (principals) to be negative and conjectural (January 2002). CNBC commentators (agents), perhaps quite justifiably, regularly criticize financial analysts (agents) for their failure to downgrade stocks in a timely manner (e.g. WorldCom during the May 2002 decline in the firm's PPS).

SUMMARY

This chapter provided for the examination of a single firm, PurchasePro, and several examples of both public and private information events. It is supplemented by a summary of news headlines (Appendix Chapter 7.1), and some examples of successful pump and dump efforts (Appendix Chapter 7.2).

It is important to realize that PurchasePro is like so many big caps, converted to small- and micro-cap stock status. As this change takes place, financial analysts cease coverage of these once big-cap stocks. These firms, therefore, are converted to neglected stock status (Chapter 4).

CHAPTER 8. DETAILED CASE STUDY 2: UNIVERSAL EXPRESS (OTC BB: USXP)

The pile of Merrill Lynch emails released by New York attorney-general Eliot Spitzer last month support his contention that the broker's internet analysts sacrificed their integrity in order to drum up business for their investment banking colleagues (Chaffin, 2002).

INTRODUCTION

Chapter 3 provided coverage of moral hazard and discussion of the structural incompatibility of analyst and underwriting functions (see Fig. 3.3). Contemporary investigations by the SEC and other regulators allege that public information releases, by financial analysts may have been misleading. They may have failed to disclose *private* information that was inconsistent with these public announcements. Their motivation, it has been alleged, was to profit from enormous underwriting fees.

These (misleading) behaviors have long been presumed to persist in the small- or micro-cap markets (e.g. OTC BB and Pink Sheets). Therefore, the researcher interested in studying contemporary big-cap stock market structures (and failures) may gain useful insights through the study of the small- and micro-cap stocks.

This chapter will use Universal Express, Incorporated (Universal Express; OTC BB: USXP), a neglected micro-cap or penny stock, to illustrate the significicant effect of information on an OTC BB or Pink Sheet stock. Universal Express (USXP), unlike PurchasePro (Chapter 7), was not a technology stock that enjoyed rapid PPS increases and big cap status during the late 1990s. USXP did, however, enjoy a relatively significant increase in PPS after a legitimate public information release relating to a favorable court judgment. Since news of this judgment, USXP has issued corporate news releases, frequently, the vast majority of which have had nothing to do with the favorable court judgment or prospects for collections of this amount. Furthermore, there has been significant dilution, through the issuance of additional shares of USXP stock.

This chapter will provide company background information and details associated with a *public* information release. It will also provide an illustration of market efficiency (or inefficiency), as the legitimate, public news release for this neglected stock was summarized and spammed via the Internet's stock-chat message boards. This case also introduces the researcher to methods of financing, commonly employed by these penny or micro-cap stocks. Finally, the topic of stock price and market maker manipulation (MMM), as well as that of "naked shorting," is introduced and a chapter summary is provided.

COMPANY BACKGROUND

Universal Express (USXP) is an integrated B2B service company. The president, chairman of the board of directors, and chief executive officer (CEO) of USXP is Richard A. Altomare.

At the end of their March 31, 2001, quarter, USXP had a negative book value, negative earnings per share, and a current ratio below 1.0. The firm's stock had a 52-week low of $0.014 and a 52-week high of $0.305. The 52-week high was achieved on July 31, 2001, after news releases relating to a $389 million judgment in USXP's favor. With a market capitalization of about $8 million, USXP had approximately 59 million shares outstanding and a float of about 54 million shares at the date of the news release. By June 2002, 15 months later, USXP had approximately 190 million shares issued and outstanding. By March 2003, USXP had approximately 346 million shares issued and outstanding and the stock was trading well below $0.01 per share.

THE NEWS

On July 26, 2001, at 12:43 a.m., a Business Wire[57] news release announced that the Circuit Court, Dade County, Florida, had awarded Universal Express damages in a favorable verdict for $389 million. The award was for fraud and conversion, failure to honor previous funding commitments and stock manipulation. This judgment was final and could not be appealed, according to the prominent Miami attorney specializing in this area of litigation. The breakdown of the $389 million (with separable amounts rounded) follows:

- $87 million in compensatory damages,
- $26 million in interest, and
- $275 million in (tripled) punitive damages.

An extremely professional table and examination of the anticipated impact of the award on the PPS of Universal Express stock was produced on August 6, 2001, at 4:56 p.m. Assuming attorney's fees of 33% and 58,250,206 shares outstanding, the PPS ranged from $0.22 (at a 5% collections rate) to $4.47 (at a 100% collections rate).

Select Capital had been found liable for their actions in a common scam played on SC and OTC companies, seeking financing through convertible debentures. They sold Universal Express's stock at $2 per share and bought it back at $0.05 to $0.07 to cover their short positions. Below is a generic illustration of how *death spiral financing* works:

A financial institution offers a company $1 million in cash in return for the right to purchase the firm's stock at a discount of 20%. The firm agrees to register these shares under an S-registration and provide them to the financial institution at the agreed upon 20% discount to the "bid" price. Since many financial institutions are also registered brokers/dealers in securities, they short the form's stock to $0.10 per share. Therefore, the financial institution, by selling shares short, has flooded the market with additional sell orders/shares of the firm's stock, depressing the stock price below that at which the firm's stock would trade at "market." At the same time, the firm is filing the S-8 with the SEC. After achieving what the financial institution believes is the lowest price possible (e.g. $0.10), they receive $1 million in shares in the firm's stock at a price of $0.08 instead of $0.10 (i.e. the 20% discount). In some cases, the financial institution may be able to use this technique to acquire control of the firm.

Those posting on the RB message board appeared to be fully aware of these facts. In the words of *Invest_tech,*[58] a convertible debenture:

> . . . *is the most desperate (sic) type of financing available to a public company. It is a last resort when all else fails.*

In the case of Universal Express, questions remained. How much (if any) of the $389 million award would be collected?

At the time of the award, Universal Express had about 50–60 million shares outstanding. Therefore, if the entire amount were collected, the judgment would result in a cash infusion of approximately $7 per share before attorney's and collection fees. At the close of trading on July 26, 2001, Universal Express stock was trading at about $0.05 per share, opening at $0.017 and closing at $0.048 per share following the initial *public* information release. Volume of shares traded on July 26, 2001, exceeded 42 million, approximately 16 times the average daily volume for Universal Express stock.

THE BROAD DISSEMINATION OF INFORMATION ON THE INTERNET

On the RB message boards, *nitehawk62*[59] noted:

> *Man did this stock get pumped on Yahoo over night. Going to be a nice GAP UP this AM.*

More than 1,000 posts of messages (below) appeared on the Yahoo! Finance (YF) investment stock-chat message boards. These posts were completed during the evening after news had been released of the $389 million judgment favoring Universal Express. A representative example of the message was posted by *new_alias_2001us*.[60] (YF did not, at the time, maintain a stock chat message board for Universal Express, per se.) The message, complete with typos and errors, follows:

> ***%1000 IN ONE WEEK***
>
> *This is a once in a lifetime chance folks. USXP is currently trading for .05. After lawyer fees and taxes there will be around $150 million left to put in the companys bank account. Based on the 50 million share float, that gives USXP a $3 a share cash value. 80 Million shares have been traded in the past two days in anticipation of the next press release. The next press release should put us well over the $1 mark and that alone is 20X your investment if you get in early. Don't wait to get shares cause a lot of people are gonna jump on this train as soon as the bell rings. Last week USXP had 18K in cash and was trading for roughly 0.015. Next week they will have $150 million in cash and should be trading around $3. What are you waiting for? The earlier you put your order in the closer to the front of the line you will be monday morning. There have been massive buy orders in the past two days, 500K at a time and even 2 million share trades. Get yours before its too late!!!!!!!!!!!!!!!!!!! USXP*

The impact of these postings appears to have been significant. Table 8.1 provides pre-open bid/ask changes for the 30 minutes prior to the 9:30 a.m. (regular trading session) open. The highest bid rose from $0.049 to $0.057 (16%) and the lowest ask rose from $0.051 to $0.058 (14%) during this 30-minute period. Figures 8.1 and 8.2 provide supplemental graphics of price and volume measures for the July 2 through July 26, 2001 period.

Table 8.2 provides the firm's reverse split and stock dividend history, while Table 8.3 provides some measures for the two-month trading period surrounding the July 26, 2001, after hours news release. Some exploratory statistics were generated to measure relations between RB stock chat message board posts (see Fig. 8.3), 4 p.m. closing prices and volume for Universal Express.

MsgPctChg is the trading day to trading day percentage change in RB stock chat message board messages, PPSPctChg is the percentage change in PPS and VolPctChg is the percentage change in the volume or number of shares traded. All three metrics are from 4 p.m. close to 4 p.m. close.

USXP: High, Low & Close and Impact of News of $389M Judgement

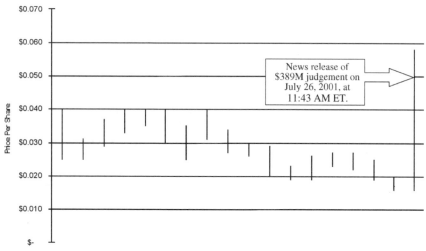

Fig. 8.1. USXP: High, Low & Close and Impact of News of 3389M Judgement.

USXP: Volume of Shares Traded

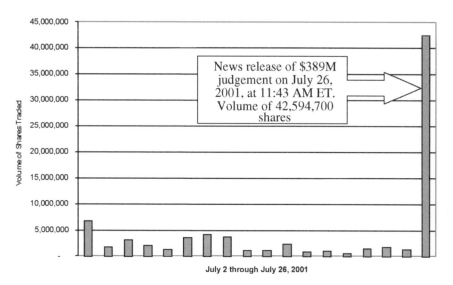

Fig. 8.2. USXP: Volume of Shares Traded.

USXP Raging Bull Messages

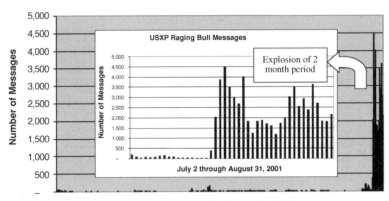

June 30, 1998 through August 31, 2001

Fig. 8.3. USXP Raging Bull Messages.

Table 8.1. July 27, 2001 Pre-Market Activity for USXP.

Time	Bid	Incremental Pct Chg – Bid	Ask	Incremental Pct Chg – Ask	Volume
9:00:43 AM	$0.049				5,000
9:19:37 AM			$0.051		5,000
9:19:49 AM	$0.050	2.04%			5,000
9:22:00 AM	$0.051	2.00%			5,000
9:22:32 AM			$0.053	3.92%	5,000
9:22:44 AM	$0.052	1.96%			5,000
9:22:57 AM			$0.055	3.77%	5,000
9:23:16 AM	$0.054	3.85%			5,000
9:24:27 AM			$0.058	5.45%	5,000
9:24:53 AM	$0.057	5.56%			5,000

Table 8.2. USXP: Reverse Split (RS) and Stock Dividend (%) History.

Amount	Ex-Date	Pay-Date	Record-Date	Announcement Date
12 to 1 RS	8-Nov-96	N/A	N/A	N/A
70 to 1 RS	30-Jun-98	N/A	N/A	N/A
4%	15-May-99	N/A	N/A	N/A
4%	18-Jul-00	15-Aug-00	20-Jul-00	20-Jun-00
8%	19-Sep-01	16-Oct-01	21-Sep-01	21-Aug-01

Table 8.3. Selected USXP Measures Surrounding USXP News Release Event Date.

MsgPctChg	PPSPctChg	Volume	VolPctChg	Date
–2.41546%	25.0000%	6773500	–41.3829%	02–Jul–01
–52.97030%	–3.3333%	1764800	–73.9455%	03–Jul–01
–62.10526%	20.6897%	3190800	80.8024%	05–Jul–01
102.77778%	8.5714%	2082000	–34.7499%	06–Jul–01
–5.47945%	0.0000%	1371800	–34.1114%	09–Jul–01
7.24638%	–13.1579%	3592400	161.8749%	10–Jul–01
85.13514%	–3.0303%	4189500	16.6212%	11–Jul–01
12.40876%	0.0000%	3771800	–9.9702%	12–Jul–01
–31.16883%	–6.2500%	1150300	–69.5026%	13–Jul–01
–5.66038%	–3.3333%	1246900	8.3978%	16–Jul–01
–50.00000%	–24.1379%	2342500	87.8659%	17–Jul–01
0.00000%	0.0000%	877900	–62.5229%	18–Jul–01
–22.00000%	18.1818%	1045200	19.0568%	19–Jul–01
–17.94872%	–3.8462%	575500	–44.9388%	20–Jul–01
–28.12500%	0.0000%	1504400	161.4075%	23–Jul–01
–13.04348%	–16.0000%	1727800	14.8498%	24–Jul–01
–35.00000%	–19.0476%	1404200	–18.7290%	25–Jul–01
2792.30769%	182.3529%	42594700	2933.3784%	26–Jul–01
443.35106%	–12.5000%	36471300	–14.3760%	27–Jul–01
89.18257%	323.8095%	71134700	95.0430%	30–Jul–01
16.06727%	–17.4157%	62480500	–12.1659%	31–Jul–01
–22.29157%	–0.6803%	27640900	–55.7608%	01–Aug–01
–14.25703%	29.4521%	15058800	–45.5199%	02–Aug–01
–10.27099%	13.2275%	19860700	31.8877%	03–Aug–01
49.70172%	–14.4860%	11147900	–43.8696%	06–Aug–01
–54.47073%	–19.1257%	13636900	22.3271%	07–Aug–01
–31.83807%	–12.8378%	8635500	–36.6755%	08–Aug–01
46.95024%	–29.4574%	14777600	71.1262%	09–Aug–01
2.89459%	36.2637%	11507300	–22.1301%	10–Aug–01
–8.59873%	–11.2903%	6210900	–46.0264%	13–Aug–01
–6.44599%	–4.5455%	3960600	–36.2315%	14–Aug–01
–26.13284%	0.0000%	3697300	–6.6480%	15–Aug–01
45.46218%	35.2381%	21178200	472.8018%	16–Aug–01
14.09590%	–1.4085%	7807800	–63.1328%	17–Aug–01
53.62025%	–12.8571%	6607600	–15.3718%	20–Aug–01
14.76599%	20.4918%	13595800	105.7600%	21–Aug–01
–26.82366%	4.7619%	8995600	–33.8354%	22–Aug–01
14.56044%	4.5455%	6412400	–28.7163%	23–Aug–01
–18.73929%	0.6211%	4885900	–23.8054%	24–Aug–01
53.28836%	–5.5556%	4909700	0.4871%	27–Aug–01
–25.79758%	–1.9608%	7623900	55.2824%	28–Aug–01
–31.69014%	–10.0000%	3059700	–59.8670%	29–Aug–01

Table 8.3.   Continued.

MsgPctChg	PPSPctChg	Volume	VolPctChg	Date
−1.95334%	−5.1852%	1690700	−44.7429%	30–Aug–01
19.75650%	9.3750%	6178200	265.4226%	31–Aug–01

$MsgPctChg \times VolPctChg = r = 0.962$; $R^2 = 0.925$ (F = 515.7; $N = 44$)

$PPSPctChg = I'cept + MsgPctChg + error$ produced R^2 at 0.223
(F = 12.1; $N = 44$)

SOME STATISTICAL MEASURES

The Pearson product moment correlation (r) between MsgPctChg and VolPctChg is very high, at 0.962 ($N = 44$), suggesting that trading volume and RB message board posts are very highly correlated. The R-squared (R^2) for these two variables is 92.5% (F = 515.7). As a predictor of change in PPS (PPSPctChg), RB messages for Universal Express (MsgPctChg) produced an R-square of only 22.3% (F = 12.1).

Recall that 42.6 million shares traded on July 26, 2001. On July 27, 2001, more than 1 million shares traded in the first minute (by 9:31 a.m.). By 9:39 a.m., the first 10 minutes of trading, 3 million shares traded. Six million shares (10% of the entire float of about 50–70 million shares) traded in the first 20 minutes (by 9:48 a.m.). And by 10 a.m., 9 million shares of Universal Express stock had traded. However, the entire July 27, 2001, trading day resulted in 36.5 million shares of Universal Express stock changing hands. Therefore, more than 25% of the day's trading (9:30 a.m. to 4 p.m.) occurred in the first 30 minutes of the trading day.

When these high volume levels are achieved, conjecture always enters into the conversations on the stock chat message boards. In the case of Universal Express, even prior to the July 26, 2001, announcement, conversations included the possibility that the Universal Express's float was increased by market makers (MMs) via "naked shorting" techniques. Both before and after the news release of the $389 million judgment, it was alleged that Knight (NASDAQ NM: NITE) was spearheading these behaviors, as a representative post by *upthbid* (RB message number 9335) suggests:

> *NITE will not let this stock run . . . MMs got killed yesterday they will short it until they can slow it down and cover.*

MOTIVATING FACTORS FOR THE INTENTIONAL GENERATION OF INFORMATION ASYMMETRY

The stock-chat message boards are filled with information. Some is truthful; some is intended to deceive or manipulate the PPS of the firm's stock. This mixture generates much "noise." The reader endeavors to correctly identify those factual informational components to be considered when buying or selling a stock.

To the extent that the *author* (agent) of the message is successful in misleading the *reader* (principal), the author(s) possess *hidden, private* or *asymmetric information*. They seek to provide *signals* to those *monitoring* the message boards, in an effort to maximize personal gains. The motivating factors for providing both negative and positive information are summarized in the following sections.

Motivating Factors for Bashing – Negative Information. Motivating factors for spreading negative information, whether factual, fabricated or comprised of a mixture of truth and fiction include:

(1) reduction of the price of the stock for a lower entry or purchase price,
(2) swing- or day-traders in the "buy" mode,
(3) personal satisfaction (i.e. ego trip) for poster,
(4) reduction of the price of the stock for profitable short covering,
(5) amusement for minors, and/or
(6) retaliation against the company for prior losses.

Motivating Factors for Hyping – Positive Information. In their study of voluntary disclosures of equity offerings, Lang and Lundholm (2000) found that firms significantly increasing disclosure activities in the six months prior to the offering experience PPS increases, but these disclosures may be used to hype the stock, and may be followed by significant PPS declines upon the issuance of these equities.

Motivating factors for spreading positive information, whether factual, fabricated or comprised of a mixture of truth and fiction include:

(1) increasing the price of the stock for a profitable sale,
(2) swing- or day-traders in the "sell" mode,
(3) personal satisfaction (i.e. ego trip) for the poster,
(4) increasing the price of the stock for a long term holder of the stock, and/or
(5) amusement for minors.

ARE PEOPLE PAID TO BASH OR HYPE STOCKS ON STOCK-CHAT MESSAGE BOARDS?

The following (late August 2001) exchange occurred on the RB stock-chat message board for Universal Express:

From kurtnv_1: msg # 68980, Wednesday, 29 August 2001.

. . . what would be the reason to bash a bad stock? . . . I have a rough time believing bashers are performing a selfless public service.

From DC-Steve: msg #69016.

. . . you are operating on the assumption that folks only post for financial gain.

From kurtnv_1: msg #69317.

I do know that paid bashers exist. . . . the last place I worked at hired them as well as hypers. Microcap_Matty may actually be having issues as a result of his alleged part in a hoax.

From DC-Steve: msg #69326.

What outfit do you know of that has hired paid bashers and pumpers?

From kurtnv_1: msg #69358.

DC: We went under the name of Marketing Direct Concepts, we use (sic) to issue a stock advisory letter called the StockUp Report we (sic) issues quarterly (more like when we wanted to pump or bash something). And our beloved imperious leader made millions on Oshman's Sporting Goods (OSH). We also covertly represented a bogus organization called the "Association for Investor Awareness Council" (AIA Council). I am so glad I was just network administrator, fixing the computers.

Do a search on Google for Marketing Direct Concepts, there are still flames out there on it.

DC-Steve: RB msg #69367.

kurt, thanks. After that association, I'd think you'd be more wary of penny stock pumps. If you know how those guys operated, surely you're aware there is a lot more energy and effort put into pumping penny stocks than bashing them.

BTW, were any of the folks you say were paid to bash stocks paid to bash penny stocks?

Kurtnv_1: msg #69386.

DC There were a number of stocks, I can't remember all of them, and I was a lot more ignorant back then. I would have to say yes, we had a huge database of fund managers and small cap brokers we worked with. Yes worked with.

Yes I am wary of pennies and this is the only one I'm playing right now. I have guarded optimism.

DC-Steve had been accused of being a "paid" basher. After a review of the posting history of DC-Steve, it was concluded that this was, in no small part, due to his own posting history and a conversation with another poster from another firm's RB message board, as follows:

Rato_Gordura[61]: msg #69918.

> *OT: Steve- did you get the email from FAKE. There's a bonus if we set another 52 week low and close below three!!*

DC-Steve: msg #69923; original post was msg #412813 (IFTP board).

> *I'm on it, Rato. I'm even calling in some markers with ERNS & NITE to make sure they help us make it happen! They owe me big time after all the help I gave them in destroying BIFT so that Sprint might survive.*

ARE MARKET MAKERS MANIPULATING STOCK PRICES?

"An early contribution to the "order-arrival" literature, Niederhoffer and Osborne (1966), drew attention to the fact that specialist market makers could make use of their knowledge of the order-arrival process as revealed by limit orders to derive monopolistic trading profits" (Dunne 1994, p. 79).

Market makers possess private (incoming order flow) information. In early June 2002, allegations of *front-running* flooded the business press and media, and SEC and NASD investigations were underway to examine trading practices at the Knight Trading Group, Incorporated (NASDAQ NM: NITE):

> Knight Trading is currently battling allegations of front-running by a former top trader at the firm . . . in a 2001 arbitration filing with the National Association of Securities Dealers, alleged that traders were making trades for their own accounts ahead of customer orders in the same stock. Knight denies the allegations of front-running, but acknowledged Tuesday that the Securities and Exchange Commission has launched an informal investigation (Cramer 2002).

Knight Trading Group handled more than 11% of all NASDAQ trading in 2000.[62] Carrel (2002) notes:

> This isn't the first time the big trader . . .has gotten into trouble. In January, an earlier NASD investigation into trading-rule violations, including failing to honor trades at publicly posted prices,[63] concluded with Knight paying a $1.5 million fine. It was the largest penalty ever imposed by the NASD for such violations. In addition, between 1997 and 2001, the Jersey City, N. J.-based firm was named in 10 NASD regulatory actions, according to the Journal, alleging violations that included attempting to trade a halted stock, failing to keep

adequate trading records and not being prompt enough in executing customer orders. Without
confirming or denying the allegations, Knight paid fines ranging from $1,000 to $50,000.

Some of the academic research has attempted to separately examine inventory
control effects (e.g. the specialist's role as a dealer, required to maintain inventories to ensure an orderly market) from asymmetric information effects (e.g.
the specialists role as an investor, attempting to generate returns from inventories).

For example, a study by Hasbrouck and Sofianos (1993) examined the trades
of NYSE specialists (MMs or dealers).[64] They concluded that the principal
source of specialist trading profits were from short-term trades. Furthermore,
those trades involving specialist participation had a higher immediate impact
when compared to trades excluding specialist participation. Hasbrouck and
Sofianos found that NYSE specialist profits were due almost entirely to the bid-
ask spread.

Madhaven and Smidt (1993) developed a model, incorporating both inventory and information effects, and tested it using inventory data from a NYSE
specialist. After controlling for inventory effects, the half-life of inventories
declined to approximately seven days. Quote revisions (toward the mean) were
negatively related to specialist trades and positively related to the information
conveyed by incoming order imbalances. Their results, with respect to the
greater informational content of nonblock orders (where *uninformed* agents are
presumed to submit block orders and *informed* agents place a series of smaller
trades), were consistent with those from Seppi (1990), Madhaven and Smidt
(1991), and Keim and Madhaven (1992). They found the specialist to be "an
active investor . . . profiting in the short term from information about impending
order imbalances" (1618).

In a study by Christie and Schultz (1994), the results of which were reported
by several national newspapers on May 26 and 27, 1994, the question of implicit
collusion (e.g. information asymmetry) among NASDAQ dealers was raised.
At issue were the wide inside (e.g. bid-ask) spreads and the avoidance of odd-
eight quotes. Using the May 27, 1994 event date, Christie et al. (1994) found
an immediate reaction to these news releases. The day following national news
coverage, dealers for Amgen, Cisco Systems, and Microsoft significantly
increased their use of odd-eighth quotes and mean inside spreads fell nearly
50%. This pattern repeated for Apple Computer the following day, as virtually
all dealers moved in unison to adopt odd-eighth quotes.

In anticipation (and support) of the NYSE move toward decimalization,
Easley et al. (1996a) investigated the incidence of what is referred to as "cream-
skimming." They tested the hypothesis that purchased order flow facilitated the
increased availability of uninformed liquidity trades, leaving information-based

trades to establish the market for a security. In their examination of both NYSE and Cincinnati stock exchanges, they identified significant, exchange-based differences in the information content of orders. Their results were consistent with cream-skimming.

In a later extension, Easley et al. (1996b examine information-based trading for both active and infrequently traded stocks. They find a lower probability of information-based trading for high volume stocks.

In a laboratory market, Bloomfield (1996) found that market makers established quotes to protect against adverse selection and to control inventory. The laboratory setting examined the behaviors of two uninformed MMs competing with heterogeneously informed investors.

SUMMARY

The case study of Universal Express, contained in this chapter, complements the case study of PurchasePro.com, contained in Chapter 7. Universal Express is a true penny or micro-cap stock.

Appendix chapters are provided to supplement this case. First, Appendix Chapter 8.1 provides examples of messages posted by the RB stock-chat message boards by someone using the Universal Express CEO's name as an alias. Appendix Chapter 8.2 provides a very small sample of some of the news releases and Universal Express announcements made by the firm. Appendix Chapter 8.3 provides the researcher with an introduction to *cybersmear* (see Cataldo and Killough 2003), a topic of increased concerns and allegedly tied to shorting and naked-shorting. These topics are coming under increased scrutiny by the SEC and, perhaps, too often, used to scapegoat brokerage firms and to explain PPS decreases in small- and micro-cap stocks. Finally, Appendix Chapter 8.4 introduces the researcher to the topic of market maker manipulation (MMM).

The above appendix chapters provide supplemental introductions to topics likely to be relevant to researchers interested in "tooling up" via study of the Universal Express case. Recall that Universal Express did, in fact, receive a favorable judgment of $389 million. Whether these monies are ever collected is interesting, but secondary. What is likely to be of greatest interest to researchers of agency theory (Chapters 2 and 3 in Section I) and capital markets efficiency (Chapters 4 and 5 in Section II) is the study and use of this case to extend and generalize future findings from studies and increase their understanding of the contemporary topics of shorting, naked-shorting, and market maker manipulation (MMM). All involve the establishment and preservation of condition of *information asymmetry*, *hidden* and *private* information. And, increasingly, these matters, which are more prevalent in the less efficient small- and micro-cap markets, are drawing the attention of the SEC and other regulators.

CHAPTER 9. CASES LISTED ON THE SILICON INVESTOR (SI) STOCK-CHAT MESSAGE BOARD[65]

> Given the large range of informational stipulations in the theory, it is surprising that so little empirical analysis of the informational structure of the lawsuits exists (Osborne, 1999, p. 399).

INTRODUCTION

From an agency theory perspective, the firm represents a series of contracts between groups of owners, managers, and employees. Each group has a unique utility function. Therefore, contracts are designed to maximize the utility for each group, but under constraints imposed by the contracts of others. The application of agency theory does not, however, require the goal of wealth maximization.

Agency theory is also applied in political science, where it is used to explain the behaviors of regulators and/or bureaucracies. Applications to the study of law are also common, where it is used as a structure to examine and explain the responsibility of unlawful behaviors.

This chapter begins with a few illustrative examples of information asymmetry. First, it provides a (rare) post on a stock-chat message board where the author admits to intentional deceit (i.e. the intentional generation of information asymmetry). Next, two examples of non-economically motivated hoaxes, perpetrated via the Internet's stock-chat message boards, will be presented. Brief summaries of the conflicting and equally desirable objectives of combating cybersmear and protecting free speech are also introduced. The remainder of this chapter is devoted to the development and examination of some descriptive statistics, relating to a non-randomly selected sample of 126 observations of litigation-related allegations of the improper generation of information asymmetry, the development of two, broad hypotheses and a brief discussion of some intuitively appealing findings.

A STOCK-CHAT MESSAGE BOARD POST ADMITTING DECEIT

The following is an atypically cruel and blatant illustration of the types of information asymmetry, seen daily on the stock-chat message boards. There is very little reason for inhibition on these boards, though anecdotal evidence suggests that some spend enormous amounts of time over extended periods to develop deceitful aliases for use and reuse. This message (#231632, dated March 26, 2002) dealt with covering a short position and was posted on the YF message boards for WorldCom stock:

> . . . I didn't sell. *I lied* (emphasis added) that I did to lure you into covering . . . YOU on the other hand posted that you covered 10K short shares at a time when the price was around $6.85. Meaning . . . you HAVE LOST approximately (and at the very LEAST) $8,500.00 . . . in less than 24 hours!
>
> . . . you could have covered at $6 just a few minutes ago . . . . . . I hate to see anybody lose money . . . especially an emotional cripple like yourself.

In June 1998, the SEC created an Office of Internet Enforcement to deal with increasing securities fraud (e.g. market manipulation) over the Internet. In August 2000, the SEC awarded employee-owned Science Applications International Corporation (San Diego, CA) a $4.9 million contract to develop software designed to detect online fraud.

THE IMPACT OF INTERNET-BASED HOAXES

In addition to the cases, summarized in Appendix Chapter 9.1, some stock-chat message board posts are nothing more than hoaxes, without profit motive. Below are brief summaries of two such cases:

PairGain. On April 7, 1999, a Southern California communications gear-maker/engineer – an employee of PairGain Technologies Limited since 1997 – created a Web site that looked like a *Bloomberg News* article, suggesting that PairGain was about to be acquired by Israeli-owned ECI Telecom Limited for $1.35 billion. Over just a few hours, the stock soared by 32% to $11.13 per share, before the story was exposed as a fake.

The FBI traced the Internet address to a 26-year old resident of Raleigh, North Carolina. He was ordered to pay $93,000 in restitution to investors who purchased the stock and sold at a loss after the company denied the report. He was also sentenced to five months of home detention and five years of probation. There was no evidence of personal gain from the hoax.

Webnode. On April 24, 1999, Business Wire (Webnode) filed a lawsuit[66] against the 38-year-old president of a Westport, Connecticut firm called Insurance Software Solutions, a web designer who put together the fictitious site and an art historian, residing in Milan, Italy, for their April Fool's gag – a phony press release, as follows:

> *WebNode.com today announced it has been granted an exclusive contract by the U.S. Department of Energy (DOE) Office of Science (formerly Office of Energy Research) to raise $4 billion in funding for the new countrywide state-of-the-art fiber optic Next Generation Internet (NGI) to replace the existing copper backbone.*
>
> *Webnode.com's contract calls for it to sell 40 million nodes on the NGI to the general public. Each node will carry an initial value of $100.*

These three were regular posters on the SI message boards. The suit alleged fraud and infringement of the *Business Wire* trademark.

The April 1, 1999, release claimed that the U.S. Department of Energy granted Webnode (a fictitious company) the exclusive right to raise funds for the next-generation Internet. The pranksters paid *Business Wire* $260 to distribute the false release. The announcement and the fictitious site (webnode.com) attracted more than 2,000 inquiries. *Wire News*, unknowingly, picked up and repeated the false press release.

The same group pulled an April Fools prank in the prior year, as well. Setting up a phony web site for FBN (Fly by Night) Associates, they concocted a false press release for the fictitious firm's product, a modified Timex watch that could detect Y2K non-compliant computers simply by being worn near them. This earlier April Fools prank included an announcement that the product had received a blessing from the pope. However, in this earlier prank, the trio did not distribute the release on *Business Wire.*

The case was settled for a $27,500 payment to *Business Wire* by Safeco Insurance, the homeowner's policy insurer (e.g. personal liability insurance) for one of the defendants.

ATTACKING CYBERSMEAR

Generally, a firm must first obtain a subpoena forcing Yahoo! Finance (YF; NASDAQ: YHOO),[67] Raging Bull (RB), Silicon Investor (SI, owned by Go2Net)), America Online (AOL), Stockhouse Media (SM) or the relevant stock-chat site, to provide the message-board users' registration information. After the firm secures a court order to force the Internet service provider (ISP) to identify those posting these messages, papers are filed in the appropriate venue/court. The Communications Decency Act of 1996[68] protects AOL and other Web sites from being sued for libelous and/or false statements appearing on their bulletin boards and stock-chat rooms.

PROTECTING ANONYMITY AND FREE SPEECH

Several organizations provide for the protection of free speech on the Internet:

The Electronic Frontier Foundation (EFF; http://www.eff.org) was founded in July of 1990. It is the leading civil liberties organization working to protect rights of free speech in general and in the digital world. Based in San Francisco, EFF is donor-supported.

The Protective Action League (PAL; Protective@erols.com) was formed by three firms, joined together to form an advocacy and protection group to protect SC firms and to combat stock bashing.

The Public Citizen Litigation Group was founded by Ralph Nader in 1971 and is a non-profit consumer advocacy organization. They have filed suits on behalf of John Does to protect the anonymity of Internet critics.

The Electronic Privacy Information Center (EPIC) was founded in 1994 and is a non-profit research group that examines free speech issues on the Internet. In the context of cybersmear, they are best known for their joint suit (joining forces with the ACLU) against YF. Prior to the suit, YF routinely disclosed the identities of users – without prior notice – in response to subpoenas.

The American Civil Liberties Union (ACLU), Americans for Computer Privacy (ACP), the Internet Free Expression Alliance (IFEA), Privacy International (Privacy.org), the John Does Anonymous Foundation (JDAF; www.johndoes.org), the Liberty Project, and lawsuits, under the heading of Strategic Litigation Against Public Participation (SLAPP), represent other organizations and acronyms to be reviewed by researchers interested in studying these cases.

THE DATA BASE

There are multiple purposes for providing the case summaries (see Appendix Chapter 9.1) of the listings contained in this chapter:

First, these summaries provide the means for classification of these observations for hypothesis development and testing.

Second, researchers and graduate students may chose to examine this same data base, add to it, and extend it as the population of observations grows or can be more fully developed from the SI message boards or additional Internet site links and other sources. The primary purpose of the case summaries is not to provide formal or legal case citations, but to classify the event for a specific application.

Finally, the objective of this listing is not to determine guilt or innocence or eventual outcome of the litigation. It is for this reason that the terms "alleged" or "allegedly" (or a derivative) have been used, liberally, as many of these cases may remain "in process" and the eventual outcome may not have yet been determined.

DATA ASSEMBLY AND RESEARCH METHODOLOGY

The methods used to select the 126 observations contained in Appendix Chapter 9.1 follow:

The first step was to summarize call letter(s)/ticker(s) using the CBSMarketWatch (and other) web site(s) and the references (or audit trail) provided in the articles examined from the SI web site. These results are summarized in Table 9.1.

Columns in Table 9.1 indicate whether the stock has been listed and traded on the New York Stock Exchange (NY), America Stock Exchange (AX), NASDAQ (NAZ), over-the-counter bulletin board (OTC BB), PinkSheets (PK) and/or a foreign exchange (For). Therefore, the call letter(s) for the publicly held firms, listed in Table 9.1, may represent those used for several (but not necessarily all) exchanges for which the firm's securities have been listed.

Hypothesis 1. One might find it intuitively appealing to hypothesize that a larger portion of the firms with information asymmetry-related problems, suggested through successful hyping or cybersmear efforts and litigation-based firm responses, might be mirco-cap or penny stocks and listed on the PinkSheets or OTC BB exchanges. These exchanges contain a relatively large number of neglected securities (see Chapter 4), have larger bid/ask spreads and, therefore, are presumed to maintain relatively high levels of information asymmetry. A quantitative framework for this hypothesis is provided by Eq. (9.1), in the alternative form, as follows:

$$NY < AX < NAZ < OTC\ BB < Pink \qquad (9.1)$$

where the number of observations on the PinkSheets would be highest, followed by the OTC BB stocks, followed by the NAZ (NASDAQ) stocks, and so on.

Table 9.1 subtotal results suggest that the largest number of stocks, from this non-randomly selected sample, were (at one time in their history) listed on the OTC BB ($n = 49$). A more precise examination might associate the legal actions with the exchange, using the commencement of the alleged information asymmetry event date, but is beyond the scope of this chapter and monograph.

Table 9.1. Summary of Observations Examined – Exchanges and Call Letters/Tickers.

Obs	Firm Name	NY	AX	NAZ	OTCBB	Pink	For	Call Letter(s)/Ticker(s)
				Exchange(s)				
1	2TheMart.com					X	X	TMRT/918319
2	4KidsEntertainment	X						KDE
3	AgriBio Tech					X	X	ABTX(Q)/900501
4	AHT				X			ADVH/AHTC(Q)
5	AirTran Holdings	X						AAIR/AAI
6	AK Steel Holdings	X					X	AKS/AKSPR/0015720/890363
7	Amazon Natural Treas.					X	X	AZNT/ANTD
8	Americare Health Scan				X			AMIT
9	AnswerThinkConsult Gp				X		X	ANSW/ANSR/914597
10	Ants Software				X			ANTS
11	Apple Computer			X			X	AAPL/6689/865985
12	Aqua Vie Beverage				X			AVBC
13	Ashton Technology			X	X		X	ASTN/912022
14	Ashworth			X			X	ASHW/885358
15	Bid.com			X			X	ADBI/ADY/917499
16	BioFiltration Systems					X		BIFS
17	Biomatrix	X					X	BXM/882548
18	BioPulse International				X		X	BIOP/BPZ/917016
19	BioShield Technologies				X	X	X	BSTIU/BSTI/924511
20	Bridge Publications	–	–	–	–	–	–	Not applicable/Privately firm
21	Brightpoint			X			X	CELLL/CELL/897867
22	Broadband Wireless Int'l					X		BBAN
23	Callaway Golf	X						ELY
24	Caremark Rx	X			X		X	CMX/CMXKO/899118
25	Carnegie Int'l		X		X	X		CGYC/CGY
26	CBQ				X			CBQI
27	Centre Capital					X		CCCX
28	ClipClop.com			X			X	CLOPF
29	Cohr			X				CHRI
30	ComputerXpress.com					X		CPXP/USAV
31	Computer'd Therm Imag			X		X		COII/CIO
32	Credit Suisse 1st Boston						X	DJAS0/922597
33	Creditrust			X	X		X	CRDT(Q)/923450
34	Cummins Engine	X						CUM
35	DelSecur				X			DLSC
36	Dendrite Int'l			X			X	DRTE/615606/896203
37	E*Trade Group	X		X			X	ET/ETJPF/various foreign
38	eConnect				X			ECNC
39	Emulex			X			X	EMLX/868379
40	Fidelity Holdings			X				FDHG

Table 9.1. Continued.

Obs	Firm Name	NY	AX	NAZ	OTCBB	Pink	For	Call Letter(s)/Ticker(s)
					Exchange(s)			
41	FinancialWeb.com					X		FWFB
42	Fischer Imaging		X				X	FIMG/909392
43	Fonix				X		X	FONX/893209
44	Fruit of the Loom	X			X		X	FTLA(Q)/35941620/892740
45	Global Telemedia Int'l					X		GLTI/GTMI
46	Golden Eagle Int'l				X			MYNG
47	Great Canadian Gaming						X	CGE/GCD
48	Gyrodyne Co. of America			X			X	GYRO/925061
49	H-Quotient				X			HQNT
50	Harbor FL Bancshares			X				HARB
51	Healthcare Recoveries	X		X				HCRI
52	HealthSouth	X					X	HRC/875508
53	Hemispherx Biopharma			X			X	HEB/HEBWS/HEMXU/ 906543
54	Diamond Hitts Prod				X			DHTT/HITT
55	Hollis-Eden Pharm			X			X	HEPH/913285
56	Hvide Marine				X			HVDM/HMAR(Q)
57	Imaging Diagnostics				X			IMDS
58	Impath			X			X	IMPH/899422
59	Imperial Sugar				X			IPSU/IPSUV/IPSUZ/IPSZV/ IHK/IPRZ
60	Informix				X		X	IFMX
61	Infotopia				X			IFTP
62	Ingram Micro	X					X	IM/903027
63	InsynQ				X			ISNQ
64	InvestAmerica				X		X	INVT/IVK/928978
65	ITEX				X			ITEX
66	Ives Health				X			IVEH
67	IXL Enterprises			X			X	IIXL/922795
68	Kellstrom Industries			X		X	X	KELL/KELLU/KELL (W)&(Q)/904734
69	Kelly's Coffee				X			KLYS
70	Labor Ready	X						LRW
71	Legacy Software	–	–	–	–	–	–	Not Identified
72	Lilly Industries	X					X	LI/BC43/various foreign
73	Liviakis Fin'l Comm	–	–	–	–	–	–	Not Identified
74	Log On America				X		X	LOA/LOAX/LOAX (E)/920790
75	Loislaw.com		X				X	LOIS/928058
76	Lucent Technologies	X			X		X	LU/LUCTP/LUCTO/899868
77	MasTec	X					X	MTZ/861257

Table 9.1. Continued.

Obs	Firm Name	NY	AX	NAZ	OTCBB	Pink	For	Call Letter(s)/Ticker(s)
78	Medinix Systems				X		X	MDNX/923849
79	MeltroniX				X			MTNX
80	M.H. Meyerson			X				MHMY
81	Medinah Energy			X				MDNA
82	Metro-Goldwyn-Mayer	X					X	MGM/909572
83	NCO Group			X			X	NCOG/918006
84	NetCurrents				X			NTCS(W)
85	New Visual Ent			X	X		X	NVEI/NWVIE/64909820
86	NYSE	–	–	–	–	–	–	Not Applicable/Exchange
87	Nutek				X			NUTK
88	Ocwen Financial	X						OCN
89	Original Media					X		OMDA
90	Osage Systems Group					X		OSE/OSYM
91	Owens Corning	X					X	OWC/872099
92	PDC Innovative Ind				X			PDCI
93	Peak Int'l		X	X			X	PEAKF/PTT*/919399
94	Philip Services			X			X	PSC/PHV/PSCD(E)
95	Phoenix International			X				PHXX
96	PhyCor				X		X	PHYC(Q)/883444
97	Presstek			X			X	PRST/877988
98	ProNetLink.com				X			PNLK
99	Quest Net				X			QNET(E)
100	Rayethon	X					X	RTNa/RTN/RTNPR/911364/ 852099
101	Remtrack			X				RENT
102	Rentech		X				X	RTK/912954
103	Rural/Metro			X				RURAL/RURLC
104	Sabratek					X		SBTK(Q)
105	SATX					X		SATX
106	SeaChange Int'l			X			X	SEAC/903655
107	Seitel	X					X	SEI/OSL
108	Shaman Pharm					X		SHPH/SHMNO
109	Shoney's	X			X			SHN/SHOY
110	Solv-Ex			X				SOLV(Q)/SVXC/SVXC(W)
111	Source Info Mgmt Sys			X				SORC
112	Sov'n Ptnrs Lmtd Ptrs	–	–	–	–	–	–	Not Identified
113	Spectrum Oil			X		X		SPUM/SPOC
114	Stampede Worldwide				X	X		STPW(Q)/STWW/SPWW
115	Star Telecom					X	X	STRX(Q)/907468
116	Steroid Inhib Int'l				X		X	STGI/920435
117	Stone & Webster					X		SWBI(Q)

Table 9.1. Continued.

Obs	Firm Name	NY	AX	NAZ	OTCBB	Pink	For	Call Letter(s)/Ticker(s)
					Exchange(s)			
118	Sunbeam				X	X		SOCW(E)/SOCW(Q)/ SOCN(Q)
119	Talk Visual				X	X		TVCP
120	Thomas & Betts	X					X	TNB/852663
121	T. K. & Co	–	–	–	–	–	–	Not applicable/Private firm
122	Titan Investments	X					X	TWI/886485
123	Wade Cook Financial				X			WADE
124	Xircom		X				X	XIRC/883819
125	ZiaSun Technologies				X		X	ZSUN/919009
126	Zixit			X			X	ZIXI/878243
	Exchange Totals	**23**	**6**	**39**	**49**	**21**	**58**	**196**
	LESS: NYSE origin	na	(0)	(2)	(3)	(0)	(15)	(20)
	LESS: AX origin	na	na	(1)	(3)	(1)	(4)	(9)
	LESS: NAZ origin	na	na	na	(4)	(2)	(25)	(31)
	LESS: OTCBB origin	na	na	na	na	(4)	(9)	(13)
	LESS: PK origin	na	na	na	na	na	(3)	(3)
	Origin Exchange (Net)	**23**	**6**	**36**	**39**	**14**	**2**	**120**

na = not applicable.

Subtotals provided at the bottom of Table 9.1 provide a surprisingly large number of (once) NYSE (NY) listed firms ($n = 23$). Of this total, 20 of these firms were also listed on other exchanges and/or lost their NYSE listing as they failed to maintain minimum PPS, net asset or other minimum requirements for continued listing on the NYSE.

There were only a modest number of American Stock Exchange listed firms ($n = 6$). All of these firms were also listed on other exchanges or lost their American Stock Exchange (AX) listing.

The subtotal counts for the NASDAQ (NAZ), over-the-counter Bulletin Board (OTC BB), and PinkSheets (Pink) stocks ($n = 39$, 49 and 21, respectively) were significant, as intuition would suggest, since these relatively thinly traded stocks might more easily fall prey to a shortage of public information or higher levels of private or hidden information (e.g. information asymmetry), PPS movements causally related to rumors and analyst neglect, and/or are more generic (see Chapter 4).

Subtotals and totals from this very preliminary analysis only partially support the first hypothesis. The largest number of observations does not originate from PK exchange stocks, but is from the OTC BB, as follows:

$$NY < AX < NAZ < OTC\ BB < Pink\ (Hypothesized) \qquad (9.1)$$

$$\begin{array}{c} AX < Pink < NY < NAZ < OTC\ BB \\ (Observed - Exchange\ Totals) \end{array} \qquad (9.1a)$$

$$\begin{array}{c} AX < Pink < NY < NAZ < OTC\ BB \\ (Observed - Origin\ Exchange\ (Net)) \end{array} \qquad (9.1b)$$

where the findings contained in Eq. 9.1a represent the sequence from "Exchange Totals" in Table 9.1 and those contained in Eq. 9.1b represent the sequence from "Origin Exchange (Net)" in Table 9.1. (Note that the results from Eqs 9.1a and 9.1b are consistent.)

The first hypothesis was not theory- or literature review-based, was only intuitively appealing, and may have required refinement (e.g. scaling of observations by the count of securities listed on each exchange). It was based on the presumption that neglected securities would provide the most likely candidates or targets for the intentional generation of conditions of information asymmetry. A complete listing of limitations of this exploratory analysis is beyond the scope of this chapter and monograph.

Generally, the firms that have been the targets of cybersmear have been "troubled." That is, they have had declining revenues, earnings, and so on. Because of this, many have been delisted from larger exchanges – with more stringent listing requirements, to smaller exchanges – with few or no requirements.

For example, a firm listed on the NASDAQ national market (NM), but failing to continue to meet minimum PPS exchange listing requirements, may be forced to trade on the OTC BB or PK, where exchange listing requirements are modest. The detailed case study of PurchasePro.com, contained in Chapter 7, represents such a case. Since the April 2000 NASDAQ "crash," many firms have experienced similar circumstances.

Alternatively, a firm with financial problems may have failed to file financial statements in a timely manner (assigned an "E" suffix), filed for Chapter 11 bankruptcy protection (assigned a "Q" suffix), issued warrants for a small ownership provision for prior equity holders after emerging from bankruptcy (assigned a "W" suffix), emerged from bankruptcy with new call letters, and so on. Generally, foreign firms (e.g. Canada) have an "F" suffix, with five letters, and other foreign firms (e.g. Xetra or Berlin exchanges) are assigned a number for identification.

Therefore, the information provided in Table 9.1 will facilitate researcher use and extensions of this data base, by providing an audit trail of both contemporary and prior call letters.[69]

The second step was to attempt to classify the 126 observations as Cybersmear (C; $n = 116$), Hyping (H; $n = 8$) or Other (O; $n = 2$). These classifications are not subject to interpretation, are mutually exclusive, and are summarized in Table 9.2.

Table 9.2. Summary of Observations – Principal, Agent and Nature of Asymmetric Information.

	Classification			[Author(s)]		Agents/Others involved		
Obs	C	H	O	Alleged Principal	M	SEC/FBI/USAtty	Intervenors	Other
1	X			?	X		EFF/ACLU	
2	X			?	X			
3	X			?	X			
4	X			Rival Firm (acquired)	X			
5			X	Insider(s)	X			
6	X			?	X		EFF/PC	
7	X			Identified	X			
8	X			Rival Firm	X			
9	X			Insider/Employee (discharged)	X	ACLU/EPIC		
10		X		?		SEC		
11			X	Insider(s)	X			
12	X			?	X			
13	X			Identified one	X			
14	X			Rival Firm	X			
15		X		Identified		SEC		
16	X			?	X			
17	X			Identified				MSD
18	X			?	X			
19	X			?	X			
20	X			?	X			
21	X			?	X			
22		X		Identified		SEC		ODS
23	X			Rival Firm	X			
24	X			Impersonator(s)/MM(s)	X			
25	X			Identified	X			
26	X			?	X			
27	X			Short(s)	X			
28	X			?	X			
29	X			Rival Firm/Insider/ Ex-employee	X			
30	X			?	X			
31	X			Short(s)/MM(s)	X			
32	X			Investor(s)? of firm evaluated	X			

Table 9.2. Continued.

	Classification			[Author(s)]		Agents/Others involved		
Obs	C	H	O	Alleged Principal	M	SEC/FBI/USAtty	Intervenors	Other
33	X			Rival Firm employee(s)	X			
34	X			Insider(s)?/Employee(s)?	X			
35		X		MM/Insider				QSC
36	X			Insider(s)?/Employee(s)?	X		ACLU/PC	
37	X			Impostor(s)	X			
38		X		Insider(s)		SEC		
39	X			Short	X	SEC/FBI		
40	X			?	X			
41		X		Identified		USAtty		
42	X			?	X			
43	X			MM(s)/?	X			
44	X			?	X		ACLU	
45	X			?	X			
46	X			Identified	X			
47	X			Identified	X			
48	X			Identified?	X			
49	X			Short(s)?	X			
50	X			?	X			
51	X			Insider(s)?/Employee(s)?	X			
52	X			Ex-employee/Employee spouse	X			
53	X			MMs/Short(s)?	X			
54	X			Reporter & News Service	X			
55	X			?	X			
56	X			Shareholder(s)	X			
57	X			Rival Firm/Ex-employee	X			
58	X			?	X			
59	X			Insider(s)/Employee(s)	X			
60	X			Insider(s)?/Employee(s)?	X			
61	X			Identified (1)/(1)?	X			
62	X			?	X			
63	X			Short(s)?	X	SEC/FBI		
64	X			Short(s)?	X			
65	X			Ex-employee(s)	X			
66		X		?		SEC		
67	X			Employee(s)?	X		PC	
68	X			?	X			
69	X			?	X			
70	X			?	X			
71	X			Investor(s)	X			
72	X			Employee(s)?	X			

Table 9.2. Continued.

Obs	Classification			[Author(s)]		Agents/Others involved		
	C	H	O	Alleged Principal	M	SEC/FBI/USAtty	Intervenors	Other
73	X			?	X			
74	X			Ex-employees	X			
75	X			Insider(s)?	X			
76	X			?	X	SEC/USAtty		
77	X			Ex-employee(s)	X			
78	X			Employee(s)?	X		EFF	
79	X			Insider(s)?/ Ex-employee(s)?	X			
80	X			Short(s)?		SEC/USAtty		
81	X			Identified	X			
82	X			Short/Imposter	X			CDC
83	X			Debtor	X	SEC		
84	X			Ex-COO/Ex-sales executive	X			
85	X			Identified	X			
86	X			Imposter(s)	X			
87	X			Identified	X	SEC		
88	X			?	X			
89	X			?	X			
90	X			?	X			
91	X			Imposter	X			
92	X			Investor	X		JDAF	
93	X			Ex-CEO	X			
94	X			Journalist/Politician/?	X			
95	X			Ex-employee	X			
96	X			Insider	X			
97	X			Short(s)	X			
98	X			Imposter	X			
99	X			MM/Ex-employee	X			
100	X			Employees	X			
101	X			?	X			
102		X		Identified		SEC		ASIC
103	X			Insider(s)	X		EFF/LP	
104	X			Short(s)	X			
105	X			?	X			
106	X			Identified (1)/?	X			
107	X			Shareholder(s)?	X			
108	X			?	X			
109	X			Shareholder?/Imposter(s)	X			
110	X			Short(s)?/MM(s)?	X			
111	X			Job applicant (not hired)	X			
112	X			Rival Firm	X			

Table 9.2. Continued.

| Obs | Classification | | | [Author(s)] | | Agents/Others involved | | |
	C	H	O	Alleged Principal	M	SEC/FBI/USAtty	Intervenors	Other
113	X			?	X			
114	X			Ex-co-worker (prior job)	X			
115	X			MMs/Imposter(s)	X			
116	X			Ex-chairman	X			
117	X			Insider(s)	X			
118	X			?	X			
119	X			Identified	X			
120	X			Identified?	X		PC	
121	X			?	X			
122	X			?	X			
123	X			?	X			
124	X			Employee Imposter	X			
125	X			Shareholder(s)	X			
126	X			Rival Firm	X			
	116	8	2	Totals	116	13	10	5

Legend: C = Cybersmear, H = Hyping and O = Other under CLASSIFICATION column; M = Management, SEC = Securities and Exchange Commission, FBI = Federal Bureau of Investigation, USAtty = U.S. Attorney, NYSE = New York Stock Exchange, EFF = Electronic Frontier Foundation, ACLU = American Civil Liberties Union, PC = Public Citizen, EPIC = Electronic Privacy Information Center, JDAF = John Does Anonymous Foundation, LP = Liberty Project, MSD = Massachusetts Securities Division, ODS = Oklahoma Department of Securities, QSC = Quebec Securities Commission, CDC = California Department of Corporations (Internet Compliance and Enforcement Division) and ASIC = Australian Securities and Investments Commission under AGENTS.

Hypothesis 2. One might find it intuitively appealing and hypothesize that management would be more likely to intervene and litigate in cases of cybersmear, when the firm's PPS may be adversely affected and at risk. A quantitative framework for this hypothesis is provided by Eq. (9.2), in the alternative form, as follows:

$$Hyping < Cybersmear \tag{9.2}$$

Of the hyping (H) observations, not even one single observation resulted in management (M) intervention. Both of the observations classified as other (O), involving insider trading, resulted in management intervention (e.g. observations 5 and 11). Therefore, hypothesis 2 is fully supported.

The vast majority of the observations involved actions (legal or otherwise) against unknown or anonymous posters (?; $n = 39$). Twenty of the posters were employees, ex-employees or alleged to be employees or ex-employees ($n = 20$), 18 were identified or alleged to have been identified ($n = 18$), sixteen were insiders or alleged to be insiders ($n = 16$), and 12 were shorting the firm's stock or alleged to be shorting the firm's stock ($n = 12$). Nine of those posting to the stock-chat message boards were imposters or alleged to have been imposters ($n = 9$) and the same number were from rival firms or alleged to have originated from rival firms ($n = 9$).

In addition to employees, ex-employees, insiders and imposters, some were identified or alleged to be MMs ($n = 6$), a topic covered in Chapter 8 and Appendix Chapter 8.4. The bashers were identified or alleged to be shareholders, ex-executives, reporters, employee spouses, politicians, a job applicant (denied employment), a debtor or even an ex-co-worker, who followed a co-worker to his new position in an effort to harm his new employer.

The reasons for increasing the level of uncertainty, via the generation of misinformation, which, by definition, constitutes information asymmetry, are varied. The largest groups of those against whom legal actions are threatened represent those associated with the firm through employment. The number of observations identified or alleged to be an employee or ex-employee ($n = 20$), job applicant denied employment ($n = 1$), an ex-co-worker ($n = 1$) or an ex-executive ($n = 3$) totals 25 observations.

SUMMARY

Information asymmetry is, perhaps, most apparent on the Internet's stock-chat message boards. Two highly publicized cases where the SEC became involved were published in Cataldo and Killough (2002). Supplemental information, suitable for content analysis and relating to these same cases, is contained in Appendix Chapter 7.2.

The case studies of a failed pump and dump effort for a formerly big-cap stock, PurchasePro.com (Chapter 7), and the contrasting small- or micro-cap stock, Universal Express (Chapter 8), were used to introduce the researcher to the potential for the generation of increased levels of information asymmetry via a contemporary medium, the Internet's stock-chat message boards.

The tabular summaries presented in this chapter have been developed from the cases summarized in Appendix Chapter 9.1. These cases represent a non-random data base of 126 observations that others may choose to use and explore for investigations more applicable to their specific research disciplines and/ or extend for use in their own research.

The major findings of this chapter are that: (1) most litigation-based challenges to the Internet-based generation of conditions of information asymmetry

occur for firms listed on the OTC BB; and (2) management appears to intervene only in those cases involving the spread of negative information or
cybersmear, but does not intervene in cases where the nature of the information is positive or what might be classified as hyping. These management-based
behaviors may, therefore, be said to be consistent with those of, for example,
Enron executives, where the financial analyst (Merrill) or auditor (Andersen)
provided positive public information signals to investors and potential investors
(see Section II and Chapters 4 and 5).

CHAPTER 10. SUMMARY

Identification of the major sources or firm-specific drivers of information asymmetry will suggest more precise (less noisy) measures of asymmetry (Aboody & Lev, 2000, p. 748).

INTRODUCTION

The Internet's stock-chat message boards have accelerated the dissemination of both information and mis-information. These message boards contain examples of hyping and bashing and may increase noise and the risks of adverse selection and moral hazard. To the extent that efforts by individuals to increase conditions of information asymmetry are successful, this Internet-based form of pubic information diverts economic resources away from productive and profitable investments and toward nonproductive or less profitable endeavors. The true nature of the information, posted on the Internet's stock-chat message boards, is private and known only to the agent or author.

SOME SUBSEQUENT EVENTS RELATING DIRECTLY TO MONOGRAPH COVERAGE

Subsequent events, relating directly to chapters and appendix chapters contained in this monograph, follow:

- In February 2003, **Merrill Lynch** (NYSE: MER) agreed to pay $80 million to settle the SEC investigation of its role in Enron (Pink Sheets: ENRNQ) transactions.
- As reported on February 21, 2003, in a Business Wire, *Global Stock Transfer Sues DTC over Electronic Exits*, announcement of a suit against the Depository Trust Company (DTC) was publicized. The suit relates to efforts to inhibit naked short selling, dubbed the "OTC rebellion." This story, in addition to one published on March 10, 2003, in a CBS MarketWatch article by John Labate, "SEC widens probe into 'death-spiral' schemes," is evolving, as this monograph goes to press. They are most closely related to naked

149

shorting, MMM, and portions of **Chapter 8**, **Appendix Chapter 8.3** and **Appendix Chapter 8.4**.

- The highly-publicized **Enron** and **WorldCom** cases have been followed by at least two additional, highly-publicized cases: (1) During February 2003, **Ahold** (NYSE: AHO), the world's largest retailer, lost approximately sixty% of it's market value after reporting that U.S. profits had been overstated. It was announced that the CEO and CFO would resign. During March 2003, **HealthSouth Corporation** (NYSE: HRC; PinkSheets: HLSH) publicized the unreliable nature of past financial statements.
- **PurchasePro.com** (PinkSheets: PROEQ), in bankruptcy, confirmed an SEC investigation in August 2002 and FBI inquiries in February 2003 (see **Chapter 7** and **Appendix Chapter 7.1**).
- The events examined in **Appendix Chapter 7.2** were followed by the establishment of an Internet- and fee-based stock-tip service/business, located at http://www.lebed.biz/.
- USXP, examined as a case study in **Chapter 8** and, in the form of news and public relations releases in **Appendix Chapter 8.2**, provided news of an additional $137 million jury award on April 23, 2003. This news resulted in a rally in the firm's PPS, but only for a few hours, unlike the original rally for the $389 million judgment.

SUMMARY

In the early months of 2003, Microsoft (MSFT) has, for the first time in their history, decided to pay a dividend to shareholders. Previously, Microsoft was the only Dow Jones Industrial Average stock that had never paid a dividend. This event occurred at a time when the elimination of the double-taxation of dividends was being promoted in a variety of Bills introduced by both executive and legislative branches. The newly created Public Oversight Board (POB) proposed an increase in the level of management responsibility for the establishment and maintenance of internal controls during this same period.

The above are consistent with structurally increasing or improving the signals (e.g. the payment of dividends and tax reductions relating to dividend payments) and monitoring (e.g. internal controls emphasis) mechanisms of publicly traded firms. These proposals appear to focus on modifying the behaviors of management and the reduction of adverse selection (Chapter 2) and moral hazard (Chapter 3), with lesser emphasis on the modification of the behaviors of external parties (e.g. auditors and financial analysts).

Demand for monitoring relates to the level of a firm's internal and external agency costs (Jensen and Meckling 1976; Simunic and Stein 1986). To discover hidden or private information, the investigator must research and monitor the subject. In the applications and cases examined in this monograph, the subject has been the financial instrument or the equity security of the firm; the investigator is the investor or prospective investor. Figure 10.1 summarizes the principal-agent relations noted or examined throughout this monograph.

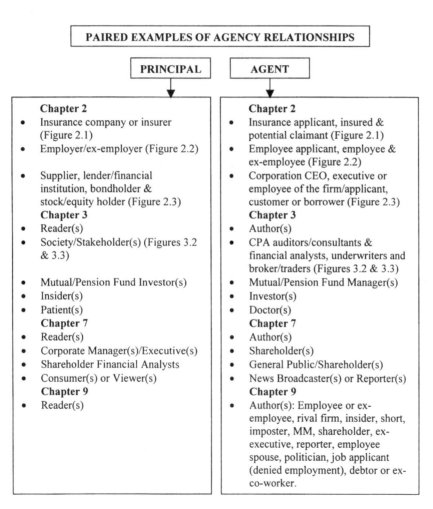

Fig. 10.1. Chapter Introductions of Information Asymmetry: Principal-Agent Relationships.

This monograph has provided evidence of linkage between financial and managerial accounting education and research. With respect to theory development, this linkage is most apparent through hidden information (managerial) and private information (financial). And, as the highly-publicized Enron case suggests, the failure of Merrill (financial analyst) and Andersen (auditor) to fulfill their fiduciary responsibilities has also blurred the distinction between external (financial) and internal (managerial) functions, though it is presumed that these relations are undesirable and they are not likely to assist the researcher in achieving technical advancements in theory development.

This monograph has also provided numerous examples of the various forms and levels of information available on the stock-chat message boards and from other Internet-based sources. For the researcher, interested in developing data bases from this relatively novel medium of information exchange, the stock-chat message boards represent a treasury of allegations convertible to testable hypotheses.

APPENDIX CHAPTERS

APPENDIX CHAPTER 7.1.
SELECTED (JANUARY 2001 THROUGH MAY 2002) PURCHASEPRO NEWS RELEASES & ARTICLES

INTRODUCTION

PurchasePro.com, Incorporated (PurchasePro; NASDAQ NM: PPRO) is the subject of the case study contained in Chapter 7. This appendix contains a summary of electronic news headlines associated with PurchasePro. They represent *public* information releases from legitimate sources and are presented in chronological sequence to provide interested researchers with a timeline of events.

BACKGROUND

These news headlines were developed from the CBSMarketWatch.com, YF and Datek (proprietary) News Center Internet sites. This is only a sample of news and public relations releases. In particular, redundant or repetitive releases have not been included (e.g. repeated law firm announcements for class action lawsuits). These public news releases will provide a summary of the chronological events facing PurchasePro.

The contents of Chapter 7 were developed, in part, from this sample of electronic news releases, as follows:

TUESDAY, JANUARY 16, 2001
- 7:13 PM: PurchasePro.com downgraded by Adams Harkness (Briefing.com).

MONDAY, JANUARY 29, 2001
- 11:40AM: Lehman bullish on PPRO (CBS MarketWatch.com).

WEDNESDAY, JANUARY 31, 2001
- 6:56AM: PPRO, AOL expand ties (CBS MarketWatch.com).

155

MONDAY, FEBRUARY 5, 2001

- 3:19PM: PurchasePro shares down 18%, or $4.66 to $20.25 on heavy volume (CBS MarketWatch.com).
- 4:30PM: UPDATE 1-PurchasePro stock drops after Barron's article (Reuters U.S. Company News).

THURSDAY, FEBRUARY 8, 2001

- 1:46PM: PurchasePro Calls Suit Groundless (Business Wire).
- 3:30PM: Purchasepro.com dropped to 'accumulate' from 'strong buy' at Prudential (CBS MarketWatch.com).

MONDAY, FEBRUARY 12, 2001

- 5:38PM: PurchasePro Achieves Cash EPS of $0.11; Revenue Exceeds Prior Three Quarters Combined (Business Wire).

TUESDAY, FEBRUARY 13, 2001

- 12:05AM: PurchasePro stock up on surprise fourth-quarter income (Reuters U.S. Company News).

FRIDAY, MARCH 2, 2001

- 10:11AM: PurchasePro cut to 'neutral' from 'outperform' at Morgan Stanley Dean Witter (CBS MarketWatch.com).

TUESDAY, MARCH 6, 2001

- 11:56AM: PurchasePro buys BayBuilder to boost auction offering (Reuters U.S. Company News).

WEDNESDAY, MARCH 7, 2001

- 8:35AM: PurchasePro sees Q1 EPS $0.09/shr, 01 EPS $0.59.shr (Reuters U.S. Company News).

FRIDAY, MARCH 9, 2001

- 6:00PM: PurchasePro.com downgraded by Lehman Brothers (Briefing.com).

MONDAY, MARCH 12, 2001

- 6:52PM: PurchasePro chairman to liquidate portion of holdings (Reuters U.S. Company News).

WEDNESDAY, MARCH 21, 2001

- 6:51AM: PurchasePro.com cut to 'hold' at Prudential (CBS MarketWatch.com).

WEDNESDAY, MARCH 28, 2001
- 7:57 PM: PurchasePro expands deal with AOL (CBS MarketWatch).

TUESDAY, APRIL 3, 2001
- 9:58AM: PurchasePro dropped to 'buy' at CS first Boston (CBS MarketWatch.com).

THURSDAY, APRIL 19, 2001
- 2:47PM: PurchasePro to Report First-Quarter Results on April 25, 2001; Will Host Conference Call the Same Day (Business Wire).

WEDNESDAY, APRIL 25, 2001
- 4:39PM: PurchasePro Reschedules First Quarter News Release and Conference Call (Business Wire).
- 5:18PM: PurchasePro delays earnings report to Thursday (Reuters U.S. Company News).

THURSDAY, APRIL 26, 2001
- 6:58PM: PurchasePro Reports First Quarter Results (Business Wire).
- 7:29AM: PurchasePro Q1 shr loss $0.02 (Reuters U.S. Company News).
- 8:20AM: PurchasePro net loss widens (Reuters U.S. Company News).
- 6:00PM: PurchasePro.com downgraded by SG Cowen, CSFB (Briefing.com).
- 6:41PM: Weiss & Yourman Files Class Action Lawsuit Against PurchasePro.com, Inc. (PR Newswire).

FRIDAY, APRIL 27, 2001
- 12:00AM & 6:00PM: RESEARCH ALERT-Prudential cuts Purchasepro.com (Reuters U.S. Company News & Briefing.com).

THURSDAY, MAY 10, 2001
- 9:24AM: Lengthy Investigation Leads to Filing of Class Action Against PurchasePro.com, Inc. by Shapiro Haber & Urmy LLP on Behalf of Defrauded Investors (PR Newswires).

WEDNESDAY, MAY 16, 2001
- 6:59PM: Richard L. Clemmer Joins PurchasePro as Chief Financial Officer (Business Wire).

MONDAY, MAY 21, 2001
- 10:59AM: PurchasePro chairman and chief executive resigns (Reuters U.S. Company News).

- 12:46PM: PurchasePro jumps after chairman quits (CBS MarketWatch.com).

TUESDAY, MAY 22, 2001
- 9:19AM: PurchasePro restates Q1 results (CBS MarketWatch.com).
- 8:51 PM: PurchasePro restates, shares tumble (CBS MarketWatch.com).

TUESDAY, MAY 29, 2001
- 2:24PM: PurchasePro revises Q1 loss once again (CBS MarketWatch.com).

TUESDAY, JUNE 5, 2001
- 1:23PM: PurchasePro.com Replaces CEO (Associated Press).

WEDNESDAY, JUNE 6, 2001
- 5:50PM: PurchasePro names COO, second executive in week (Reuters U.S. Company News).

THURSDAY, JUNE 14, 2001
- 2:02PM: PurchasePro Charged With Securities Fraud, Says The Pomerantz Firm (Internet Wire).

MONDAY, JUNE 18, 2001
- 6:27PM: PurchasePro Chief Resigns (Associated Press).

MONDAY, SEPTEMBER 17, 2001
- 3:50 PM: PurchasePro restructures AOL deal; ends payments (Reuters).

TUESDAY, OCTOBER 9, 2001
- 5:42 PM: PurchasePro asks shareholders to protect company stock (Reuters).

THURSDAY, NOVEMBER 29, 2001
- 2:05 PM: PurchasePro execs to purchase co's stock (Market Pulse).
- 5:24 PM: PurchasePro says auditors resign (Reuters).

MONDAY, DECEMBER 17, 2001
- 6:12PM: PurchasePro Engages Grant Thornton as Independent Auditors (PrimeZone Media Network).[70]

FRIDAY, DECEMBER 21, 2001
- 3:04PM: PurchasePro Secures Commitment For $15 Million of Equity Financing (PrimeZone Media Network).

TUESDAY, JANUARY 29, 2002

- 2:12PM: PurchasePro Releases Open Letter to CNBC (PrimeZone Media Network).

THURSDAY, FEBRUARY 14, 2002

- 8:55AM: PurchasePro completes $6 Million Financing: Company Says Financing Requirements Now Complete (PrimeZone Media Network).

MONDAY, MARCH 11, 2002

- 8:00 AM: PurchasePro Retail Shareholders Release Research Analysis On Company (PrimeZone Media Network).

THURSDAY, MAY 2, 2002

- 7:26 PM: PurchasePro Announces 1-for-5 Reverse Stock Split (PrimeZone Media Network).

SUMMARY

The public information from the selected headlines contained in this appendix provides a summary of many of the major events affecting PurchasePro from January 2001 through May 2002. Four of the six events examined in Chapter 7 can be directly linked to the public information releases alluded to in the headlines contained in this appendix.

APPENDIX CHAPTER 7.2.

ILLUSTRATIONS OF ASYMMETRIC INFORMATION: SUCCESSFUL RELEASES OF PRIVATE MISINFORMATION LEADING TO STOCK PPS INCREASES

INTRODUCTION

Chapter 7 contains the summarized details of an unsuccessful attempt to increase the PPS of PurchasePro's stock (Table 7.2). This appendix will provide researchers with a series of examples of relatively successful, thought short-lived, efforts. The content of this appendix chapter represents an extension of Cataldo and Killough (2002).

Unlike cybersmear, a topic covered in greater depth in Chapter 9, hyping, touting or pumping endeavors, and the release of misinformation and/or asymmetric, hidden or private informational release patterns associated with efforts to increase a firm's PPS are examined in this appendix chapter. Also, unlike Appendix Chapter 7.1, this appendix chapter does not deal with public information from legitimate sources, though illustrations of efforts to signal a PPS increases through the use of seemingly legitimate and external sources of both public and private information are presented.

An SEC action was the source of information used for the development of this appendix chapter. However, the common practice of using aliases on the stock-chat message boards precludes the identification of the person or persons initiating or engaged in the dissemination of information (or misinformation), leading to the illustrated PPS increases. For example, it is not uncommon for those observing the release of what is characterized as *private* and favorable information to knowingly participate, presumably for personal gain.

Therefore, the operational definition of the investor/trader capable of seeing the private information presented in this appendix as an opportunity to generate trading profits is a sophisticated investor. This operational definition differs from that used for the sophisticated and unsophisticated investor in the financial economics literature.

The sophisticated investor possesses private information, operationally defined as the knowledge of spamming patterns and behaviors, and techniques useful for the detection of these schemes. With this knowledge, the sophisticated investor/trader is able to assess the risks associated with adverse selection – the decision to participate or not participate in the scheme, as well as the level of participation (e.g. active assistance or inactive participation). The unsophisticated investor does not possess this information (or expertise), but is reacting to what is presented as private - soon to become public information or misinformation, as the specific case may suggest.

BACKGROUND

On September 20, 2000, the SEC issued Release No. 7891:[71]

> On eleven separate occasions between August 23, 1999 and February 4, 2000, (name) engaged in a scheme on the Internet in which he purchased large blocks of thinly traded micro cap stocks and, within hours of making such purchases, sent numerous false and/or misleading messages, or "spam," over the Internet touting the stocks he had just purchased. (Name) then sold all of these shares, usually within 24 hours, profiting from the increased price his messages had caused. During the course of the scheme, (name) realized a total net profit of $272,826.

> Almost all of the stocks that are part of this scheme were traded on the NASD Over the Counter Electronic Bulletin Board, with the balance traded on the NASDAQ National Market. (Name) conducted his trading in custodial accounts at two broker-dealers. Although these accounts were in his father's name, (name) made all of the trading decisions.

This SEC cease-and-desist-order listed nine stocks, identified as manipulated, over the August 23, 1999 through February 4, 2000 period, as follows:

(1) Manchester Equipment Company, Incorporated (MANC),
(2) Fotoball USA, Incorporated (FUSA),
(3) Yes Entertainment, Incorporated (YESS),
(4) Just Toys, Incorporated (JUST),
(5) Firetector, Incorporated (FTEC),
(6) Man Sang Holdings, Incorporated (MSHI),
(7) West Coast Entertainment, Incorporated (WCEC(E)),
(8) Classica Group, Incorporated (TCGI), and
(9) Havana Republic, Incorporated (HVAR).

The SEC disclosed the trading details associated with only one of these stocks. Man Sang Holdings, Incorporated (MSHI). The other eight stocks, in addition to Man Sang, are briefly examined in this appendix.

For each of the stocks featured in this appendix, both price and volume charts for the August 23, 1999 through February 4, 2000 period specified by the SEC "cease and desist" order are provided.[72] These eighteen figures are supplemented by five additional figures.[73] A summary of findings is provided at the end of this appendix.

Tables 7.2.1 and 7.2.2 provide descriptive measures of the 52-week high and low PPS and the number of stock-chat messages contained on the RB message boards for each of the nine stocks examined in this appendix, in sequence. This information is provided for two reasons.

The first table (Table 7.2.1) provides a reference point – the historical PPS for each stock. This range can be associated with the PPS activity generated by the information posted on the message boards.

The second table (Table 7.2.2) provides an example of the measures easily developed from information available to researchers for explanatory model development and predictive model testing. For example, a measure of stock price or stock volume volatility may be correlated to the number of messages posted to a message board for a particular stock. An illustration, using a basic regression model, is provided in Chapter 9.

Exhibit 7.2.1 provides a very different analysis. Using the time period and other information made available in the SEC release, and the information devel-

Table 7.2.1. Selected Descriptive Measures of the Nine Stocks Listed in the Securities and Exchange Commission "Cease and Desist" Order.

Ref	Firm Name	Stock Ticker or Call Letters	52-week price range as of September 30, 2000	
			Low	High
1	Manchester Equipment Co	MANC	$2.93750	$9.12500
2	Fotoball USA	FUSA	$2.93750	$8.90625
3	Yes Entertainment	YESS	$0.02000	$0.03800
4	Just Toys	JUST	$0.37500	$5.31250
5	Firetector	FTEC	$1.12500	$4.93750
6	Man Sang Holdings	MSHI	$1.00000	$5.12500
7	West Coast Entertainment	WCEC(E)	$0.05000	$0.72000
8	Classica Group	TCGI	$1.00000	$9.28125
9	Havana Republic	HVAR	$0.04000	$0.26000

Table 7.2.2.   Selected Descriptive Measures from the Raging Bull (RB)
Message Boards.

Ref	Stock Ticker or Call Letters	Raging Bull Message Number 23-Aug-99 Begin	4-Feb-00 End	Inclusive Message Count	9-Mar-01 Message Count	Date of first available Message
1	MANC	56	200	145	281	11-Jan-99
2	FUSA	2	72	71	82	4-Aug-98
3	YESS	2,961	3,394	434	3,642	4-Mar-99
4	JUST	1	467	467	671	26-Oct-99
5	FTEC	54	150	97	189	18-Feb-99
6	MSHI	1	251	251	1,108	10-Jan-00
7	WCEC(E)	195	481	287	757	7-May-99
8	TCGI	1	52	52	163	20-Jan-00
9	HVAR	4,448	7,049	2,602	10,619	19-Jun-98

oped in this appendix, this exhibit examines the feasibility that a single trading
account could be fully invested and used to trade each of the nine stocks. None
of these stocks were marginable. The conclusion is that a single (cash) trading
account could, in fact, have been used for each of the spamming events identified in this appendix.

Discussion of each of the nine stocks listed in the SEC "cease and desist"
order follows:

1. MANC

Figure 7.2.1 illustrates the high, low, and closing prices for Manchester
Equipment Company, Incorporated (MANC). There are several spikes in this
price chart.

Figure 7.2.2 illustrates the volume of shares traded. The relatively modest
spikes in price, from Fig. 7.2.1, are extremely easy to detect (and are labeled)
in this volume chart. A review of the stock chat on one message board revealed
the following post:

YF msg #1825, August 13, 1999 at 9:07 p.m.
Maybe someone can give Stock Dogs a call? They might run this thing back up to $9????

Research efforts revealed that *Stock Dogs* (aka *Stock-Dogs.com*) was an advisory
service provided by someone using the alias, *Jonathan Lebed.*[74] The (above)

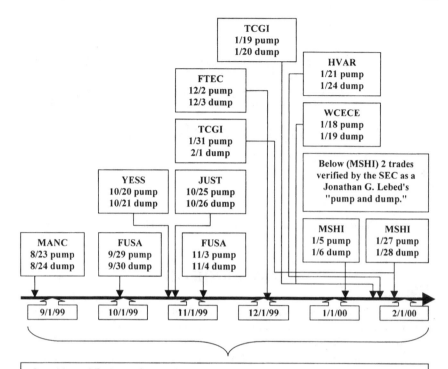

Exhibit 7.2.1. Forensic Results – Profit-Maximizing and Sequential Trades of the Nine Securities Identified in the SEC "Cease and Desist" Order.

stock-chat message board poster got his/her wish . . . only 10 days later.[75] Representative examples of some of the August 23–24 messages posted on the Manchester Equipment Company message boards follow:

RB msg #65, Monday, August 23, 1999 at 11:31 p.m.
KEEP YOUR MANC SPAMMERS OFF OTHER BOARDS!

RB msg #66, Monday, August 23, 1999 at 11:47 p.m.
I read about MANC on another board and logged on out of curiosity. I see that today you finally got off of your 52 week low and are already going bananas. The spammer said that MANC was making millions. The P/L of 4/30/99 showed a revenue increase of 10% to 165.7M and a net profit drop of 41% to 938K. Someone on your board has not done their DD[76] before visiting other boards and shouting MANC's virtues.

RB msg #67, Tuesday, August 24, 1999 at 2:29 a.m.

Classic pump and dump. I see the rumor mills churning and it is irrelevant at this point whether or not the fundamentals are fact or fiction. You will see MANC skyrocket to anywhere from the 6 to 9 level within a week.

One week later MANC will be back at 2.5. It does not matter if MANC merits a higher valuation or not. The day-traders will make it thus. Watch for volume to surpass 500K tomorrow and 1 million on Wednesday.

I will be watching and learning, but not profiting or losing.

Note that RB message number 67 (above) suggests that a sophisticated investor has chosen to both: (1) disclose the (low) quality of the information; and (2) disclose his/her intention to not participate. This case is analogous the Enron case, where the financial analyst, also a sophisticated investor/advisor, was discharged after his firm failed to agree with his decision to downgrade Enron stock. Similarly, those providing negative commentary on the stock-chat message boards are "fired" (e.g. placed on "ignore").

The share price of MANC increased from a range of $2.50 through $3.125 to a range of $3.4375 through $4.50 on August 23 and August 24, 1999, respectively. Volume also increased, from a low of 700 shares on August 20, 1999 to 123,700 shares on August 23, 1999 to 804,500 shares on August 24, 1999. Figure 7.2.3 focuses on the price of Manchester Equipment Company stock on the August 23-24, 1999, trading days.

MANC

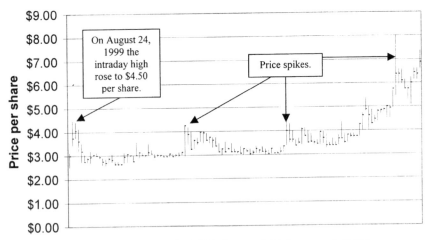

August 23, 1999 through February 4, 2000

Fig. 7.2.1.

MANC Volume

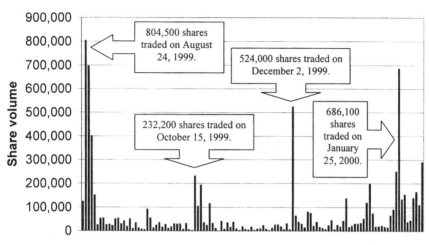

Fig. 7.2.2.

MANC

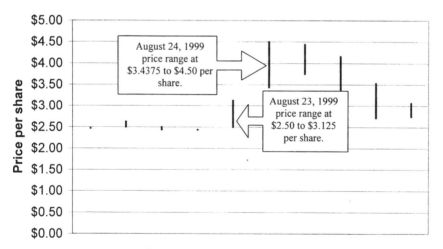

Fig. 7.2.3.

Finally, one post comments on the SEC "cease and desist" order and the trading range for MANC stock:

YF msg #4027, October 4, 2000 at 3:52 a.m..
Since the kid is gone MANC has become really boring. The true value now shows. This stock is a buy under $3 and a sell at $4. It's like fishing without a hook.

The August 13, 1999, post on the YF stock-chat message boards suggested that *Stock Dogs* be contacted to hype the stock. Responses to hype (these actual spamming posts were removed and were not available) were identified 10 days later, on August 23–24, 1999, a period consistent with a price spike. Some of the stock-chat messages referred to significant errors/inaccuracy of the financial measures contained in the hype.

2. FUSA

Figure 7.2.4 illustrates the high, low, and closing prices for Football USA, Incorporated (FUSA). Two stock price spikes, where one trading day's price was followed by an apparent gap (i.e. a stock price low in excess of the prior trading days high).

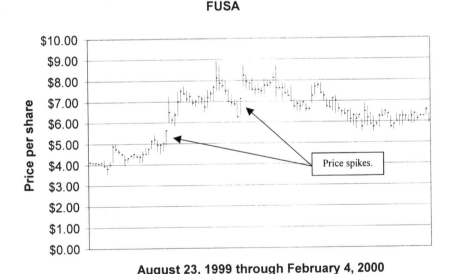

FUSA

August 23, 1999 through February 4, 2000

Fig. 7.2.4.

FUSA Volume

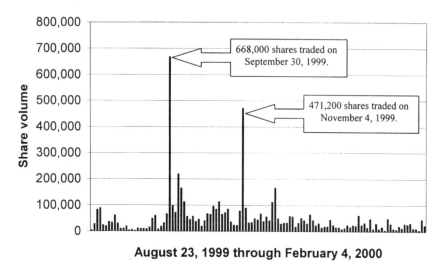

668,000 shares traded on September 30, 1999.

471,200 shares traded on November 4, 1999.

August 23, 1999 through February 4, 2000

Fig. 7.2.5.

Figure 7.2.5 illustrates trading volume for the same period. The two significant volume increases are consistent with the stock price increases exhibited in Fig. 7.2.4. Again, the volume chart provides stronger (visual) evidence of some form of news on these trading days.

On Thursday, September 30, 1999, there was a 1,000% volume increase in Football USA stock; from 66,500 shares at a range of $4.875 through $5.625 per share on September 29th to 668,000 shares at a range of $6 through $7.25 per share on September 30th. Two posters make suggestions to two different stock-chat message board communities on the Football USA message boards:

RB msg #16, Thursday, September 30, 1999 at 7:42 a.m.
We would appreciate it if you would have "eucdlv" or whatever his other alias is, stop spamming other boards. We don't care about this stock and you wouldn't want us spamming your board. EOM!!!!

YF msg #389, September 29, 1999 at 9:56 p.m.
There is an individual with more than 160 identical messages today on various boards. I'm sure I missed some . . . Be careful out there, as hype might increase volume and price, but who wants to hold the bag. Check the most known boards and you'll see (message follows): "Be sure to write down this symbol . . ." FUSA

Nobody has found this out yet, but FUSA management is in Hong Kong right now signing a deal to produce POKEMON products!!! Take a look at what GRIN and KIDE have done thanks to POKEMON deals. FUSA is a much stronger situation, and looks like it will be the next company to TAKE OFF.

UFSA's EPS is on track of reaching $0.90 for this year. The average company in this industry trades with a PE of 36 . . . WHICH WOULD VALUE FUSA AT $32+. FUSA is ready to make a HUGE RUN!!!

FUSA's products can be found at stores such as Walmart, Footlocker, J. C. Penney, K-mart, Toys R Us, Modell's, Sears, and The Sports Authority. Besides POKEMON . . . FUSA has major licensing deals with the NFL, NHL, MLB, NCAA, ESPN, Rugrats, Blues Clues, Charlie Brown, and many more.

I am also hearing that a number of other huge contracts are soon going to be announced including a major deal with Disney.

This is the BIGGEST OPPORTUNITY that I have ever found!!! I am buying all the shares I can at these levels! Take the time to do research on this company . . . YOU WILL NOT REGRET IT . . ."

YF msg #412, September 30, 1999 at 9:18 a.m.
FUSA has been OVERSPAMMED!
Just gotta laugh. It was probably some kid with a couple hundred shares trying to make a few bucks.

The second series of spamming occurred on November 3-4, 1999:

YF msg #642, November 4, 1999 at 2:16 a.m.
I found this in the RAZF area, posted by kduy7:
"CHECK THIS STOCK OUT!!! FUSA . . .
I have been told by the company that they are working on a huge Pokemon contract!
Pokemon is going to be the hottest toy this year.
Once we get the news on this . . . FUSA is going to explode. KIDE went from a few dollars to $80 thanks to Pokemon. FUSA is making a lot more money than KIDE . . . and is expected to be the next stock to take off!
FUSA is definitely the most undervalued stock on the entire NASDAQ. When 1999 is all said and done . . . it looks to me like EPS profits should reach $1.50 for the year. For a company growing as fast as FUSA is, in such a strong industry . . . I would consider a PE of 40 to be fair.
This would value FUSA at $60. Currently, FUSA is trading for only $7.
Besides Pokemon, FUSA has huge contracts with Warner Brothers, United Media, Disney, Nikelodeon, Major League Baseball, the NFL, NHL, and over 300 NCAA colleges.
You can find their products at many major stores such as Toys R Us, Modells, Sports Authority, K-Mart, and WalMart. You will even see their items frequently sold on QVC.
Don't miss out on FUSA! This is a rare ground-floor opportunity! FUSA is going to breakout and make a huge run an the days/weeks to come!!!!!

Posts were made and referred to "160 identical messages" spamming this firm's stock. An example of the actual hype was not deleted and was available for review.

3. YESS

Figure 7.2.6 illustrates the high, low, and closing prices for Yes Entertainment, Incorporated (YESS). Fig. 7.2.7 illustrates the volume of shares traded.

Trading volume for Yes Entertainment Inc. was 5,200 and 7,500 shares on October 15 and 18, 2000, respectively. On October 19, 2000 volume increased to 127,000 shares. By October 27, 2000, volume declined to 78,900 shares. Figure 7.2.8 illustrates the October 20 and 21, 1999, price activity, for what appears to have been a single and extremely successful spamming effort.

This price and volume response appears to have benefited from posts suggesting: (1) his/her discovery of insider information; and (2) a distancing of the poster from the actual insider information post or "news" release. This information proved to be inaccurate.

One of the posts from the stock-chat message boards on October 20, 1999 follows:

RB msg #3165, Wednesday, October 20, 1999 at 10:00 p.m.
JUST GOT THIS OFF OF YAHOO!
Just found this take for what it is worth no way to confirm it right know (sic) so any one who can find out let us know.

YESS

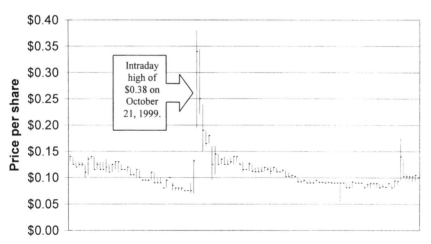

August 23, 1999 through February 4, 2000

Fig. 7.2.6.

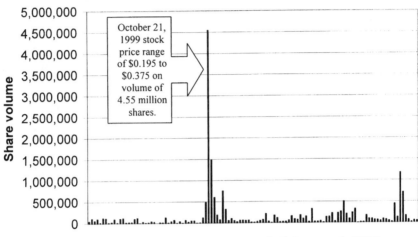

Fig. 7.2.7.

THE NEXT STOCK TO GAIN 1000% . . .
by: (alias)[77] BE SURE TO WRITE DOWN THIS SYMBOL, "YESS."
YESS is currently trading for only $0.13. I predict that it will be over $1 by the end of the
month. How come???
I just got off the phone with the World Wrestling Federation. They have signed a HUGE
LICENSING DEAL with YESS!!!
The news hasn't been announced yet by YESS . . . but now that the WWF has IPOed, a
press release will likely be out shortly. YESS is going to make a HUGE RUN!!!
The experts are predicting that WWF merchandise will be THE HOTTEST ITEMS this
season. WWF is the MOST POPULAR THING right now, much BIGGER than anything
else including POKEMON.
YESS was over $5 not too long ago. The WWF deal may be what the company needed to
turn itself back around!
Thanks to the WWF deals, THQI took off from just a few bucks to over $40 . . . as did
JAKK. There is a good chance that YESS will be next!
YESS's products are being sold at MANY MAJOR STORES such as TOYS R U.S. and
KAYBEE. The company also makes such well-known products as Teddy Ruxpin and Yak
Bak Pens.
This is probably the biggest opportunity I have ever found!!! Don't miss out on YESS!

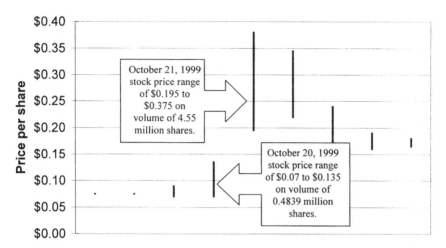

Fig. 7.2.8.

Apparently, a different poster from the stock-chat message boards on October 21, 1999:

RB msg (YESS) #3166, Thursday, October 21, 1999 at 8:16 a.m. EDT.
*Someone posted this on the ORXX boards. Probably just a rumor. HUGE NEWS IS COMING
. . . BE SURE TO WRITE DOWN THIS SYMBOL, "YESS" . . . YESS is currently trading
for only $0.13. I predict that it will be over $1 by the end of the month. How come??? I
just got off the phone with the World Wrestling Federation. They have signed a HUGE
LICENSING DEAL with YESS!!! The news hasn't been announced yet by YESS . . . but
now that the WWF has IPOed, a press release will likely be out shortly. YESS is going to
make a HUGE RUN!! The experts are predicting that wwf merchandise will be THE
HOTTEST ITEMS this season. WWF is the MOST POPULAR THING right now, much
BIGGER than anything else including POKEMON. YESS was over 45 not too long ago.
The WWF deal may be what the company needed to turn itself back around! Thanks to
WWF deals, thqi took off from just a few bucks to over $40 . . . as did JAKK. There is a
good chance that YESS will be next! YESS's products are being sold at MANY MAJOR
STORES such as TOYS R U.S. and KAYBEE. The company also makes such well-known
products as Teddy Ruxpin and Yak Bak Pens. Don't miss out on UESS! This is probably
the biggest opportunity I have ever found!!!*

Some of the established members on the board provided fair warning to the uninformed:

RB msg #3177, Thursday, October 21, 1999 at 9:22 a.m.
This NEWS bull-shitt (sic) has been used 3 other times before this year. YESS is a Pump/dump!!!!!! Beware . . . I was already caught up in it.

RB msg #3178, Thursday, October 21, 1999 at 9:24 a.m.
These pump and dumps are cyclical – this WWF "news" was used a few months ago. If you buy and get burned just hold on – they'll eventually do it again!

In this case, a "look what I found" approach proved to be a very effective. The hype was effectively distanced from the poster and included references to: (1) insider (private) information; (2) what appeared to be (public) news; and was (3) associated with the well-known World Wrestling Foundation (WWF). The WWF had recently had a highly publicized and very successful initial public offering (IPO).

4. JUST

Figure 7.2.9 illustrates the high, low, and closing prices for Just Toys, Incorporated (JUST). Figure 7.2.10 illustrates trading volume.

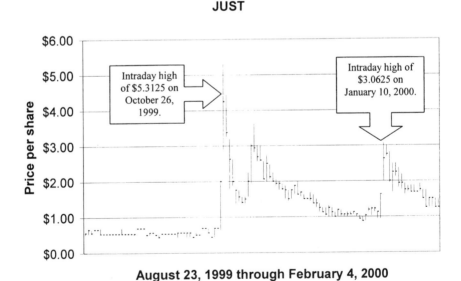

Fig. 7.2.9.

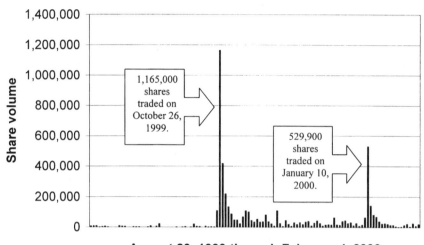

Fig. 7.2.10.

Each of the abrupt PPS peaks in the figures was examined for spamming or references to on the stock-chat message boards. Note that the WWF (World Wrestling Foundation) association, successfully used in the YESS spam just one week earlier (October 20–21, 1999), was used again.

Several of the posts from the stock-chat message boards on October 26, 1999 follow:

RB msg #3, Tuesday, October 26, 1999 at 10:52 a.m.
. . . it's hot . . . expected to hit $20.00 soon.[78]

RB msg #5, Tuesday, October 26, 1999 at 10:53 a.m.
I think we are seeing blockbuster news for this company . . . just go read the news. **WWF** *(emphasis added), and others plus sales in the WalMart and toys are us. The company has more value than the stock issued. This is a good mark for a takeover. Regards.*

A response follows:

RB msg #6, Tuesday, October 26, 1999 at 10:53 a.m.
expected only by the HYPSTERS ALL OVER THE BOARDS! Of which I am sure you are one of.

But the efforts to rally the stock continued:

RB msg #9, Tuesday, October 26, 1999 at 10:57 a.m.
I saw on another board, that some OTC stock has moved from 0.50 to 5.25 in two days on account of a buyout rumor. I am not too sure whether it's this one. I happened to see this symbol just today as it was posted by someone . . . that watchout for this stock (JUST) WHICH WILL SOON ROCKET TO 20$, like it happened to JAKK OR SOMETHING. I have spent the last one hour to see who this individual was but no luck. Seemed like he was pretty confident about his statement.

RB msg #10, Tuesday, October 26, 1999 at 10:57 a.m.
STOCKMASTER = This stock will hit 20$ by the end of week.

RB msg #21, Tuesday, October 26, 1999 at 11:58 a.m.
And the float is less than 3 mil? 68 employees? God!! What else needs to be said . . .

RB msg #31, Tuesday, October 26, 1999 at 12:34 p.m.
. . . look at the support line, hasn't dropped below 4.00 for about 2-3 hours. MMs[79] won't let it. It opened at 5.25. There is something going on here. Too many buyers between 4–5 range. I guarantee u (sic) guys it won't close below 3.75. This will open at 4.75 tomorrow if the stock price is around the 4.00 range. I believe that this is a buyout play and some great news will be released soon. Watch and see. Good luck all . . .

A response from a lucid investor followed:

RB msg #34, Tuesday, October 26, 1999 at 1:42 a.m.
I think you're an idiot . . . do u (sic) know what a support line is, read a book on stocks or something. Try "How to get started e-day trading" first and learn about bids/asks and support lines and etc. by your profile u (sic) don't play with the big stocks, you're a bb man, wow.

But the commentary continued:

RB msg #40, Tuesday, October 26, 1999 at 2:22 p.m.
How can you short a stock with **WWF** *(emphasis added) products THAT is HOT and XMAS around the corner . . .*

RB msg #43, Tuesday, October 26, 1999 at 2:49 a.m.
Hello, it's anybody's guess on the support level. On this little firecracker. it appears as if all bets are off as far as historical data goes. We shall see what we shall see. Cryptic, eh?

RB msg #54, Tuesday, October 26, 1999 at 3:39 p.m.
Wow . . . is this stock strong or what. Should gap up nice tomorrow, I still won't sell, something is up with "just" afternoon run, do u (sic) guys like what u (sic) see. I do . . . nuff (sic) said, sorry I was a dick earlier, just was tired of people talking out of their @ss (sic) . . . good luck.

JUST

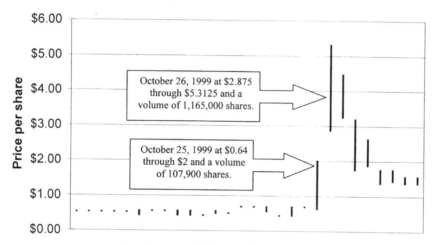

Fig. 7.2.11.

RB msg #56, Tuesday, October 26, 1999 at 3:56 p.m.
I already jumped in this morning, I am having the time of my life! Not boring at all!! Go baby GO!!!

On October 18, 2000 zero shares of Just Toys traded. The October 15, 1999 high and low was at $0.6875 at 3,500 shares. From September 28 through October 22, 1999, shares traded at a high of $0.6875. On October 25, 1999 the price ranged from $0.64 through $2 at a volume of 107,900 shares. On October 26, 1999, price ranged from $2.875 through $5.3125 at a volume of 1,165,000. These stock price ranges are represented in Fig. 7.2.11.

Building on the success of the WWF association in the Yes Entertainment (YESS) case, approximately one week earlier (October 20-21, 1999), the WWF association was also used to hype Just Toys on October 26, 1999.

5. FTEC

Figure 7.2.12 illustrates the high, low, and closing prices for Firetector, Incorporated (FTEC). Figure 7.2.13 illustrates the volume of shares traded.

In addition to the price and volume measures for Firetector illustrated by Figs 7.2.12 and 7.2.13, respectively, Fig. 7.2.14 (FTEC(1)) illustrates what

FTEC

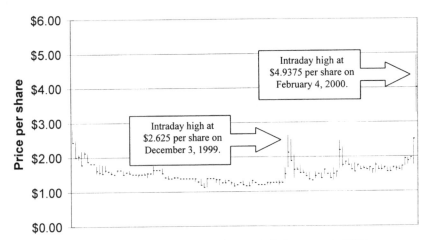

August 23, 1999 through February 4, 2000

Fig. 7.2.12.

FTEC Volume

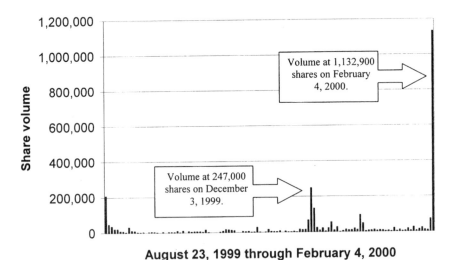

August 23, 1999 through February 4, 2000

Fig. 7.2.13.

FTEC (1)

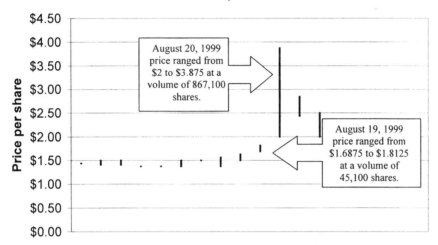

August 6 through August 31, 1999

Fig. 7.2.14.

appears to have been the results of spam over the August 19 through August 20, 1999 period. Some of the message board posts from August 19, 1999 follow:

RB msg #7, Thursday, August 19, 1999, at 9:00 p.m.
Not only is FTEC making huge profits . . . but this entire industry is about to take off. FTEC belongs $5-$10. No downside risk here . . . we are under book value.

RB msg #9, Thursday, August 19, 1999, at 11:22 p.m.
All I can say is that when we get the awaited news, with only 200K in the float, FTEC is going to take off! $0.17 EPS profits already this year . . . this is a great opportunity!

RB msg #17, Friday, August 20, 1999, at 10:17 p.m.
FTEC Will Close Over $3 Today . . .
Float is gone and more players will be in quickly on this.
Legalized gambling is in vogue!

RB msg #36, Friday, August 20, 1999, at 11:25 a.m.
We'll Be Over $4 Today! EOM
Cautionary statements were also available. Examples follow:

RB msg #8, Thursday, August 19, 1999, at 11:11 p.m.
All revenues . . . no profit margin . . . only $3,000 in the bank . . . I'll pass!

RB msg #26, Friday, August 20, 1999, at 10:38 a.m.
This one has "tank fast" written all over it . . . a good stock to use a stop loss order on,
as much as I hate to use those kinds of orders . . .

Finally, the "dump":

RB msg #39, Friday, August 20, 1999, at 11:34 a.m.
Bought A. M. @ 2 1/32 – Out 3 11/16 . . . I love this country!
And the aftermath commentary:

RB msg #49, Saturday, August 21, 1999, at 10:51 p.m.
Classic pump and dump.
More dumping at the opening on Monday.
Such high volume for no apparent reason . . . always a bad sign.

RB msg #67, Sunday, August 29, 1999, at 3:26 p.m.
Who can say what the heck is going on here. Certainly looks as if it was manipulated a
few days ago. More trades than shares. When FTEC did the reverse split to avoid de-listing
from the NASDAQ it diminished the total amount of shares in the float, thus leaving it prey
to day-traders. Keep an eye on this one and be nimble about getting out if another unwar-
ranted spike hits it.

RB msg #71, Friday, September 10, 1999, at 9:28 a.m.
I have no idea why I bought this stock – other than it was spammed to me from some
investment midget. But I own it now!

As illustrated in Figs 7.2.12 and 7.2.13, the February 3–4, 2000 period is the
focus of Fig. 7.2.15. History repeated in early February 2000, but to a more
informed audience.

RB msg #98, Friday, February 4, 2000, at 12:56 a.m.
If you click on the "Igivegoodtips" (or what ever his name is) name you will see that he
spammed the FTEC stock to TONS OF OTHER boards. People don't like this kind of thing.
I think he did the same thing before. He was a busy camper on 2/3/2000. Last time I saw
something like this, I came back the next day and all trace of that spam post was gone.
Except for posts like mine talking about this crap. Makes you wonder, eh?

But the "pumping" continues even after the above post:

RB msg #99, Friday, February 4, 2000, at 7:17 a.m.
$20 easy very soon.
FTEC is one of the most undervalued companies I have ever discovered. Huge deals are
being worked on. Small float. This thing will fly very soon.

FTEC (2)

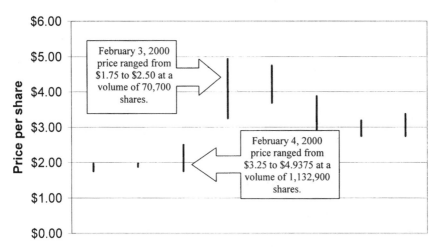

February 1 through February 10, 2000

Fig. 7.2.15.

The discussion and analysis of spam continues:

RB msg #71, Friday, February 4, 2000, at 8:30 a.m.
*Yes, it's a spammer. 2 weeks ago he did it with **WCEC** (emphasis added), using exactly the same kind of text . . . for 2 days WCEC rocketed. It's now back and under the price of before the spam. People tend to react to this kind of spam and lose in the end. If you like a risky play, you can buy at the opening and sell at day's end. I'll bet we'll see the same as with WCEC.*

RB msg #110, Friday, February 4, 2000, at 12:03 p.m.
This is a pump and dump. I would sell and buy back in at a cheaper price next week.

Then, the spammer is directly confronted:

RB msg #114, Friday, February 4, 2000 at 1:41 p.m.
rlassis you must be the king of pump and dump!!
After looking at your record every stock I looked at had gone down since you started screaming strong buy . . . RSAS, BTWS, NVXE, LITH.

RB msg #127, Friday, February 4, 2000 at 3:13 p.m.
Mikeygold spamming the same stocks as rlassis.
How's that strong buy of LITH at $2 going to $10? NOW AT $1!

Your message:
"LITH will break $2 today . . . on the way to 10 dollars. When LION IPOs don't expect
anything less than $60 on the first day of trading. This market is huge . . . batteries
included!!!!!! E-cars, E-commerce huge market this century . . ."

Apparently, the spammer told one of the posters to "get a life." This message illustrates the confidence that comes with the anonymity associated with an alias:

RB msg #129, Friday, February 4, 2000 at 3:34 p.m.
I got a life and now I have your money . . . it went down after I sold . . . thanks a bunch.
I think you are all a bunch of parasites . . . YOU/rlassis and your 2 other names that you
just started posting today.

And further comments are made on the pattern of the stock's price:

RB msg #135, Friday, February 4, 2000 at 4:53 p.m.
Isn't that amazing . . . doubling again on a Friday . . . same as August 23rd and December
3rd?

Firetector is a particularly interesting case, because of the reaction to the hype. The original messages were removed from the boards, but several of those posting on the message boards "saved" the spamming history in the body of their posts. This prevented the loss of the audit trail, if and when complaints of the hype led to the elimination of these posts hyping Firetector stock.

February 4-5, 2000, posts suggested that the spammer could not use another alias or email address to complain about the hype – resulting in its removal:

RB msg #136, Friday, February 4, 2000 at 4:56 p.m.
FTEC SPAMMER:
Just thought I'd preserve the FTEC SPAMMER history of posts. He'll delete them
shortly . . .
Posts by carthy11 (9 posts): hyping FTEC on boards for HVAR, TCGI, EBID, AFIN, &
ABET.[80]

RB msg #138, Friday, February 4, 2000 at 6:27 p.m.
Rlassis . . . here . . . I'll save your spam for you:
Posts by rlassis (95 posts): hyping FTEC on boards for BTWS, FTEC, MCLL, MIGS, ASDS,
NVXE, & NAVR.[81]

RB msg #140, dated Friday, February 4, 2000 at 6:33 p.m.
When FTEC goes back to $2 I will be able to buy back twice as much . . . THANKS SPAM-
MERS.

In this case, some long-term investors (or individuals damaged from earlier hype) decided to save the posting history of hype in the body of their own, independent messages. This preserved the audit trail, in the event that these spamming posts were later removed from the message boards. This case also illustrates the use of fundamental financial information used to support recommendations to buy (e.g. low book value and low float).

6. MSHI

The trades relating to Man Sang Holdings, Incorporated (MSHI) were specified in the SEC "cease and desist" order. Figure 7.2.16 illustrates the high, low, and closing prices for Man Sang. Figure 7.2.17 illustrates the volume of shares traded.

7. WCEC(E)

Figure 7.2.18 illustrates the high, low, and closing prices for West Coast Entertainment, Incorporated (WCEC(E)). Two separate PPS peaks occurred for West Coast Entertainment. The first was on January 5, 2000. On January 4 the stock price for West Coast Entertainment rose to an intraday high of $0.25. On January 5 the intraday high rose even further to $0.49. On January 6 the intraday high declined to $0.40.

The second PPS increase on this stock occurred two weeks later. On January 14 West Coast Entertainment had an intraday high of $0.315 per share. For January 18 the intraday high was $0.71 per share. For January 19–20, 2000 the intraday high rose further, to $0.72 per share, before the decline began on January 21 (with an intraday high of $0.67).

Figure 7.2.19 illustrates the volume of shares traded for West Coast Entertainment over this same period. The highest volume days were on January 5 at 1,354,900 shares and January 18–20, with three consecutive trading days of heavy volume ranging from 1.28 through 5.57 million shares traded.

The message boards for this trading period contained both cautionary comments of spamming and the actual spam. At least two insightful investors noticed the use of two aliases by a single person:

RB msg #232, Tuesday, December 28, 1999, at 10:56 p.m.
Note . . .that SMARTGUY and FRAUDBUSTER are quite possibly one and the same.

RB msg #249, Wednesday, January 5, 2000, at 9:42 a.m.
. . . this stock is getting pumped.

One message poster began his/her posts on January 15 and concluding posting on January 17, never to be heard from again. Recall that on January 18–20

MSHI

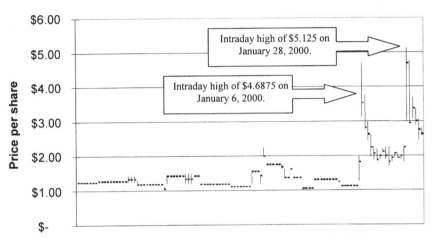

August 23, 1999 through February 4, 2000

Fig. 7.2.16.

MSHI Volume

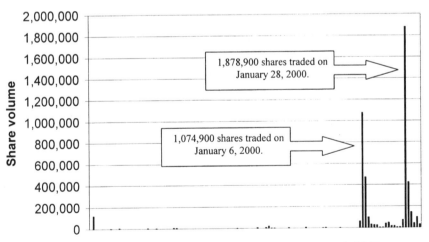

August 23, 1999 through February 4, 2000

Fig. 7.2.17.

WCECE

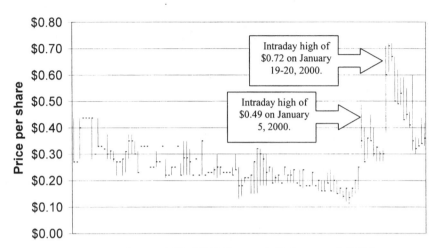

Intraday high of $0.72 on January 19-20, 2000.

Intraday high of $0.49 on January 5, 2000.

August 23, 1999 through Febraury 4, 2000

Fig. 7.2.18.

WCECE Volume

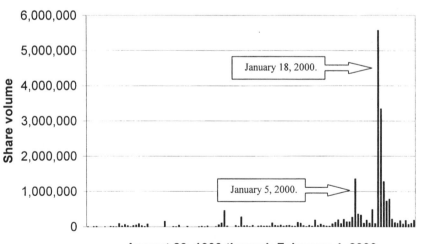

January 18, 2000.

January 5, 2000.

August 23, 1999 through February 4, 2000

Fig. 7.2.19.

West Coast Entertainment stock peaked at $0.72 per share. Portions of some this these posts follow:

> RB msg #340, Saturday, January 15, 2000, at 7:03 p.m.
> *WCECE is extremely undervalued.*
>
> RB msg #341, Saturday, January 15, 2000, at 7:13 p.m.
> *. . . looks to be at least 10X undervalued.*
>
> RB msg #343, Saturday, January 15, 2000, at 8:59 a.m.
> *. . . this stock should be priced substantially higher . . .*
>
> RB msg #347, Sunday, January 16, 2000, at 10:09 a.m.
> *WCECE is a tremendous value . . .*
>
> RB msg #362, Monday, January 17, 2000, at 6:55 p.m.
> *There is tremendous upside potential . . .*

Another poster also began posting on January 15 and concluded on January 17, also never to be heard from again:

> RB msg #337, Saturday, January 15, 2000, at 4:01 p.m.
> *Once the investment community takes notice to WCECE you won't be seeing WCECE at these dirt-cheap prices.*
>
> RB msg #348, Sunday, January 16, 2000, at 10:20 a.m.
> *WCECE is probably an acquisition candidate . . . a cheap way for BBI to expand their business.*

Next, a posting representing what might be referred to as the "look what I found" technique, similar to the one used on FUSA:

> RB msg #357, Monday, January 17, 2000, at 4:40 p.m.
> *Look at this sales pitch I found on the YAHOO message board for MSFT.*
> ******WCECE******
> *No one knows about WCECE yet, this is the biggest gem which I have ever uncovered.*
> *Currently WCECE is at around $0.30 . . . these are ground floor prices! I feel that we will se it over $5 very easily in the upcoming days/weeks . . .*
> *Huge news is coming . . . Huge deals are being signed! WCECE is going to take-off to MUCH HIGHER LEVELS!!!*
> *I personally see little risk when buying WCECE for anywhere under $5, as WCECE has a book value near $5.*
> *WCECE is making over $110 million in sales. The average company in the industry trades at 4 1/2X sales. With 14 million shares outstanding, this would value WCECE at $35.*
> *Again . . . I am sure that $35 will eventually come, but since I would like to remain very conservative . . . my short-term target price on WCECE is still $5.*

Besides Blockbuster, WCECE is probably the most well-known company in the entire industry. It is unbelievable that we can buy shares of WCECE right now for under 1/2 dollar . . . as they have over 376 stores nationwide!

WCECE is starting to position their business more and more into the DVD market. I am hearing that very soon . . . DVD stocks are going to become the huge play, just like cellular and linux stocks have been in recent weeks. WCECE is one of the biggest players in this booming industry.

WCECE also has a major Internet presence. They operate what I consider to be the best video/DVD e-commerce website on the entire Internet!

The only other 2 companies I know of that have Internet video/DVD e-commerce websites which even come close to being as good as WCECE's site . . . are RENT and BGST. And by the way . . . RENT and BGST are both already trading at around $7.

Be sure to take the time to do your research on WCECE! I have never found something with such HUGE POTENTIAL in my entire life! This is probably the biggest opportunity you will ever come across . . .

Finally, on January 18, 2000, someone posts the spam originating from a variety of additional stock-chat message boards:[82]

RB msg #368, Tuesday, January 18, 2000, at 7:52 a.m. and continued on #369 for the same date.
Be very careful here investors . . . spamming is in full force . . .

RB msg #379, Tuesday, January 18, 2000, at 8:55 a.m.
. . . remember, when a pump and dump happens the "regular" investor who has been scammed into buying a stock NEVER gets out fast enough. The crash happens so fast they cannot react.

RB msg #390, Tuesday, January 18, 2000, at 11:59 a.m.
Get out while u can . . . this was a spammed pump and dump!!! Do your own DD and check out IVOC . . . I'm not telling you to buy, just to look at it and do some DD . . .

RB msg #393, Tuesday, January 18, 2000, at 12:42 p.m.
I've been investigating this stock. The spam job on 38 boards earlier today seems to be part of a massive Internet spam job.

And the following message explains how capital formation might be adversely affected by hype:

RB msg #396, Tuesday, January 18, 2000, at 1:46 p.m.
I took advantage of the unexplained increase and sold all of my holdings today. Probably will not go back in ever.

And since it worked on one stock, and a large group of readers are available, an attempt to redirect these readers to another stock is initiated.

RB msg #403, Tuesday, January 18, 2000, at 3:55 p.m.
THIS ONE IS HOT, BUT IVOC IS ON FIRE!!
DON'T WAIT!!

RB msg #416, Wednesday, January 19, 2000, at 9:09 a.m.
ADOT is going to rock! Hurry!

In this case, posters on the message boards were able to specifically identify
the same poster using multiple aliases for spamming. The "look what I found"
technique, so useful in the case of Yes Entertainment (YESS), was repeated
and used to lend credibility to the content of the spam. A rarely seen message
was also identified. One long-term investor indicated that he sold all shares and
would never re-purchase the firm's stock, because of the spamming.
Immediately after the "pump and dump" had concluded, investors/speculators
were led to other stocks that were being hyped.

8. TCGI

Figure 7.2.20 illustrates the high, low, and closing prices for Classica Group,
Incorporated (TCGI). Fig. 7.2.21 summarizes trading volume for the same
period.

TCGI

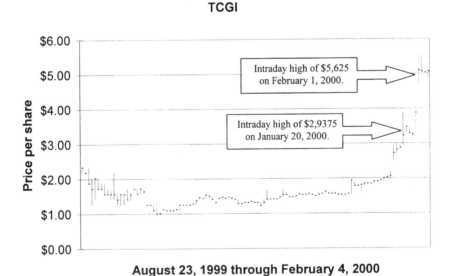

August 23, 1999 through February 4, 2000

Fig, 7.2.20

TCGI Volume

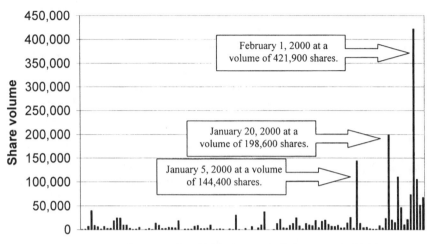

August 23, 1999 through February 4, 2000

Fig. 7.2.21.

On January 20, 2000, with volume at 198,600 shares, the following stock-chat board posts appeared:

> RB msg #4, Wednesday, January 20, 2000, at 12:50 p.m.
> *Classic P&D with this one* . . .[83]

And another on January 31, 2000:

> RB msg #12, Monday, January 31, 2000, at 9:26 p.m.
> *TCGI is being pumped up all over these boards. It's a classic pump of a stock that trades very little so a little buying power can give it a lift. Once it moves up a little more the dump will come sending it back down.*

And a post referring to JUST, also on January 31, 2000:

> RB msg #18, Monday, January 31, 2000, at 11:02 p.m.
> *. . . try to buy into a volatile stock that has been DUMPED. Don't buy on the PUMP. Look at the chart for **JUST** (emphasis added). It has POPPED twice in the last 3 months and is near the bottom of a DUMP. Time to buy slowly!!!! Don't blow your was all at once, it could drop down to a dollar. But when the PUMPing begins, it usually hits $3+!*

Finally, the spam and P&D is discovered:

RB msg #19, Monday, January 31, 2000, at 11:49 p.m.
Everyone check out this guys past post . . . you're a busy guy!

RB msg #22, Monday, January 31, 2000, at 11:59 p.m.
He certainly was busy, eh? Sheesh. That's just pure sickening to see. I wonder what his other name is?

RB msg #29, Tuesday, February 1, 2000, at 7:47 a.m.
Hey dbevan (this alias had been removed from the RB message boards) . . . you spam'd this stock on 50 boards . . . not to worry . . . I will stop in on as many as I can and warn them.

RB msg #36, Tuesday, February 1, 2000, at 12:48 p.m.
What was the name of the guy who spammed over 20-30 other Raging Bull boards? He spammed something like ". . . this is a sure thing . . . BUY BUY BUY." His name has been removed from your post. I'm just curious how this could be done? I'm guessing this guy . . . cancelled his "new" account name.

The following post clearly illustrates a common technique used to determine the credibility of an alias used on the message boards:

RB msg #50, Thursday, February 3, 2000, at 10:42 p.m.
IgiveSTKtips (this alias had been removed from the RB message boards). Interesting. You just signed up today and have already posted to over 30 different boards.

RB msg #51, Friday, February 4, 2000, at 1:43 a.m.
See Post #8 (this post was removed). Notice any spamilarities?

The spamming, in this case, was met with reviews of posting histories. This feature is available on the RB message boards. New aliases with high volumes of posts hyping this firms stock were well-documented by others.

9. HVAR

Figure 7.2.22 illustrates the high, low, and closing prices for Havana Republic, Incorporated (HVAR). Fig. 7.2.23 illustrates trading volume for the same period.

Havana Republic appears to have been one of alias Jonathan G. Lebed's oldest and favorite stocks. This alias first began posting on this firm on the Silicon Investor (SI) stock-chat message boards. This alias, listing occupation as "The Great One," also listed the firm name as Jonathan G. Lebed, Inc.

This appears to have been a repeat of a stock referred to by the alias, Jonathan Lebed, in the August 2, 1998 message, touting his ability to identify under-valued firms. It is common for some stocks to be "pumped and dumped" repeatedly. Therefore, conditions of information asymmetry persist.

HVAR

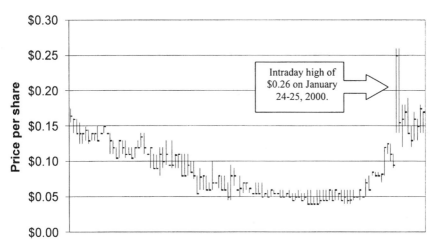

August 23, 1999 through February 4, 2000

Fig. 7.2.22.

HVAR Volume

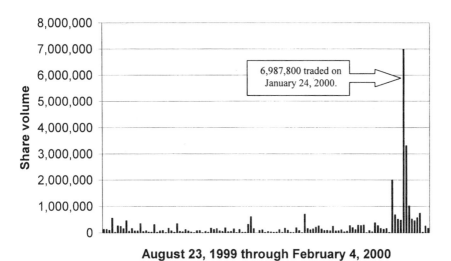

August 23, 1999 through February 4, 2000

Fig. 7.2.23.

ANALYSIS AND SUMMARY

The reference to *Stock Dogs* in YF message #1825, contained in the discussion section of Manchester Equipment Company (MANC), was an important one.

Recall, first, that many of the messages in Chapter 7 (Table 7.2) used a variation of the spelling, referring to a group as the *dawg pound*.

Second, the word *dawg* was included in the body of many of the messages summarized in Table 7.2.[84]

Finally, in the process of examining the stock-chat message board posts for this appendix and the monograph as a whole, an August 2, 1998 message by *Stock-Dogs.com* was identified. The alias used in this message[85] bore similarities to that referenced in the SEC "cease and desist" order, but preceded the period examined by the SEC.

This message noted four stocks, three of which had also shown a dramatic increase in PPS in the past. For those researchers interested in replicating my review of the message board posts contained in this appendix, and related message board posts, graphical representations of these 3 stocks are provided in Figs 7.2.24 (GLOW), 7.2.25 (RMGG) and 7.2.26 (HVAR). Recall that

GLOW

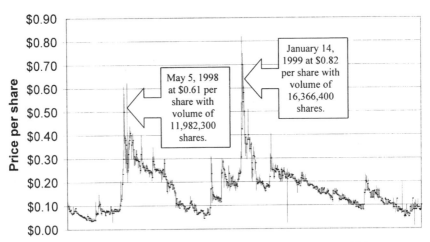

January 2, 1998 through February 4, 2000

Fig. 7.2.24.

RMGG

August 31, 1998 high at $0.92 per share at a modest volume of 543,400 shares.

November 29, 1999 high at $0.48 per share at a volume of 6,758,800 shares.

January 2, 1998 through February 4, 2000

Fig. 7.2.25.

HVAR

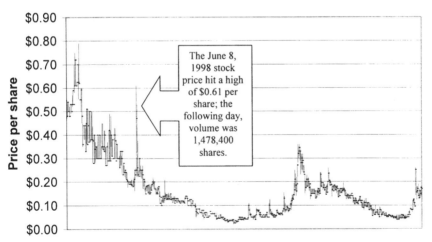

The June 8, 1998 stock price hit a high of $0.61 per share; the following day, volume was 1,478,400 shares.

January 2, 1998 through February 4, 2000

Fig. 7.2.26.

HVAR, Havana Republic, Incorporated, was included in the SEC "cease and desist" order and examined in Figs 7.2.23 and 7.2.24.

Exhibit 7.2.2 provides a theoretical framework, using the hidden information and hidden action model introduced in Chapter 3. As the stock-chat messages contained in this appendix suggest, some of those posting on these message boards were unaware of the legitimacy of the source of information posted (adverse selection in Chapter 2) and their failure to investigate the credibility

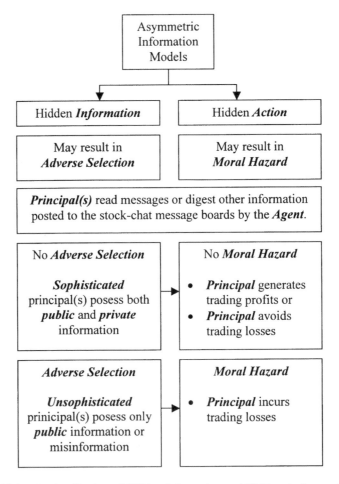

Exhibit 7.2.2. An Application of Hidden Information and Hidden Action to Stock-Chat Message Boards.

of these sources resulted in losses (moral hazard in Chapters 2 and 3). Recall that those reading and acting on these stock-chat message board posts are principals and those posting are agents, within the framework of agency theory.

This appendix contained some detail informational stock-chat message board posts for the nine stocks listed in an SEC "cease and desist" order. The supplemental price and volume charts and stock-chat message board posts contained in this appendix provide detailed insights into the manner in which information is disseminated on the stock-chat message boards and the effects on PPS and volume measures. It is important to note that, **in all cases**, a review of the messages on the same stock-chat message boards on which the spamming was posted, prior to investing, would have revealed warnings posted by those suggesting that the increase in PPS would not be sustainable.

It is likely that many made their decisions and purchased these stocks based solely on the incomplete information contained on these message boards (e.g. rational ignorance). Whether those choosing to participate are sophisticated or unsophisticated investors has not been examined. Others, as some of the messages in this appendix chapter suggests, recognized the excitement and PPS rise as unsustainable, but either contributed to the hype to participate in the gains or failed to participate, observing and attempting to warn others.

APPENDIX CHAPTER 8.1.
MESSAGE BOARD POSTS –
ALLEGEDLY FROM THE CEO
OF UNIVERSAL EXPRESS

> . . . executives have gone to the [stock-chat message] boards . . . to win the support of at least a portion of the online community (Elstein, 2000).

INTRODUCTION

Under the alias *R_Altomare*, allegedly the CEO of Universal Express, posts were made to the Universal Express RB stock-chat message board. This poster's registration information provided for a real name of *Richard Altomare* from *Plainview, New York*, with registration dated *March 30, 1999*.

There can, of course, be no assurance as to the actual identity of a person posting these messages (e.g. identity theft). However, it is also not uncommon for executives to post on the stock-chat message boards, particularly for small cap (SC) or penny stocks, where public relations news releases[86] may prove to be cost-prohibitive for these thinly capitalized firms.

STOCK-CHAT MESSAGE BOARD POSTS

A preliminary, exploratory correlational analysis resulted in a slightly positive relation between the number of posts on the RB message board for Universal Express and the posts by the alias *R_Altomare* ($N = 15$), but this relationship was not statistically significant.

Below are the 15 posts by *R_Altomare*, with dates and topics, as follows:

- March 30, 1999 (msg #1168): Addressed criticisms of the (70-to-1) reverse stock split (RS) of June 1998.[87] RS had to be done to prevent convertible

By: doweceo $
01 Mar 2002, 11:51 AM EST
HARD UPDATE
Many of you have been seeking information about our company. I am Dan Dowe, the
CEO of your company and it has always been my pleasure to inform you about
developments in our company. For the quarter ending February 28th our sales will be at
20+% over the same quarter last year which is consistent with our overall sales
performance this fiscal year. Our ability to grow is directly attributable to our ability to
finance our operations. We are considering a sale leaseback of our facility in Clifton,
New Jersey to pay off bank debt that is due and trade payables, while leaving us some
funding to operate better – essentially to increase our order flow and ship on time.
Delayed shipments are a recurring problem with our company which must be resolved
soon if we are to increase sales beyond 20% per annum.

Overall, and despite the daily pressures of operating in an undercapitalized position, we
are advancing opportunities to grow our company. We are working with the makers of
Sakrete to have our Fiberforce product distributed nationally: this program is currently
being executed at 35 Home Depot stores. We are working with a sales group that will
help us secure national representation to promote our products to major distributors of
building materials. This group will cover retail outlets like Home Depot and Lowe's and
commercial distributors like Fastenal, Grainger and Ferguson. Our sales of Sta-Dri and
Dash Patch products are turning at Home Depot and we hope to have more stores soon:
we have 30 stores for Dash Patch, 15 stores for Sta-Dri and 35 stores for Fiberforce.
Our Sta-Dri products will be part of a full-page advertisement and new product
promotion in the April issue of a leading paint dealer publication – Paint and Decorating
Retailer. Our second largest customer Orgill Bros. Distributors will be doing a 1/2 page
colored ad in its April news magazine that goes out to all its 5,000 dealers. A manufac-
turer of building materials with annual sales of $280 million is considering having us
produce our Sta-Dri products on a private label basis.

We are considering the prospects of acquiring two companies that will be merged into
our New Jersey facility. However these opportunities are early stage since financing will
be a contingency to both deals.

On the down side, our bank has a demand on the notes we have outstanding and cash
flow is still tight. Hopefully, the sale/leaseback on our property will remedy all our cash
flow problems. If you know of any commercial property investors please direct them to
us. We can be reached at 973-777-2307.

We continue to work hard each day at developing a new opportunities to increase sales
which will eliminate our biggest obstacle — tight cash flow. Thanks for your interest and
support.

Exhibit 8.1.1.   Letter from HARD CEO.

debenture (CD) holders from bankrupting the firm. Allegations were made
that MMs short Universal Express stock (see Appendix Chapter 8.4).
• October 15, 1999 (msg #1952): Responses to message board questions.
• December 28, 1999 (msg #3126): Comments on a private postal system.

- April 18, 2000 (msg #3770): Responses to recent personal attacks.
- July 26, 2000 (msg #4627): Comments on continued attacks by those "hiding" behind their message board aliases.
- September 22, 2000 (msg #4946): Comments on anonymous criticisms relating to the June 1998 RS (see March 30, 1999 msg #1168).
- December 13, 2000 (msg #5515 & #5518): Critical posts.
- December 15, 2000 (msg #5562): Extended re-post (from another author) on cybersmear and bashing (addressed in Appendix Chapter 8.3).
- August 27, 2001 (msg #64320): Clarification on the Wednesday, August 22, 2001 *Business Wire*, relating to the Universal Express support for the Dick Barbour Racing Team (see Appendix Chapter 8.2).
- September 7, 2001 (msg #80708 & 80875): Bashers concern over the September 6, 2001 *Business Wire*, misspelling of the word "bullion" (see Appendix Chapter 8.2).
- September 7, 2001 (msg #81732): Regarding sponsorship for the Dick Barbour Racing Team (see Appendix Chapter 8.2).
- September 21, 2001 (msg #94212): Regarding "recent flurry" of messages and reference to "paid bashers" (see Appendix Chapter 8.3).
- March 19, 2002 (msg #188660): General message.

SUMMARY

The samples of stock-chat message board posts, using the name of the CEO of the firm or representing posts by the CEO, in fact, are not uncommon for micro-cap stocks. For example, a series of posts by an alias known as *doweceo* (a.k.a. Dowe CEO for Novex Systems International, Incorporated; OTC BB: HARD) provides regular weekly updates on the RB message board (see Fig. 8.1). The most recent post was made on February 28, 2003.

This appendix chapter was included to provide researchers (and regulators) interested in the distinctions between public and private information and market efficiency with a sample of the types of stock-chat message board posts that corporate executives might make, from time to time. These posts would appear, on their surface, to represent a violation of SEC Regulation FD.

APPENDIX CHAPTER 8.2.
SELECTED (JANUARY THROUGH SEPTEMBER 2001) USXP NEWS RELEASES & ARTICLES

INTRODUCTION

Universal Express, Incorporated (OTC BB: USXP) is the subject of the case study contained in Chapter 8. This appendix contains a summary of only a very small portion of the electronic news headlines associated with Universal Express. They represent public information releases originating from legitimate sources and are presented in chronological sequence.

BACKGROUND

These news headlines were developed from the CBSMarketWatch.com, YF and Datek (proprietary) News Center Internet sites. Redundant or repetitive releases have not been included (e.g. repeated law firm announcements for class action inclusion) and the below represent only a small fraction of the news releases and PR announcements filed by USXP. The contents of Chapter 8 were developed, in part, from this judgmentally selected sample of electronic news releases, as follows:

TUESDAY, JANUARY 9, 2001
- 8:32AM: Universal Express, Inc. – USXP – Sells Interest in Skyworld International (Business Wire).

TUESDAY, JANUARY 23, 2001
- 11:13AM: Universal Express, Inc.'s Subsidiary PBC Network.com Announces Beginning of Telemarketing Campaign (Business Wire).

WEDNESDAY, JANUARY 24, 2001
- 11:00AM: Universal Express' – USXP – WorldPost Division Expansion (Business Wire).

THURSDAY, FEBRUARY 15, 2001
- 12:07AM: New insider trade data for USXP.OB (First Call).

WEDNESDAY, FEBRUARY 21, 2001
- 12:53AM: Universal Express, Inc. – USXP – Announces Quarterly Financial Results (Business Wire).

MONDAY, MAY 21, 2001
- 4:26PM: UNIVERSAL EXPRESS INC/ – Quarterly Report (SEC form 10QSB) (EDGAR Online).

TUESDAY, MAY 29, 2001
- 10:53AM: Universal Express, Inc. – USXP – Announces Expanded Offices in Florida and WorldPost Update (Business Wire).
- 11:45AM: Universal Express, Inc. – USXP – Sells Manhattan Concierge Subsidiary (Business Wire).

TUESDAY, JUNE 19, 2001
- 10:27AM: Universal Express, Inc. Subsidiary WorldPost.com announces Newest Web Site at www.worldpostnetwork.com (Business Wire).

FRIDAY, JUNE 29, 2001
- 10:03AM: Universal Express, Inc. Subsidiary, Postal Business Center Network, Signs Agreement with E*TRADE Access (Business Wire).

TUESDAY, JULY 10, 2001
- 10:01AM: Universal Express Inc. Announces New Corporate Locations (Business Wire).

WEDNESDAY, JULY 11, 2001
- 11:03AM: Universal Express, Inc. To Offer Free Software From Disney, Simon & Schuster, IBM, Grolier, Rand McNally, Edmark and Learning Company (Business Wire).

THURSDAY, JULY 12, 2001
- 7:32AM: The International Investment Group to Provide $5.8 Million Investment to Universal Express (Business Wire).

TUESDAY, JULY 17, 2001
- 7:59AM: Universal Express, Inc. – USXP – Engages Wall Street Firm Chapman, Spira & Carson, LLC (Business Wire).

THURSDAY, JULY 19, 2001
- 9:49AM: Universal Express, Inc.'s – USXP – CEO Richard A. Altomare Interviewed on CEOCAST.com (Business Wire).

TUESDAY, JULY 24, 2001
- 8:05AM: Universal Express, Inc. – USXP – Introduces New Luggage Division – Luggage Express (Business Wire).

THURSDAY, JULY 26, 2001
- 12:43AM: $389 Million Dollar Jury Award to Universal Express – USXP – (Business Wire).
- [????]: Universal Express Wins $389 Million in Fraud Case (Update 2) (Bloomberg).

MONDAY, JULY 30, 2001
- 9:47AM: Universal Express Expects to Collect on Record $389 Million Jury Award (Business Wire).

WEDNESDAY, AUGUST 1, 2001
- 8:06AM: Universal Express – USXP – Commences Execution Steps on $389 Million Judgment (Business Wire).
- 10:54AM: Universal Express, Inc. Subsidiary WorldPost.com to Offer International Shipping Territories to Postal Business Center Network Members (Business Wire).
- 1:02PM: IVIP Acquires Prepaid Telephone Card System – Breakthrough for International Travel Industry (Canada NewsWire).

FRIDAY, AUGUST 3, 2001
- 10:00AM: Emerging Company Report – Business of Small Market ISP; $389 Million Court Judgment Spotlights Company (PR Newswire).[88]
- 10:58AM: Universal Express – USXP – Outlines Steps to Collect $389 Million Judgment (Business Wire).

WEDNESDAY, AUGUST 8, 2001
- 10:07AM: Universal Express – USXP – to Expand Enforcement of $389 Million Dollar Judgment (Business Wire).

THURSDAY, AUGUST 9, 2001

- 9:37AM: Universal Express – USXP – $389 Million Dollar Judgment Reported in the National Law Journal (Business Wire).

THURSDAY, AUGUST 16, 2001

- 10:32AM: Universal Express – USXP – Commences Seizure Steps on $389 Million Judgment (Business Wire).

FRIDAY, AUGUST 17, 2001

- 10:00AM: The Emerging Company Report Television Program, Weekend of 8/17–19 (PR Newswire).

TUESDAY, AUGUST 21, 2001

- 7:31AM: Universal Express, Inc. – USXP – Declares 8% Stock Dividend (Business Wire).
- 9:31AM: Universal Express, Inc. to Repurchase Some of Its Outstanding Common Stock (Business Wire).

WEDNESDAY, AUGUST 22, 2001

- 9:33AM: Universal Express, Inc. – USXP – Pays-off Previous Debt (Business Wire).
- 3:11PM & [3:45PM]: [REPEATING] Universal Express, Inc. – USXP – Sponsors Dick Barbour Racing Team (Business Wire).

THURSDAY, AUGUST 23, 2001

- 7:31AM: Universal Express – USXP – Signs Letter Of Intent To Acquire Virtual Bellhop, Inc. (Business Wire).

FRIDAY, AUGUST 24, 2001

- 1:01PM: Universal Express, Inc. – USXP – Announces Payment Date and Plan of Distribution for 8% Stock Dividend (Business Wire).

TUESDAY, AUGUST 28, 2001

- 2:18PM: Universal Express – USXP – Announces Further Collection Steps On $389 Million Judgment (Business Wire).

THURSDAY, AUGUST 30, 2001

- 9:43AM & 11:19AM: Universal Express, Inc. – USXP – Announces New Corporate Web Site (Business Wire).

* 1:10PM: Universal Express to Join American Airlines, Canon Film – USA – and Anheuser Busch as Sponsors for Richard Dent/Venetian Resort Hotel and Casino Celebrity Golf Invitational (Business Wire).

FRIDAY, AUGUST 31, 2001
* 10:00AM: Emerging Company Report: 250th Show Profiles Direct Marketing; Gold Success in a Low Price Market (PR Newswire).
* 10:30AM: Universal Express' President & CEO Follow-up Appearance On Television Program of Emerging Company Report (Business Wire).

THURSDAY, SEPTEMBER 6, 2001
* 12:59PM: Universal Express Announces Further Locations On $389 Million Judgment (Business Wire).
* 12:58PM: Universal Express Corrects Spelling in First Graph (Business Wire).

FRIDAY, SEPTEMBER 7, 2001
* 12:34PM: Universal Express – USXP – Engages Rubenstein Associates as P. R. Council (Business Wire).

SEPTEMBER 18, 2001
* 11:16AM: Universal Express, Inc.'s Chairman Announces Buying of Stock (Business Wire).

THE CONVERSION OF *PRIVATE* INFORMATION TO *PUBLIC* INFORMATION

In addition to the public information contained stock-chat message board posts, alleged to originate from officers of the companies (see Appendix Chapter 8.1), and the sample of public news releases contained in this appendix, it is not uncommon for those posting to the message boards to post emails, or portions of emails, alleged to be personal emailed communications with officers of the company (e.g. USXP RB message #'s 69368, 69757, 79168, 73265, 78261, and 99369).[89] These posts, if truthful, represent the conversion of private information to public information through an intermediary, and may also take the form of representations made regarding personal telephone conversations to the firm (e.g. USXP RB message #'s 74129, 79691 and 79676).[90]

It is also a common practice for updated posts, complete with links to public information available on other Internet sites, to contain relevant due diligence (DD) for those drawn to further investigate a company by seeking this additional information from the stock-chat message boards (e.g. USXP RB message #'s 71477 and 73542).

SUMMARY

The public information from the selected headlines contained in this appendix provides a summary of some of the events affecting Universal Express from January through September 2001. Initially, these news releases related to the $389 million judgment in Universal Expresses favor. However, numerous public information releases followed and failed to mention the judgment or collection efforts. Researchers interested in the effects of public information releases on stock prices in these small- or micro-cap stocks may wish to review these and more contemporary news releases for Universal Express in association with PPS and volume.

APPENDIX CHAPTER 8.3.
INFORMATION AND MISINFORMATION SIGNALS IN THE FORM OF CYBERSMEAR

. . . the secretary/treasurer of a . . . small publicly traded retailer claimed to spend 30 minutes to one hour, daily, monitoring . . . YF [stock-chat message board] . . . to identify disgruntled employees or ex-employees, and his efforts had identified . . . six . . . (o)nly one required some form of legal threat/action . . . (Cataldo & Killough, 2003).

INTRODUCTION

Chapter 4 introduced the position, developed by Arbel (1985), that information asymmetries are greater for neglected or generic stocks. Investors may find it intuitively appealing to significant effects from rumors and the instability associated with successful stock price manipulation for small- or micro-cap or generic stocks. Investors may not anticipate the same information asymmetries to result in the successful manipulation of big-cap or brand name stocks.

It is through the study of the techniques used to generate conditions of information asymmetry for these micro-cap stocks, that insights may be developed for applications to big-cap stocks. Never-the-less, this section on cybersmear begins with some big-cap stock examples.

The following examples are presented in an extremely summarized form. More fully developed and detailed examples have already been provided in Appendix Chapter 7.2. The posts summarized in this appendix chapter remained on the YF message boards immediately following the rumors relating to General Motors Corporation.

Following these examples from the YF stock-chat message board is a frequently re-posted list of techniques used to generate uncertainty (risk) and manipulate information and the price of a stock.

CONDITIONS OF INFORMATION ASYMMETRY
GENERATED BY RUMORS

On the morning of Thursday, June 27, 2002, a rumor resulted in a trading halt
for General Motors (NYSE: GM) stock. These rumors followed the very recent
public information releases of downward earnings restatements for both
WorldCom (WCOM(E); approximately $4 billion for the prior 5 quarters) and
Xerox (NYSE: XRX; approximately $6 billion, up from a previously acknowl-
edged amount of $3 billion, for the prior 5 years).

With approximately 561 million shares outstanding, the $4.25 PPS decline
in the price of General Motors common stock, prior to the trading halt, resulted
in an intraday market capitalization decline of approximately $2.4 billion dollars.
The trading halt was timely, and the price of General Motors stock recovered
to close at $51.50 per share. Additional recovery occurred on Friday, June 28,
2002, when the PPS for General Motors common stock closed at $53.45.

Some summarized excerpts from the posts by a user alias known as *myrecommendation*, from the General Motors stock-chat message board for YF,
follow:

- Fraudulent pension accounting at GM.
- GM stock halted again. Rumors are true. Sell now.
- GM rumor is not a rumor now. $26 billion fraud. On CNN now. This is the
  end of the market.
- Fraud charges prepared for GM on news. Will keep everyone updated on
  GM crimes against investors.
- Cover up rumor within GM surfaces. Something bad is about to happen to
  another American company. Sell on rumor. This is going to be ugly.
- Fraud certain at GM says *WSJ*. Page A2. GM is next WCOM. There is
  absolutely no doubt about this. (Name excluded) discovered an internal memo
  revealing the fraud and will present it to the SEC.

Similar posts were made by a user alias known as *truthdisclosurecanon*, also
from the General Motors stock-chat message board for YF, many of these posts
are in response to those from *myrecommendation* and implicate International
Business Machines (NYSE: IBM), General Electric Company (NYSE: GE) and
the *Wall Street Journal* (*WSJ*; a legitimate and well-respected source of public
information), as follows:

- $10.2 billion fraud at IBM. IBM's fraud dwarfs WorldCom's.
- GE & *WSJ* are partners in crime.

The volume of negative or bad news posts, in this case, were modest. More credible posts were significant and available to those visiting the YF stock-chat message board for General Motors. However, it warrants mention that highly inflammatory "strong sell" ratings were posted by at least two aliases with the same *2002* suffix used by those posting to the PurchasePro site in an earlier stock manipulation effort (see Chapter 7 and related appendix chapters).

REFERENCES TO SPECULATOR AND MARKET MAKER MANIPULATION

The RB stock-chat message boards for Universal Express (see Chapter 8) contained many suggestions that the firm's stock PPS was depressed as a direct result of off-shore short-selling (e.g. RB message #'s 68368, 69854, 69864, 70665, 71714, 71717, 72851, 74624, 76083, and 102563). In the case of Universal Express, Knight Trading Group, Incorporated (OTC BB: NITE) was the alleged culprit (e.g. RB msg #71353).[91] Recall that Knight Trading had recently been implicated in a SEC investigation (see Chapter 8). And, of course, the legendary nature of DAWGs (see Chapter 7 and Table 7.2) resulted in a reference on the Universal Express stock-chat message boards (e.g. USXP RB message #52690).

CYBERSMEAR/BASHERS HANDBOOK[92]

Perhaps the most significant public release of bashing is Talk Visual (see Chapter 9).

In the academic literature and the context of corporate governance conflicts, bashers may be characterized as dissidents.[93] The following has been posted (and re-posted) on many stock-chat message boards for (at least) several years. The substance of the content has been retained, but in a summarized format:

- Bashers never bash a bad stock. They are never present on the stock-chat message boards for stocks without any potential. Their (frequently, well-choreographed) objective is to bring the price down for: (1) a lower entry price; or (2) to cover a short at a profit.
- Bashers always bring up old news that you have heard many times. Most startup companies have some bad news in the past. Bashers will post this information over and over again. Some unsophisticated bashers will even attempt to change dates (to freshen up old news), in a clear effort to deceive.

- Bashers post many times a day. They try to control the tone or sentiment of the message board and attempt to bash every bit of positive news. Their objective is to wear you down.
- Bashers will lie – their objective is merely to plant the seed of doubt.
- Bashers know you can't verify their statements. They rely on you to be too lazy to verify the information they post. They often work in packs and often validate or support each other.
- Bashers play on your lack of patience. The basher is at his best when you tire of waiting for a gain.
- Bashers bring the price of the stock down. Their objective is to wear down the faithful and scare away any new or potential investors.

RULES FOR SUCCESSFUL CYBERSMEAR-BASED MANIPULATION[94]

According to the theories presented below, the "Grade A" basher can spend up to 80 hours per week bashing a stock. The most skilled of bashers post lots of old news (with links), never respond to being called a "basher," and never post on another stock-chat message board with the same alias. Presumably, the keys to becoming a successful basher follow:

- Be anonymous. Use two or more aliases to stimulate discussion. Three or four aliases can dominate a board and wear down the longs. Use multiple ISPs, handles and aliases.
- Use 10% facts and 90% suggestion; the facts will lend credibility to suggestions.
- Develop alliances . . . let others help you find out about the stock before beginning to bash the stock. Enter with humor and reply to all who reply to you.
- Identify foes (longs). Use them to your advantage. Lead them. Do not follow their lead. Bait the longs into personal debates to wear them down. If others share your concerns, show concern and extend discussion.
- Increase bashing efforts as your position begins to gain momentum, but only bash until the momentum of the stock's price turns. Then, let doubt carry this momentum.
- Give the appearance of being open-minded.
- Be bold in your statements. People follow strength.
- Write headlines in caps with catchy statements.
- Ignore posts that label you as a "basher." New investors will not be aware of your posting history.
- When identified, put up a brief fight, and then back off. Return in 1 hour.

- Your goal is to limit the momentum of the run, not to tank the company or create a plunge. Be subtle and consistent.
- Kill the dreams of profits, not the company or the stock.
- Use questions to control the discussion and to generate critical thinking. Use statements to reinforce facts.
- Avoid lies, name-calling and the use of profanity.
- Encourage people to call the company. Most won't. They'll take your word for claims made. If they do call, find something that is inaccurate in how they report their findings.
- Discourage people from believing positive or favorable Press Releases.
- Compile a list of data prior to beginning bashing efforts. Continually post any negative press releases.
- Always cite low stock volume, even when it isn't low.
- Promote other stocks that would-be investors can buy. They may sell the stock you are bashing, reducing the PPS to a level for entry.
- Do not respond to challenges about the ethical nature of your bashing behavior.

REGARDING MEMBER MARK RATINGS ON THE RB MESSAGE BOARDS

The Raging Bull (RB) and Yahoo! Finance (YF) stock-chat message boards, both, maintain systems for rating posts. These ratings systems are not unlike those by Moody's for bonds or those buy stock analysts to buy, sell or hold a stock.

The RB board provided for those approving of the information content of a posted message to "member mark" the poster with dollar signs (e.g. $, $$, $$$, $$$$ and $$$$$). Dollar signs may also be reduced, as a poster is placed on "ignore." However, this system, and the information content of these member marks, can be manipulated (e.g. RB msg #74329). For example, through the creation of multiple aliases, a single individual may member mark themselves.

The YF system merely provides the option to "recommend" a specific message or place all information posted by a particular alias on "ignore." In contrast with the RB system, the favorable attention associated with prior posts from an alias produces no cumulative advantage, but each individual message is either recommended or not recommended.

SUMMARY

Several techniques are used by sophisticated users of the stock-chat message boards to identify potential stock price manipulation efforts through the public dissemination of seemingly private information, itself, the generation of conditions of information asymmetry. The easiest is to check the registration date of the alias by the person posting a message. However, some bashers may use multiple aliases, allowing some of these to remain dormant for long periods of time. Therefore, it may be necessary to scan the content of their prior posts, increasing the monitoring cost of information – in terms of time expenditures.

Consider that a basher may have multiple aliases and feign conversations with others (in reality, themselves). Their objective may be to reduce the PPS of a stock to provide for a more profitable entry price. They achieve this objective by signaling to those unsophisticated users of the message boards. This is more difficult to detect, but most of us have key words that we prefer in daily conversation. This sometimes leads to the detection of those engaged in the temporary establishment of negative sentiment and/or information asymmetry.

APPENDIX CHAPTER 8.4.
MARKET MAKER MANIPULATION (MMM)

I found out how Michael's making his money. We're selling stock for companies that don't exist (Giovanni Ribisi aka Seth Davis in the film, *Boiler Room*).

INTRODUCTION

Market maker manipulation (MMM) is a common complaint on the stock-chat message boards. Used primarily as a scapegoating strategy, MMs are blamed for a broad variety of real and imagined injuries. Still, there are clear and observable cases of MMM, correctly monitored and interpreted by those posting on the stock-chat message boards.

Because so many investors/traders have access to the Level 2 (L2) quotes, a system allowing all to see and monitor the line-up of bid and ask blocks by MM, it is common for those posting on the stock-chat message boards to discuss this highly visible information (i.e. information symmetry). Researchers interested in MMM, and willing to acquire expertise in the use of the L2 quotation system, will find that the stock-chat message boards are filled with a variety of MMM-related commentary, assistance, and testable hypotheses. A sample listing of the acronyms or call letters, comparable to a ticker symbol for a stock and used to identify and keep track of the behaviors of a MM, are summarized in Table 8.4.1.

This appendix chapter provides some brief examples of starting points for researchers interested in further investigation the topic of MMM. First, an example of a petition to boycott the OTC BB is provided. These petitions appear, from time to time, on a variety of both big-cap and small- or micro-cap stock-chat message boards. Second, two examples of the types of techniques used by (or associated with) MMs, as provided on at least one web site, are provided. There are a broad variety of web sites providing this type of information, which attempts to train investors/traders to monitor and correctly interpret the signals provided by MMs. Finally, some actual cases, involving NASD intervention, are provided. These are the most extreme of examples, and

Table 8.4.1.   A Listing of Selected Active Market Makers.

L2[1]	Active Market Maker[2]	Parent/Corporate Name	Ticker[3]	Web Site: www.
ABSA	Alex Brown & Sons[4]	See Deutsche Bank AG	Subsidiary	AlexBrown.DB.com
AGSI	Aegis Capital Advisors LLC[5]	Charles Schwab Corp	NY:SCH	AegisCapital.net
BEST6	Bear Sterns	Bear Sterns Co's Inc	NY:BSC	BearSterns.com
BRUT	Brass Utility LLC, The[7]	Brut ECN,[8] LLC	Affiliated	Ebrut.com
BTSC6	BT Alex Brown[9]	See Deutsche Bank AG	Subsidiary	AlexBrown.DB.com
CANT	Cantor Fitzgerald LP	Cantor Fitzgerald LP[10]	Proprietary	CantorUSA.com
COWN	Cowen & Co	Société Générale Group[11]	Subsidiary	Cowen.com
DAIN	Dain Bosworth[12]	See RBC Fin'l Group	Subsidiary	DainRauscher.com
DEAN	Dean Witter	See Morgan Stanley	Affiliated	MSDW.com
DLJP	Donaldson, Lufken & Jenrette	See Credit Suisse Group[13]	Merger	Merger
DMLG	Deutshe Morgan Grenfell	Deutsche Bank AG (DeAM)[14]	OTC: DTBKY	Deutsche-Bank.com
FACT	First Albany Corp	First Albany Co's Inc	NAZ:FACT	Fac.com
FAHN	Fahnestock & Co	Fahnestock Viner Hldgs Inc	NY:FVH	Fahnestock.com
FBCO6	Credit Suisse/First Boston	Credit Suisse Group[15]	LSE: CSGZnq.L	CSFB.com
FPKI	Fox-Pitt, Kelton[16]	Swiss Re Immo	ZRH:SRIZ.S	FoxPitt.com
GSCO6	Goldman Sachs	The Goldman Sachs Group Inc[17]	NY:GS	GS.com
HRZG	Herzog, Heine, Geduld Inc	See Merrill Lynch	Subsidiary	Herzog.com
JBOC	JB Oxford & Co	JB Oxford & Co[18]	NAZ(SC):JBOH	JBOxford.com
JEFF	Jefferies Co	Jefferies Group Inc	NY:JEF	JefCo.com
JPMS	JP Morgan Securities	J.P. Morgan Chase & Co.	NY:JPM	Chase.com
LEHM	Lehman Brothers	Lehman Brothers Hldgs Inc	NY:LEH	Lehman.com
LEGG	Legg Mason Wood Walker Inc	Legg Mason Inc	NY:LM	LeggMason.com
MASH	Mayer Schweitzer	Schwab Capital Markets LLP[19]	NY:SCH	MASH.com
MHMY	MH Meyerson & Co Inc[20]	M.H. Meyerson & Co Inc	NAZ(NM):MHMY	MNMeyerson.com
MLCO6	Merrill Lynch	Merrill Lynch & Co Inc[21]	NY:MER	ML.com
MONT6	Montgomery Securities	Bank of America Corp[22]	NY:BAC	BankAmerica.com
MSCO6	Morgan Stanley	Morgan Stanley Dean Witter & Co[23]	NY:MWD	MSDW.com
NEED	Needham & Co	Needham & Co[24]	Proprietary	NeedhamCo.com
NITE	Knight Securities LP[25]	Knight Trading Group Inc	NAZ:NITE	TriMarkSecurities.com
NMRA	Nomura Securities Int'l	Nomura Hldg America Inc	LSE:8604q.L	Normura.com
OLDE	Olde Discount[26]	H&R Block Fin'l Advisors Inc	NY:HRB	HRBlock.com
OPCO	CIBC Oppenheimer	CIBC[27]	NY:BCM	CIBCOpCo.com
PERT	Pershing Trading[28]	See Credit Suisse Group	LSE:CSGZnq.L	Pershing.Com
PIPR	Piper Jaffray[29]	U.S. Bancorp	NY:USB	PiperJaffray.com
PRUS	Prudential Securities	Prudential PLC[30]	NY:PUK	Prudential.com
PWJC	Paine Webber Jackson Curtis	See UBS Securities	Subsidiary	Subsidiary
RPSK	Rauscher Pierce Refsnes[31]	See RBC Fin'l Group	Subsidiary	DainRauscher.com
SBSH6	Salomon Smith Barney Inc	Salomon Smith Barney Hldgs Inc[32]	NY:C	SmithBarney.com
SELZ	Furman Selz Cap Mgmt LLC[33]	ING Group NV	NY:ING	IFSAM.com
SILK	Spear Leeds & Kellogg	Spear Leeds & Kellogg[34]	Subsidiary	SLT.com
SNDV	Soundview Financial	SoundView Technology Group Inc	NAZ:SNDV	WitSoundView.com
SWCO	Schroder Wertheim & Co	See Salomon Smith Barney[35]	Merger/Sale	Merger/Sale
TUCK	Tucker Anthony	RBC Fin'l Group[36]	NY:RY	RoyalBank.com
UBSS	UBS Securities	UBS[37] AG[38]	NY:UBS	UBS.com
WSLS	Wessels Arnold & Henderson[39]	See RBC Fin'l Group	Subsidiary	RBCDRW.com

Notes:

[1] This 4-character symbol is depicted on the NASDAQ Level II (L2) trading/monitoring system. This symbol is not the same as and should not be confused with that of a stock ticker symbol or call letters. This table was designed with the objective of organizing these MM symbols alphabetically.

[2] This table represents the integration of lists from several web sites (e.g., www.daytradingfirms.com/market.html; theexecutioner.com/mmaker.html; www.daytraderproducts.com/mm_ecn.html; www.acas-online.net/international/spanish/Market/market. html; and www.electronicdaytrader.com/indextop.html). In addition to the selection of market makers for which detailed information is provided in this table, researchers will find it of interest to gain an understanding of the breadth of MMs for research design purposes. These listings change, quite literally, daily.

Table 8.4.1. Continued.

---

[3] Where NY = NYSE = New York Stock Exchange, LSE = London Stock Exchange, NAZ = NASDAQ = National Association of Security Dealers Automated Quotation system, and ZRH = Zurich stock exchange.

[4] Deutsche Banc Alex. Brown represents the investment banking activities of Deutsche Banc Alex Brown, Inc. (U.S.) and Deutsche Bank Securities, Ltd. (Canada). They are subsidiaries of Deutsche Bank AG. Alex, Brown & Sons, organized in 1800, and are the oldest NYSE member firm still doing business under the same name. The runners-up are 1818 Brown Brothers Harriman & Co., 1849 Lazard Freres & Co., and 1850 Lehman Brothers, Inc.

[5] Aegis Capital Advisors, LLC is affiliated with U.S. Trust Corporation (UTC), a wholly-owned subsidiary (June 2000-) of Charles Schwab Corporation.

[6] According to one web site (http://theexecutioner.com/mmaker.html), these market makers are "elephants" – they carry the greatest weight in trading activity.

[7] Founded in 1998, Brut ECN (formerly The Brass Utility) offers its BRASS trade-routing software for market makers; it also trades stock as an electronic communications network (ECN). In this capacity Brut serves as a hybrid broker, stock exchange, and market maker (matching trade orders in a certain stock). The ECN serves market makers and institutional investors, automatically executing matching orders for a small fee. SunGard Data Systems owns approximately 20% of Brut; other minority shareholders include Merrill Lynch, Morgan Stanley Dean Witter, Goldman Sachs, Lehman Brothers Holdings, Bear Stearns, Knight Trading, and Salomon Smith Barney.

[8] Brass Utility LLC is an ECN (Electronic Communications Network). A listing of this and other ECNs from several web sites (e.g., www.electronicdaytrader.com/mm2.html; www.daytraderproducts.com/mm_ecn.html; and theexecutioner.con/mmaker.html) follows: ARCA Archipelago/Terra Nova Trading LLC; ATTN Alltech/Attain; BRUT Brass Utility LLC; BTRD Bloomberg; INCA Instinet/Instinet Corp; ISLD Island/Island Corp; REDI Redibook/Spear Leeds & Kellogg; NTRD NexTrade; MKXT Tradescape; and STRK Strike Technologies.

[9] Deutsche Bank Alex Brown is traded on the London Stock Exchange (LSE) under the call letters DBKGnq.L.

[10] Prior to their initial public offering (IPO) in December 1999, eSpeed® (NASDAQ NM: ESPD) was a wholly-owned subsidiary of, and conducted operations as a division of, Cantor Fitzgerald Securities, which in turn is a 99.5%-owned subsidiary of Cantor Fitzgerald, L.P. (collectively with its affiliates, Cantor). We commenced operations as a division of Cantor on March 10, 1999, the date the first fully electronic transaction using eSpeed® system was executed. Cantor had been developing systems to promote fully electronic marketplaces since the early 1990s. Since January 1996, Cantor has used the eSpeed® system internally to conduct electronic trading.

Perhaps the hardest hit firm in the New York City World Trade Center terrorist attack, Cantor Fitzgerald specializes in fixed-income securities, institutional equities, derivatives, and foreign stocks. The TradeSpark product (TradeSpark, LP is a fast, efficient, market-neutral electronic marketplace created by seven companies in September 2000) is a leading energy trading marketplace powered by eSpeed® technology.

[11] A subsidiary of Société Générale Group (sg-ib.com).

[12] Formed by the 1997 merger of Dain Bosworth and Rauscher Pierce Refsnes and bought by RBC Financial Group (formerly Royal Bank of Canada) in 2001, the company and its subsidiaries provide brokerage services in the western US and investment banking services to government and corporate clients nationwide. The firm has offices in nearly 30 states. RBC Dain Rauscher underwrites security placements, serves as a market maker for nearly 500 companies, and clears and settles trades for some 170 brokerage firms. The firm attributes nearly 60% of its net revenues to its Private Client division.

[13] The Credit Suisse Group completed a merger with Donaldson, Lufkin & Jenrette (DLJ) in November 2000.

[14] Deutsche Bank Asset Management (DeAM) was formerly Morgan Grenfell Asset Management.

[15] A subsidiary of Swiss bank Credit Suisse Group.

[16] Fox-Pitt, Kelton is a wholly-owned subsidiary of Swiss Re.

[17] Goldman Sachs owns Spear, Leeds & Kellogg, one of the largest specialist firms on the NYSE.

[18] JB Oxford agreed to pay the SEC some $2 million in 2000 to settle a case involving alleged illegal market manipulation by previous management (April 2, 2001 Annual Report & 10-K FYE: 12/31/2000):

On February 14, 2000, the Company reached a settlement with the Los Angeles office of the United States Attorney's Office (the "USAO") in connection with the USAO's investigation of the Company's prior management. While the Company maintains its innocence, it agreed to pay a total of $2.0 million over three years to settle the USAO matter and to reimburse the USAO for the substantial expense associated with the two and a half-year investigation. The agreement with the USAO stated that if on or before February 14, 2001 the Company enters into a settlement with the SEC that involves a payment of $1.0 million or more to the SEC, the USAO has agreed that the Company's obligation to the USAO would be reduced by $500,000. Discussions are ongoing with the USAO regarding extending this agreement, based upon the proposed SEC settlement. On October 12, 2000, the Pacific Regional Office of the SEC advised the Company that it is recommending that the SEC accept the Company's $1.5 million offer to settle the SEC's investigation. If the proposed settlement is accepted, JBOC will also agree to a censure, to refrain from any violations of securities laws, and to take certain actions to ensure continued compliance with federal securities laws. The Company paid $500,000 of the USAO settlement amount in the first quarter of 2000, $500,000 in the first quarter of 2001, and the remainder will be paid in equal annual installments over two years. If the SEC accepts the regional office's recommendation, payments to the

Table 8.4.1. Continued.

USAO and SEC would total $3.0 million. This amount has been accrued and included in accounts payable and accrued liabilities. The Company does not believe that current management was the subject of the investigation and the USAO did not bring charges against the Company.

[19] Making markets in over 5,000 OTC securities for broker-dealers and institutions.

[20] The broker/dealer's market making activities for more than 4,000 NASDAQ and OTC securities. M.H. Meyerson transferred its 54% stake in online retail brokerage service eMeyerson.com to brokerage ViewTrade Holdings in exchange for stock in ViewTrade. It also owns about half of TradinGear.com, which provides order-input technology to eMeyerson.com.

[21] Market leader competing against Morgan Stanley Dean Witter & Co.

[22] The purchase of Montgomery Securities by Nations Bank (NationsBanc Capital Corp.) was approved by the Federal Reserve on September 11, 1997. BA Capital Company, L.P. was formerly known as NationsBanc Capital Corporation.

[23] Market leader competing against Merrill, Lynch & Co., Inc. The "Dean Witter" component is dropped from the name (for advertising and promotional purposes). Subsidiaries include Jiway Holdings Limited and Van Kampen Investments, Incorporated.

[24] Their web site indicates that they have eight position traders and eleven sales traders, and have developed strong relationships with the major buyers and sellers of emerging growth stocks. Claiming to be a leading market maker in aftermarket trading, Needham & Company makes markets in approximately 210 stocks.

[25] Knight Securities, L.P. is a subsidiary of Knight Trading Group, Inc. Knight Securities, L.P., is a market maker in NASDAQ securities. Knight Capital Markets LLC holds a market position in the Nasdaq Inter-Market, the over-the-counter market in exchange-listed equity securities, primarily those listed on the New York Stock Exchange and the American Stock Exchange. Knight Financial Products LLC is a market maker in listed options on individual equities, equity indices and fixed-income futures instruments in the United States and Europe. The Company also maintains an asset management business for institutional investors and high net-worth individuals through its Deephaven Capital Management subsidiary.

[26] H&R Block acquired Olde Discount Corporation in 1999. In late 1998, Olde Discount Corporation and some executives agreed to pay $7 million in fines to settle charges that the brokerage allowed fraudulent sales practices, ran improper advertising, and violated other securities regulations. The SEC alleged the firm's compensation, production, hiring and training policies "created an environment" that encouraged brokers to deceive customers. The firm and three executives agreed to pay $5.15 million to settle the SEC's allegations. Olde and the firm's chairman Ernest J. Olde agreed to pay a total $1.85 million to resolve separate allegations by the NASD. In the SEC's case, the agency alleged that Olde brokers lied to customers, and engaged in unauthorized trading, trading in securities that weren't suitable for their customers, and unnecessary trading to generate commissions. "This case should send a very strong message that abusive practices will be vigorously punished and that officials at all levels will be held accountable," said SEC Chairman Arthur Levitt. The NASD charged Olde Discount with improper advertising, failure to supervise its brokers and failure to cooperate with the regulatory inquiry. The firm, under its settlements with both the NASD and the SEC, neither admitted nor denied wrongdoing. Ernest Olde was suspended from the securities industry by the NASD for 18 months. The SEC suspended him for 12 months. The NASD suspension will overlap the SEC's action, so Olde will be barred from the securities industry for 18 months. Olde Discount, which has more than 150 branch offices throughout the U.S., agreed to pay a $4 million fine to the SEC. Ernest Olde agreed to pay a $1 million fine and be suspended for a year. In the SEC's case, Stanley A. Snider, the firm's former director of sales, agreed to pay $100,000, and Daniel D. Katzman agreed to pay $50,000. Both Snider and Katzman also were barred from the securities industry with the right to reapply for admission in a non-supervisory capacity in five years (Friday, September 11, 1998 by Neil Roland, Bloomberg News; http://www.naplesnews.com/today/business/d373966a.htm).

[27] CIBC Oppenheimer is the U.S. Private Client Division of CIBC World Markets, the global marketing name of the investment banking and securities businesses of the Canadian Imperial Bank of Commerce (CIBC).

[28] The Pershing Division of Donaldson, Lufkin & Jenrette Securities Corporation is a Credit Suisse First Boston company.

[29] On Dec. 15, 1997, Piper Jaffray Companies Inc. announced its acquisition by U.S. Bancorp. The acquisition closed on May 1, 1998. On March 1, 1999, the company changed its name to U.S. Bancorp Piper Jaffray to reflect its partnership with parent company U.S. Bancorp.

[30] Prudential Securities is a subsidiary of the Prudential Insurance Company of America.

[31] Formed by the 1997 merger of Dain Bosworth and Rauscher Pierce Refsnes and bought by RBC Financial Group (formerly Royal Bank of Canada) in 2001, the company and its subsidiaries provide brokerage services in the western US and investment banking services to government and corporate clients nationwide. The firm has offices in nearly 30 states. RBC Dain Rauscher underwrites security placements, serves as a market maker for nearly 500 companies, and clears and settles trades for some 170 brokerage firms. The firm attributes nearly 60% of its net revenues to its Private Client division.

[32] A subsidiary of Citigroup.

[33] Furman Selz is an independent division of Aeltus Group and an indirectly-owned subsidiary of ING Group (i.e., ING Furman Selz Asset Management = IFSAM).

[34] A subsidiary of The Goldman Sachs Group, Inc., Speer, Leeds & Kellogg, is one of the top specialists (or market makers) on the NYSE and AMEX exchanges, where it deals in more than 400 and 200 listed stocks, respectively. The firm lines up buyers and sellers of stock at fixed prices (i.e., "making a market") and buys or sells stocks to offset wide price fluctuations. Its SLK

Table 8.4.1. Continued.

Capital Markets division maintains markets for some 7,000 NASDAQ and smaller Bulletin Board (BB) stocks. The company is an investor in REDIBook, a leading electronic communication network (ECN), which provides fast trade execution over the Internet.
[35] Schroder Wertheim & Co. sold its investment banking business to Citigroup's Salomon Smith Barney, leaving Schroder to carry on as an asset management concern.
[36] RBC Financial Group (formerly Royal Bank of Canada) is the holding company for Tucker Anthony in Boston and Sutro & Co. in San Francisco.
[37] UBS = Union Bank of Switzerland.
[38] UBS Warburg (formerly Warburg Dillon Read) purchased investment broker Paine Webber to increase its presence in the U.S.
[39] Minneapolis-based Dain Rauscher Corp. purchased privately held Minneapolis-based Wessels, Arnold & Henderson in early 1998.

these public information releases are often posted and re-posted to stock-chat message boards, fueling the fires of negative investor sentiment and still further claims of both actual and imagined cases of MMM.

AN APPEAL AGAINST MMM

Petitions are not uncommon on the stock-chat message boards. Links for the following petition (www.petitiononline.com/mm12/petition.html), complete with errors in grammar, etc., were posted on a variety of stock-chat message boards over the weekend of September 8–9, 2001:

To: Market makers

ATTENTION INVESTORS IT IS TIME TO SAY ENOUUGH IS ENOUGH!!! TIME TO TAKE A STAND BOYCOTT of the OTCBB Effective Sept 24th to 26th, 2001 If your tired of Market Maker Manipulation (MMM) . . . seasoned OTCBB traders know that MMM is absolutely out of control . . . [t]he Naked shorting has gone on tracked for too long . . . consider joining with us on imposing a Boycott on the OTCBB for A period of 3 days . . . we are tired of all the endless Naked shorting, the 100 share prints at the bid, the ridiculous spreads. Are you tired of seeing a stock sit for days with a.03 x.05 bid and ask and the moment someone finally decides to buy at.05 cents seconds later they lower it. All the walk downs on small volumes, move on no prints, can't buy when you want, can't sell when you want, are you ready to say enough is enough? If so join us on September 24, 2001 through September 26, 2001 during which time we will cease all trading on the OTCBB, we will be alerting every media stream possible to have our voice heard . . . What do we hope to achieve? 1. We want our voice heard that Naked shorting without any requirement to cover has to stop. 2. That a electronic trading system be implemented ASAP. 3. That we are tired of the games . . .

Sincerely,

The reference to "100 share prints at the bid" is an example of an error in the perception of what is referred to as "automated executions." When placing a market or limit order, without specifying all-or-none (AON) for the order, an immediate automated or partial execution of 100 or 200 shares is common (e.g. a 50,000 share buy order for a penny stock, resulting in an immediate 100 share partial fill for the order). Overtly claimed as a procedure designed to increase participation in the trading for a particular security, this process is broker-specific and increases order flow and commissions to the broker. Therefore, observations of these 100 and 200 share trades does not in and of itself constitute MMM, but illustrates a lack of sophistication on the part of the individual placing the order and the monitoring individuals, misreading these partial fills as a signal to require a complex explanation.

TECHNIQUES FOR MMM

The MMs job is to fill customer's orders to buy and sell stocks, and, at the same time, to make a profit for their firm from their own inventory. A contemporary example was that of Knight, contained in Chapter 8. At least one web site,[95] devoted to exposing some of the MM "games" (e.g. head fakes, shake-outs, fading, and so on), suggests that MMs manipulate stock prices with great frequency. This sentiment is common on the stock-chat message boards.

It should be pointed out that these behaviors are not without support. After all, these behaviors represent nothing more than a variation in the form, but not in the substance, of window dressing (see Chapter 3).

The overtly stated objective of those maintaining this web site is to educate individual investors in some of these techniques, so that the investor might learn to think like (or "paint") the market maker, avoiding the pitfalls that they suggest are present. Their suggestion, of course, is that these profit-maximizing market maker behaviors involve MM trading for their firm's accounts. These behaviors can often be explained by trading behaviors that do not involve MM manipulation (MMM), but result from the actions of day-traders or other retail trader behaviors. Two examples of MMM follow:

Technique Number 1: Shaking (the Tree) to Rattle "Weak Hands"[96]

The first technique, and the one that most often used to explain the decline in the price of a stock, is the MM "shake." The strategy to combat this manipulation is to watch when the market maker is buying or accumulating shares. The MM will move to the inside bid (i.e. the highest bid price), buy shares, then back off from the inside bid. A few minutes later s/he will buy shares, again, but at a lower price. This process is repeated. Each time the MM is buying at successively lower prices.

The MM may have first offered to sell (ask) with a large quantity of shares. This provides the illusion that the stock is experiencing weakness, when, in fact, the MM was generating the illusion of weakness for the stock, while buying at declining prices to increase inventory.

A few minutes, hours, or even days later, when the stock price recovers/rises, the MM will sell shares accumulated at the lowered or manipulated price. These sales will generate a profit, as s/he fills his client's buy orders with his low-cost inventory.

The web site suggests that once you realize that a MM is accumulating, and after the MM has finished creating and then buying into the weakness, the day-trader/investor should buy.

Technique Number 2: The Pre-Market Run Up

Market makers are often accused of running a stock price up in the pre-market (e.g. 7 a.m. or 8 a.m. to 9:30 a.m. on trading days). This is referred to as "gapping." Then, they sell these shares, after establishing a short-lived momentum of a price rise. This latter behavior is referred to as "shorting."

The pre-market stock gap is followed by a shift of MMs from the bid to the ask, offering to sell large quantities of the stock, making the stock look weak, panicking those recently purchasing and/or holding the stock, and bringing the stock price back down. An investor buying at the high price, immediately before the price decline, is referred to as having been caught "flat."

According to the web site, a key indicator for this type of MMM is to watch for a lack of support, on the bid or run-up of the stock price, by a MM or an ECN. Recall, however, that the attempt to cause a "run up" in the PPS of PurchasePro (see Chapter 7 and Table 7.2) was by a small group of (admittedly, inept) individual investors.

NASD REGULATION AND SANCTIONS FOR MMM

The following are the result of a NASD site keyword search, conducted through September 2001.[97] They have been briefly summarized. Search results for the key word, *manipulation*, follow:

> *(1) Royal Hutton Securities Corp. (CRD #14489, New York, New York) submitted an Offer of Settlement in which the firm was fined $20,000 . . . expelled from NASD membership . . . consented to sanctions and to findings that it engaged in stock **manipulation** (emphasis added) and fraudulent sales practices, in connection with the sale of house stocks, made material misrepresentations, received excessive commissions, failed to inform purchasers*

that they were receiving these excessive commissions, and discouraged the sale of the stocks (NASD Case #CAF000042).

House stocks are (typically) those stocks in which the broker-trader firm holds a large inventory, for the purpose of trading and profiting from trades for the firm's account, and/or stocks that the broker-trader firm has underwritten for the purpose the IPO. It is common (and legitimately so) for the commissions for these *in house* or *house* stocks to be higher than those for stocks that the broker-trader firm does not maintain a market (or inventory) of, as these other stocks involve other broker-traders and, therefore, additional transfer costs or friction (i.e. commissions) to the selling broker-trader firm.

Smaller and younger companies are less likely to go public. Both adverse selection (pre-purchase) and moral hazard (post-purchase) are present in IPOs, and information asymmetry adversely affects the prices for which shares are sold. The post-IPO relation between operating performance and ownership is often negative (Leland and Pyle 1977 and Chemmanur and Fulghieri 1995).

*(2) J. Alexander Securities, Inc. (CRD #7809, Los Angeles, California), Richard Leon Newberg (CRD #346857, Registered Principal, Golden Beach, Florida), and Dennis Jay Sturm (CRD #1407180, Registered Principal, Coral Springs, Florida) . . . participated and acted as underwriters of an unregistered shell company and surviving entity securities . . . trading, including matched trades and trades in the securities of the shell **companies created the false appearance of trading volume and market interest . . . induced other market makers to enter quotes . . . allowed the respondents to artificially affect the market price** (emphasis added) . . . (t)hey engaged in **manipulative** (emphasis added) or deceptive devices to induce the purchase or sale of securities by means of **manipulative** (emphasis added), deceptive, or other fraudulent devices and aided and abetted the **manipulative** (emphasis added) trading of others.*

*[They had] financial interests in accounts at other firms, failed to disclose these financial interests . . . [one individual] provided false testimony during the NASD investigation. The firm failed to supervise . . . trading and market making activity . . . or . . . for **manipulation** (emphasis added) (NASD Case #CAF010011).*

*(3) Falcon Trading Group, Inc. (CRD #30361, Boca Raton, Florida), Sovereign Equity Management Corp. (CRD #20016, Deerfield Beach, Florida), and Glen Thomas Vittor (CRD #1565323, Registered Principal, Deerfield Beach, Florida) were fined $1 million, jointly and severally . . . expelled from NASD membership and Vittor . . . barred from association with any NASD member in any capacity . . . respondents **effected short sales for the firms' own accounts . . . failed to make an affirmative determination that the firms could borrow the securities or otherwise provide for delivery of the securities by the settlement date** (emphasis added) . . . the respondents, in cooperation with others, attempted to obtain stock at below-market prices through the use of threats and coercion, and . . . through **naked short sales** (emphasis added) and extortion, the respondents participated in a **manipulation** (emphasis added) of the market for those securities (NASD Case #CAF980002).*

(4) NASD Regulation Hearing Panel Orders Josephthal & Co, Inc., Two Execs To Pay $3.3 Million In Fines And Restitution For Fraud And Unfair Dealing With Customers . . . more than 360 customers defrauded in a scheme using what the Panel called "tactics typically associated with 'boiler room' operations . . . "

As the underwriter of VictorMaxx's initial public offering and dominant market maker for the stock, Josephthal supported the stock from August 1995 until the beginning of May 1996 by continuing to buy up available amounts in the marketplace *(emphasis added). By mid-May 1996 . . . the firm had suffered actual losses trading the stock of more than $2.5 million, with another $1.3 million in unrealized losses . . .*

In an effort to cut its losses . . . [they] decided to sell the position to the firm's customers . . . [t]o induce the sales force to move the stock, Purjes and Fitzgerald made the stock available to them at a quarter-point below the then-current bid of $1.75 . . . result(ing) in gross commissions of about 29% . . . (creating) a "stampede" on the part of the sales force . . . from May 17 to May 31, 1996, Josephthal's sales force aggressively recommended VictorMaxx stock . . . using "tactics typically associated with 'boiler room' operations," including baseless price predictions, failing to disclose their huge compensation arrangement, unauthorized trades, and other sales practice abuses . . . confirmations received by customers indicated that the stock was being sold without any markup.

During . . . 10 business days . . . [they] . . . sold almost one million shares in over 400 transactions at an average price of $2.10 per share . . . nearly 36% of the tradable shares . . . [the] sales force continued selling, going short another 277,000 shares . . . [w]ithin a month, it was below $1, and continued to fall even more . . . was delisted . . . an investor who purchased . . . and held . . . incurred more than a 50% loss.

*. . . ordered to hire a qualified independent consultant . . . to review . . . compliance with Regulation M, the federal anti-**manipulation** (emphasis added) statute, and to adopt and implement any proposed changes . . . (NASD Case #C3A990071).*

*(5) NASD Regulation's National Adjudicatory Council Sanctions Former Monitor Investment Group Executives. NASD Regulation's National Adjudicatory Council (NAC) affirmed . . . (t)he bar . . . based on . . . **manipulation** (emphasis added) of the market in connection with . . . sale of . . . stock . . . [participation] in a fraudulent stock **manipulation** (emphasis added) scheme . . . NAC imposed the following sanctions for the **manipulation** (emphasis added) and other violations:*

*   *. . . former acting president . . . fined $90,000;*
*   *. . . former trader . . . fined $91,000;*
*   *. . . former research analyst . . . fined $90,000.*

*. . . [one individual] failed to take any action to detect, prevent, or remedy the **manipulation** and . . . failed to testify truthfully . . . assisted in the falsification of order tickets . . . NAC imposed . . . a two-year suspension . . . a $25,000 fine . . . [under appeal] to the SEC (NASD Case #?????????).*

*(6) NASD Regulation Bars John Fiero, Expels Fiero Brothers, Inc., and Imposes $1 Million Fine For Illegal Short Sales, Market **Manipulation and Extortion** (emphasis added) . . . for engaging in a **fraudulent short selling, extortion and manipulation** (emphasis added) scheme.*

*On February 6, 1998, NASD Regulation filed a complaint against Fiero and other co-conspirators alleging that **they colluded to drive down the price of 10 Nasdaq securities** (emphasis added) . . . during January 1995, and February 1995, through illegal short selling . . . This "bear raid" scheme involved Fiero and others obtaining nearly 1 million shares, units, and warrants from Hanover Sterling at below market prices through the use of threats and coercion to cover their illegally-created short positions. Ultimately, **the short selling scheme led to the failure of Hanover Sterling on Feb. 24, 1995, which was quickly followed by the collapse of its clearing firm, Adler, Coleman Clearing Corp.** (emphasis added), and the appointment of a Security Investors Protection Corporation trustee for Adler Coleman.*
. . . Fiero . . . [purchased] . . . $12.1 million of securities . . . at prices $866,500 below the then-prevailing market price . . . [and] . . . used these securities to cover his firm's short positions . . . resold the rest, primarily to other short sellers involved in the scheme.
*. . . Fiero violated short selling rules from Jan. 20 through Feb. 23, 1995 by failing to make the required affirmative determinations prior to engaging in short sales . . . **NASD rules restrict "naked" short sales, that is selling a stock short without ensuring that the stock can be borrowed or otherwise provided for by settlement date, also known as an affirmative determination** (emphasis added) . . . Fiero was not entitled to the market maker exemption from the affirmative determination rule during the time his firm was registered as a market maker because it was not engaged in bona fide market-making transactions. Fiero **manipulated** (emphasis added) the market . . . through his purchases and resale of the extorted stock and his illegal, naked short selling.*
The respondents have appealed this matter . . . [98]

As is always the case in these matters, the above provided for the opportunity for an appeal within a 45 day window. The details of the above case appeared, in the form of a January 8, 2001, NASD Press Release, and literally hundreds of times on a variety of stock-chat message boards.

*(7) Robert Alden Thayer (CRD #874129, Registered Principal, Colorado Springs, Colorado) submitted a Letter of Acceptance, Waiver, and Consent in which he was suspended from association with any NASD member in any capacity for two years . . . no monetary sanction has been imposed. Thayer failed to implement an effective system for monitoring his member firm's equities division to prevent price **manipulation** (emphasis added) of a private placement, **failed to monitor the activities of an individual** (emphasis added) . . . failed to establish, maintain, and enforce procedures reasonably designed to achieve compliance with the penny stock rules and failed to disclose the control relationship between his member firm and a security . . . suspension began January 2, 2001, and will conclude on January 1, 2003 (NASD Case #CAF000031).*

SUMMARY

Researchers interested in investigating the topic of market maker manipulation (MMM) may wish to begin tooling up for this area by watching the recent popular film, *Boiler Room*. Broad access to Level 2 has increased visibility and significantly reduced the potential for unobserved MMM (e.g. information asymmetry), but cases continue to occur. These cases are monitored by those on the stock-chat message boards and can be identified, for example, using keyword searches on the YF web site.

On an anecdotal level, cases of MMM appear to continue to occur for both big-cap and small- and micro-cap stocks, though more blatant examples of greater duration (e.g. days and even weeks) are prevalent only for thinly traded, generic, small- and micro-cap (e.g. OTC BB and PinkSheets) stocks. To conduct this type of research, the investigator will have to gain access to and monitor L2, perhaps requesting the assistance of those on the stock-chat message boards to learn to interpret the signals representing regular trading vs. market maker manipulation.

APPENDIX CHAPTER 9.1.
NON-RANDOMLY SELECTED
SUMMARIES OF 126 CASES

Companies big and small, from high tech to retail, have made John Doe one of the most sued men in America[99] (Howard Mintz, November 28, 1999).

Funny, never have seen a penny CEO complain about unfounded and untrue hype on message boards (USXP RB msg #69600).

INTRODUCTION

This chapter provides brief summaries of litigation (or threats of litigation) relating to allegations of stock price manipulations. These cases originate from the stock-chat message boards. They were also summarized in Table 9.1. Researchers interested in developing a data base for hypothesis testing will find these summaries useful as a starting point.

This appendix chapter summarizes 126 case studies. It is, however, not a comprehensive listing. By the time this monograph is published, this number is likely to approximate twice this number. The cases are summarized, below:

Observation No. 1 – Allegation of Cybersmear. In January 1999, the shares of 2TheMart.com, Incorporated (2TheMart) soared from less than $2 to $50 in one week. A graphical representation is provided in Fig. 9.1.1.

This rise in stock price was preceded by a January 20, 1999, press release, the day before the stock PPS peaked, reporting that the firm intended to establish a web site to compete with eBay, Incorporated (NASDAQ NM: EBAY). According to the press release, the site would be *operating* by June 30, 1999. However, the contract with International Business Machines Corporation (NYSE: IBM) to undertake the 6-month project to develop the site was not *signed* until June 1999. The site was finally launched in November 1999, but the company was ineffective in their efforts to operationalize the web site. A class action lawsuit against the firm alleged that they made materially false and misleading statements.

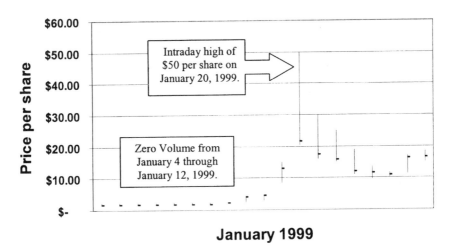

Fig. 9.1.1.   2The Mart.com, Incorporated Price per share.

2TheMart filed its own lawsuit against *Bear Down* and *Movant*, two of the 23 aliases posting critical comments on the SI web site, to learn their identities from the site's registration data. According to an April 20, 2001, EFF press release, EFF and the ACLU successfully defended the rights (i.e. motion to quash) of the twenty-three John Does to continued anonymity.[100]

Observation No. 2 – Allegation of Cybersmear. 4KidsEntertainment, Incorporated (4Kids) filed a cybersmear lawsuit in June 2000, against defendant, *Booper 34145*. Additional filings were made in August 2000, and appeared to relate to the issuance of a subpoena for the discovery of the identity of the message board poster. A status conference was scheduled for December 11, 2000, but in December 2000, a request for dismissal was granted and filed, without prejudice, by the attorneys for 4Kids.[101]

Observation No. 3 – Allegation of Cybersmear. AgriBio Tech, Incorporated alleged that a YF cybersmear campaign by *aahOOOgah* and *secman_98* suggested that the director and co-founder of the firm were about to be indicted and that owners were shorting the firms stock, respectively. These posts appeared to have adversely affected the PPS (down approximately 20%) of the firm's stock. A suit was not filed, but in August 1998, the firm's CEO held a conference call to reassure investors and analysts.

Observation No. 4 – Allegation of Cybersmear. According to a June 16, 1999, *Business Wire*, two brothers were alleged to have posted several hundred messages under a variety of aliases on the YF message boards. The brothers were the chairman/president and secretary, respectively, of a shell corporation previously acquired by AHT Corporation (AHT). It was alleged that their objective was to influence the outcome of two previously disclosed court cases in their favor by depressing AHT's stock price. However, the judge vacated the preliminary injunction granted for these cases on May 13, 1999 on grounds that the plaintiffs' hands were "unclean" due to cybersmear. AHT and the shell corporation settled the related cases in August 1999.

Observation No. 5 – Allegation of Disclosure of Insider Information. AirTran Holdings (formerly known as ValueJet) filed a suit in Boston on July 20, 2000, alleging that at least one and as many as six persons were posting confidential information (e.g. "misappropriation of trade secrets . . . ") on the RB message boards. Selected stock-chat message board posts from one of the aliases follows:

> *Post No. 10990 by JulietAlpha dated Monday, 1 May 2000 at 4:01p.m.*
> *Here it is: Load factor for Apr: 67.5 Cust. flown: 630934 Also, new pass privledges (sic) announced today for employees: USAir ID90s for FL EMPS and pass eligible dependants. More info soon . . . . JA*

And, in response to another poster's accusations of posting "bogus" information:

> *Post No. 10996 by JulietAlpha dated Monday, 1 May 2000 at 5:59p.m.*
> *Bogus? I guess you will see when it is officially released, now won't we?*

Observation No. 6 – Allegation of Cybersmear. A "Jane Doe" lawsuit was filed to identify Ohio-based aliases on both YF and AOL message boards. An executive of AK Steel Holdings (formerly known as Armco Steel) claimed that the posts were disparaging, threatening, and defamatory. At least one comment, contained in an EFF alert dated October 17, 2000, was directed at a specific executive of the firm, and was a commentary on his litigious nature: "(Name) will litigate the time of day. OOPS I will be in court."[102]

Observation No. 7 – Allegation of Cybersmear. Amazon Natural Treasures, Incorporated (Amazon) filed a lawsuit in January 2000. The suit named an American art historian who lived and worked in Italy for the prior two decades. Also named was the owner of a small manufacturing business in Wisconsin. A Connecticut software programmer and the owner of a New York public relations firm, claiming that a collection agency was suing Amazon for about $7,000 still owed for work completed for Amazon, were also named in the suit. "John Doe" co-conspirators were also named as defendants.

The suit alleged slander, defamation, libel, the intent to inflict emotional distress, tortuous and negligent interference with contracts and prospective economic advantage, and illegal shorting of non-marginable securities.

Amazon alleged that false and defamatory statements followed a rise in the firm's stock price to an April 8, 1997, 52 week high of $3.56 per share. Amazon also alleged a causal relation between these statements and the subsequent decline in the firm's stock price to approximately 12 cents per share, which, in turn, led to de-listing from the OTC BB to the PinkSheets. Messages were posted on SI and RB message boards.[103]

Observation No. 8 – Allegation of Cybersmear. Americare Health Scan, Incorporated (Americare) published a press release on June 18, 1999, disclosing the details of a libel lawsuit filed against Technical Chemicals and Products, Incorporated (NASDAQ: TCPI), the chairman/president of Technical Chemicals, and a Technical Chemicals stockholder and personal friend of the chairman/president of Technical Chemicals (posting anonymously on the YF bulletin board). According to the press release, Americare's investigation began on February 26, 1999, when they issued a subpoena to YF to disclose the identity of *Plusticker* (and 17 other aliases). Some of these aliases were later identified.

The Americare press release further stated that Americare had an ongoing patent infringement case against Technical Chemicals and had previously obtained a judgment for $328,350 against Technical Chemical and for $500,000 against the president and chairman of Technical Chemical, for the misappropriation of Americare's trade secrets.

Observation No. 9 – Allegation of Cybersmear/Disclosure of Inside Information. On February 23, 2000, Answer Think Consulting Group filed a lawsuit against YF poster, *Aquacool_2000*. The suit alleged that these posts contained defamatory remarks and contained illegally disseminated confidential information. YF disclosed the registration information for *Aquacool_2000* to Answer Think, without any prior notification to the defendant.

On May 11, 2000, a follow-up suit, against YF, charged that *Aquacool_2000* was a former Answer Think employee, was fired in March 2000 and was denied a significant cash payment and a large block of stock after Answer Think learned of his identity from YF. The ACLU and EPIC assisted *Aquacool_2000* (a name selected after the water cooler in the poster's office), in this suit against YF, in defending his/her right to remain anonymous. The suit included complaints for invasion of privacy, breach of contract, negligent misrepresentation, and unfair competition and false advertising. They sought compensatory and punitive damages, attorneys' fees, and an injunction against any future disclosures without prior notification of the registered parties.

In August 2000, the case against YF was dismissed with prejudice. YF chose not to seek to recover its attorney fees.

Observation No. 10 – Allegation of Hyping. The PPS of the stock for Ants Software, Incorporated (Ants; changing its name from Chopp Computer Corporation, the year before) rose from 88 cents on August 12 to a high of $55.63 on December 23, just before Christmas (1999). After reaching this price, Ants stock fell to $5.50 in just four days. The firm's SEC filings noted that it had no revenues from 1996 through 1999, but anticipated some revenues in 2000.

The SEC announced the formal commencement of its investigation on January 7, 2000. More than 4,000 RB message board posts reiterated the firm's claims that it had developed a technology to significantly accelerate computer data processing.

Observation No. 11 – Allegation of Disclosure of Insider Information. In early August 2000, Apple Computer, Incorporated disclosed the details of their civil suit against up to 25 persons posting insider and secret information and images of Apple's new dual-processor G4 PowerMac and its new oval-shape optical (ApplePro) mouse. The images were posted and available on the Internet on or about February 16, 2000. The official product release date was July 19, 2000.

Observation No. 12 – Allegation of Cybersmear. On February 17, 2001, Aqua Vie Beverage Company publicly disclosed that it filed a suit against 10 John Does for posts made on the RB message boards. The suit sought damages for defamation and injurious falsehoods against the Company and/or its officers, directors and products.

Observation No. 13 – Allegation of Cybersmear. An executive of Ashton Technology Group, Incorporated, in an interview, disclosed that a suit had allegedly been filed against the Internet alias, *mmmary* and 5 other John Does.[104]

Observation No. 14 – Allegation of Cybersmear. It was alleged that the vice president of a Seattle-based golf- and leisure-apparel company and a competitor of Ashworth, Incorporated, posted disparaging and untrue statements on the YF message boards under the alias of *goattrail*. The posts occurred between 1998 and 2000.

The settlement, including the apology posted on the same YF message board, follows:

Retraction, dated April 6, 2001 at 8:21 p.m. by: goattrail, msg: 3571
Between 1998 and 2000, under the name "goattrail," I posted a number of messages on
this board without revealing that I am Andrew Hilton, Vice President and National Corporate

Sales Manager of Cutter & Buck (as you know, Cutter is one of Ashworth's competitors). My messages were unfairly negative, and I regret that I posted these messages about one of Cutter's competitors in this fashion. I posted the messages without knowledge or approval of Cutter & Buck. On behalf of Cutter & Buck and myself, I apologize to Ashworth and it employees, as well as the readers of this message board, for doing so.
(Name removed)

Vice President and National Corporate Sales Manager
(Name removed)

Observation No. 15 – Allegation of Hyping. On July 8, 1999, a message, appearing to be an official *PR Newswire* release, announced a strategic alliance between AOL and the Canadian auctioneer, Bid.com International, Incorporated (Bid.com acquired ABD Systems International on October 2, 2001). This release replicated a similar *Reuter's* news agency announcement of an $89 million strategic alliance between AOL and drkoop.com, Inc. (OTC BB: KOOP(E)).

The announcement was posted on the YF message boards by *Jag 98* at 12:53 p.m. Four minutes later, after warnings of misleading posts by others on the same message board, twenty-five year-old *Jag 98* retracted the statement, suggesting that this was what he "hope(d)" would happen. At the time of the post, *Jag98* was a wholesale tool dealer living in Chicago.

Even after the retraction, Bid.com's shares rose from $8.50 to as much as $9 per share is less than one hour and volume surged from 154,000 shares per hour to more than 950,000 shares between 1:30 p.m. and 2:30 p.m. The SEC charged *Jag98* and he plead no contest. The fine was waived, but *Jag98* agreed to be subject to stiffer sanctions in the event of a similar occurrence.

Observation No. 16 – Allegation of Cybersmear. During August 2000, the CEO of BioFiltration Systems, Incorporated, announced the firm's intention to seek SEC and federal law enforcement assistance to investigate recent cybersmear posts on stock chat message boards. In anticipation of a dramatic number of new contract signings for a computer-enhancing device, the firm's stock had risen from $0.25 per share to $2.25 per share.

On a single day, August 16, 2000, the CEO alleged that BioFiltration's stock was *bashed* down to $0.50 cents per share. The stock chat message board posts alleged that BioFiltration had only one patent, an aircraft de-icer.

Observation No. 17 – Allegation of Cybersmear. Three persons, alleged to have posted "clearly libelous" messages on the YF message boards, were found guilty of posting more than half of the thirty-three thousand messages (e.g. the CEO was a Nazi SS doctor and that the firm's products to treat arthritis kill people) about Biomatrix, Incorporated. Posts were also made on the boards for two Genzyme subsidiaries (NYSE/NASDAQ NM: GZSP and GZTR). The three firms were about to release news of a merger.

These messages were posted for more than one year, beginning in the spring of 1999. Their aliases included *voteREP, VoteREPBLCN, vote_republican_2000, vr_is_back, od_438, cd_43eight, meddra_man, Jenti_is_very_pro_life, missyx_20000, mouth2857, onecutelittlegirl, bfriendly2me2, allergictochickenbits,* and others.

The August 3, 2000, court ruling was the first case where online posts were found to be libelous. Shortly after this decision, on August 21, 2000, the Enforcement Section of the Massachusetts Securities Division (MSD) moved for a temporary cease and desist order against those posting these messages.

Observation No. 18 – Allegation of Cybersmear. BioPulse International, Incorporated issued a *PR Newswire* on February 13, 2001, to respond to negative posts on the (unidentified) message boards.

Observation No. 19 – Allegation of Cybersmear. On September 2, 1999, BioShield Technologies, Incorporated, published a press release in a *Business Wire*, announcing that it would be taking legal action against *FraudFinder1, TeSquared,* and *theskepticds1* for posting defamatory and fraudulent statements on the YF message boards.

Observation No. 20 – Allegation of Cybersmear. Attorneys for Scientology's privately held Bridge Publications served AT&T WorldNet, an ISP, with a subpoena to force them to identify *Safe,* the alias for an online critic.

Observation No. 21 – Allegation of Cybersmear. In an unusual case, Brightpoint filed a "John Doe" suit, anonymously, seeking the identities of those posting on AOL. The court approved the order on August 11, 1999. AOL contested the suit, due to the anonymity of the firm, filing a motion to quash on October 15, 1999. AOL's motion to quash was denied, but AOL appealed. The Virginia Supreme Court remanded the matter to the lower court to proceed. The firm was required to provide its identity, due to its failure to provide evidence of its position that revealing the firm's name would cause economic harm to the company. The firm, Brightpoint, agreed to dismiss the case in mid-March 2001.

Observation No. 22 – Allegation of Hyping. The SEC and the Oklahoma Department of Securities (ODS) filed coordinated enforcement lawsuits in federal and state district courts to halt an alleged pump and dump stock manipulation involving Broadband Wireless International Corporation. On August 11, 2000, the assets of defendants were ordered frozen.

A convicted felon and Broadband's president, the latter having plead guilty and still on probation from a prior SEC lawsuit in 1990, posted false SEC documents and made false statements on the RB message boards. From late 1999 through February 2000, these efforts resulted in an increase from $0.12 to $12 per share for Broadband Wireless stock. The stock was sold for estimated profits of $5 million.

Figure 9.1.2 provides a graph of the closing PPS for Broadband Wireless stock from September 16, 1999, through September 15, 2000.

Observation No. 23 – Allegation of Cybersmear. For 18 months, the CEO of a rival golf club company, La Jolla Club used 27 aliases to post 163 messages on the YF message boards that were critical of Callaway Golf Company. During the period of the posts, he bought, sold and even shorted shares of Callaway stock. He posted on apology on the YF message board:

> *Apology 02/24/00 03:14 p.m. by: stevencade Msg: 5820 of 9134*
> *My name is (removed). I am the Chief Executive Officer of a golf company in Carlsbad, California, that competes directly with Callaway Golf. From April 1998 to October 1999, I posted 163 messages on this board using 27 pen names. Many of the messages were critical of Callaway Golf and its management. Many of you have known me as Encinitas Ranch. I also posted under the names of Craigleifer, StanleyLevine, Sportsmygame2, and CarlsbadSurf. Under two names, biggolfretailer and golfmart100, I posed as Callaway Golf retail accounts. Other identities under which I posted messages are as follows:*
> *Stocks30plus, NowTJ, SurfsUpNow, nowannabe, WELUVGOLF, Stockinvestorplus, Imvacationing, Sportsmygame, jackofthistrade, stockbuyernow, Rminorstlouis, GeeWizardWow, BostonSurfNow, NJGolf, RichLewissaysHello, floridaGolf, thebeststocks, IKnowgolf, IknowNike and PGAGolf Pro.*
> *I regret that I did this. Posting messages under so many aliases certainly misled the Board's readers by creating the impression that there were twenty seven board participants who held similiar (sic) critical views about the Callaway Golf Company and its management when in fact all 163 messages reflected only my own views. I apologize to all participants of the ELY Board, to the Callaway Golf Company, its employees, and shareholders. In the future, I will not be writing on this board . . .*

Observation No. 24 – Allegations of Cybersmear. Caremark Rx, Incorporated (formerly MedPartners, Incorporated), filed a suit against posters posing as the firm's CEO on an Internet stock-chat board in May 1998. One defendant was accused of sending e-mail, posing as the CEO, to a major Caremark shareholder. A Boca Raton, Florida, hedge fund was alleged to have misrepresented corporate information to certain state officials and to have planted false and misleading information with financial and other news reporters. Co-conspirators, not named in the suit but under further investigation, included a California-based investment banking firm-broker-dealer, a Cayman Island firm, an LLC based in New York City, and a California general partnership.

Observation No. 25 – Allegation of Cybersmear. Messages posted by a Texas businessman, a Maine lawyer and a California Internet user (*Indianhead*) claimed company officials at Carnegie International Corporation were engaged

Broadband Wireless

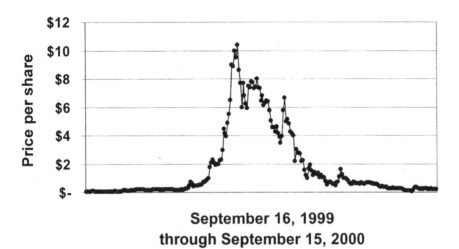

September 16, 1999
through September 15, 2000

Fig. 9.1.2.

in insider trading and attempted to convince shareholders to file a major class-action lawsuit.

Carnegie's May 28, 1999, suit alleged the posting of false and misleading messages about the handling of more than 1 million shares of Carnegie stock. These negative messages, and the response/suit from Carnegie, followed a SEC examination and an April 29, 1999, trading halt for Carnegie shares.

As a result of the SEC action, Carnegie agreed to restate earnings for 1997 and 1998. The earnings restatement required the cancellation of the bonus shares awarded to Carnegie executives and officers.

These Carnegie executives and officers filed SEC reports that they had sold (or otherwise disposed of) these shares just two days before the related SEC trading halt. The YF message board posts questioned the coincidental nature of the timing of these *dispositions*.

On February 29, 2000, Carnegie filed suit to force YF to disclose the identities of *Centralscrutiner999*, *Devilsdunce*, and *Fagnum_p_i*. A $2.1 billion suit was also filed against Grant Thornton LLC, its former accounting firm, alleging fraud, negligence and defamation.

Observation No. 26 – Allegation of Cybersmear. A February 12, 2001, a *Business Wire* release announced that CBQ, Incorporated, was taking steps to address and investigate a 10-month long cybersmear campaign. This campaign seemed to coincide with the firm's decision, in March 2000, to not acquire 1stinhealth.

The cybersmear campaign began in April 2000. The firm's stock price had declined from a high of $16.50 in January 2000 to a low of 19 cents per share. By the end of October 2001, the firm's stock price had declined further, to 4 cents per share.

Observation No. 27 – Allegation of Cybersmear. In a July 25, 2000, *PR Newswire*, Centre Capital Corporation announced that they were not aware of any insider short-selling of stock. This statement by Centre Capital was a response to rumors spread on Internet stock-chat message boards.

Observation No. 28 – Allegation of Cybersmear. Negative messages posted on SM and RB (by *WaveyDavey*, *Wavey*, *garpike*, *Montero* and *Cook81*) message boards resulted in the filing of a November 26, 1999, suit against SM, RB and 5 John Does by ClipClop.com Enterprises, Incorporated (formerly, Promark Software). The unflattering messages were posted to these boards on August 9 and from November 15 through November 22, 1999. According to a December 2, 1999, a news release, the judge in this case ordered SM and RB to remove the unflattering messages and to forbid these persons from further posts.

Observation No. 29 – Allegation of Cybersmear. Cohr, Incorporated believed that its former COO posted negative messages about the firm on YF under the alias, *ex_cohr*. The former COO had been asked to resign from the ex-COO had accepted a position as the president of a competitor, but denied writing the messages, suggesting online identity theft.

The suit included charges of breach of contract, misappropriation of trade secrets, and fraud. Cohr believed that the messages were defamatory, malicious, and were posted to drive away customers and investors.

Observation No. 30 – Allegation of Cybersmear. In a series of suits, beginning on June 11, 1999, ComputerXpress.com, Incorporated predecessor, CostPlusfive.com, Incorporated, filed suits alleging that *undestone* and *ogravity* were publishing false and disparaging messages on the RB stock-chat boards. In an August 17, 2000, *PR Newswire*, ComputerXpress announced that defense attorneys had failed to have a March 30, 2000 suit dismissed under SLAPP statutes.

Observation No. 31 – Allegation of Cybersmear. Seeking information from those posting on the RB message boards, Computerized Thermal Imaging, Incorporated, posted letters demanding that an identified alleged short-seller of the firm's stock retract earlier (mid-June 2000) statements and post an apology on the SI message board.[105]

Observation No. 32 – Allegation of Cybersmear. A retired scientist and a resident of Colts Neck, N. J., who now gives piano lessons over the Internet (alias, *binisello88*), *LA-Broker*, *Splaylaywahtheepi*, *peadir-og*, *biopharma444*, *initq*, *HealthCareChick*, and others were sued by Credit Suisse First Boston for allegedly libelous messages posted on the YF stock-chat message boards. A commercial real-estate broker in Washington who participated in the YF board (not named in the suit) was trying to raise money for a legal-defense fund.

The messages were critical of one of Credit Suisse's stock analysts. The $1 million suit was filed on July 12, 2000. On December 28, 2000, Credit Suisse filed a notice of dismissal of the suit, without prejudice.[106]

Observation No. 33 – Allegation of Cybersmear. In a suit filed on April 5, 2000, Creditrust alleged that an employee of Enhance Financial Services Group (NYSE bond: EFS6C03), a competitor at the time, used *mcnooder* and *blowhard2000* as aliases, and posted messages on the YF stock-chat boards in an effort to interfere with Creditrust's capital-raising efforts. At the time of the suit, there were 21 messages, beginning in February 1999.

Observation No. 34 – Allegation of Cybersmear/Disclosure of Inside Information. In May 2000, Cummins Engine Company, Incorporated, filed a suit against eight YF critics of Cummin's decision to extend insurance coverage to gays and unmarried couples. Twenty-one messages were posted by the eight aliases, including *nsider_47201*, in April and May 2000.

Observation No. 35 – Allegation of Hyping. The Quebec Securities Commission (QSC) confirmed, in early August, 2000, that it was investigating a possible case of stock price manipulation by a broker. The posts were by the alias, *Patrick Gravel*. Message board posts suggested that the U.S. National Security Agency (NSA) would hold a press conference to make an important announcement about DelSecur Corporation's anti-hacking technology on Webfin (owned by a Montreal Internet firm, Netgraphe was a small, French-language stock-chat message board).

The firm moved quickly to distance themselves from the source of these posts. A former investment advisor was accused of posting the false messages in July 2000. He was discharged on August 4, 2000.

Observation No. 36 – Allegation of Cybersmear. In May 2000, Dendrite International, Incorporated filed a lawsuit claiming that at least four persons revealed company secrets and/or were engaged in libelous Internet message board posts. It was alleged that false statements about the company were made by three of the defendants, three published secret company information and two identified themselves as employees of Dendrite, violating their contractual agreements to not criticize the company.

The company requested that YF provide the identities of *ajcazz, gacbar, xxlrr* and *implementor extrodinaire*. Previously, on June 20, 2000, the Superior Court judge ordered that Dendrite post its intentions on the same YF board used by the defendants, as follows:

d_villanueva_2000

YF message No. 867, June 23, 2000

Notice of Order to Show Cause

Please take notice that the following order has been entered with respect to "implementor_extrodinaire", "ajcazz", "xxplrr", and "gacbar":
Michael S. Vogel
ALLEGAERT BERGER & VOGEL LLP, 475 Wall Street,   Princeton, New Jersey 08540, (609) 688-9700
Attorneys for Plaintiff DENDRITE INTERNATIONAL, INC., a New SUPERIOR COURT OF NEW JERSEY Jersey corporation, MORRIS COUNTY CHANCERY DIVISION – Plaintiff, GENERAL EQUITY PART DOCKET NO. MRSC-129-00 v. Civil Action JOHN DOES Nos. 1 through 4 and DOES 5 through 14, inclusive, ORDER TO SHOW CAUSE Defendants.
WHEREAS, this matter been brought before the court by Michael S. Vogel, Esq., of Allegaert Berger & Vogel LLP and Robert L. Weigel, Esq., and David A. Zonana, Esq., of Gibson, Dunn & Crutcher LLP, counsel for plaintiff Dendrite International, Inc. ("Dendrite"), on application for an Order To Show Cause why an Order should not be entered granting plaintiff leave to conduct limited expedited discovery, including issuance of a commission to take discovery out-of-state, for the purpose of obtaining information sufficient to identify defendant's John Does No. 1 through 4 and serve them with the Complaint in this action; and WHEREAS, the Court has reviewed the proposed Order To Show Cause, Memorandum of Law, Verified Complaint, Certification of Michael S. Vogel, and Certification of David A. Zonana; and WHEREAS, Defendants John Does Nos. 1 through 4 are named as defendants under fictitious names pursuant to R. 4:26-4 because their names are unknown to Dendrite; and WHEREAS, it appears that the most effective and appropriate means of providing actual notice to Defendants John Does Nos. 1 through 4 of the present application is for this Court to authorize posting of this Order to Show Cause on Yahoo – Finance Home Message Board: DRTE not later than June 23, 2000; and WHEREAS, good cause exists for the entry of this Order; IT IS on this 20th day of June 2000, ORDERED as follows:
1. Defendants John Does No. 1 through 4 are directed to appear before this Court on July 5, 2000, at 4:00 p.m. in the afternoon, at the Superior Court of New Jersey, Morris County, Chancery Division, Morris County Courthouse, Washington and Court Streets, Morristown, New Jersey, and show cause why this Court should not enforce a commission granting plaintiff leave to conduct limited expedited discovery, including discovery out-of-state, for the purpose of obtaining information sufficient to identify defendants John Does Nos. 1 through 4 and serve them with the Complaint in this action.
2. Defendants John Does 1 through 4 shall file their opposition papers, if any, with the Court and serve them so as to be received by counsel for the plaintiff no later than June 30, 2000.

3. Plaintiff shall file its reply papers, if any, with the Court and serve them so as to be received by counsel for Defendants John Does 1 through 4 no later than July 3, 2000.

If you cannot afford to pay an attorney, call a Legal Services Office. An individual not eligible for free legal assistance may obtain a referral to an attorney by calling a county lawyer referral service. These numbers may be listed in the yellow pages of your phone book. The phone numbers for the county in which this action is pending are: Lawyer Referral Service, (973) 267-5882, Legal Services Office, (973) 285-6911.

Please also take notice that "implementor_extrodinaire", "ajcazz", "xxplrr", and "gacbar" may obtain copies of the court papers relating to this order by contacting (name and phone removed).

Public Citizen and the ACLU filed to oppose the identification of the YF posters in July 2000. These organizations said that Dendrite should, first, demonstrate that economic harm resulted from the posts.

In late November 2000, the judge affirmed the Internet critic's right to privacy. Dendrite had failed to prove that the messages were harmful to the firm.

Observation No. 37 – Allegation of Cybersmear. During November 2000, E*Trade Group, Incorporated filed suit against an unidentified person using the CEO's name to post messages to a stock-chat board. During October 2000, *Christos_Cotsakos* and *christoc_m_cotsakos* posted messages apologizing for shareholder losses and claiming to have made a killing on put or short stock options for the firm's stock. Messages were also posted under the name *jerry-gramaglia*, the firm's president and COO.

YF posters were served with subpoenas in February 2000. One of the posters, *Gus*, was a 40-year-old transport company employee. He sold his 10,000 E*Trade shares when the stock climbed to $15 per share. Another (i.e. *Christos_Cotsakos* and *Kathy_Levinson*) agreed to post an apology and to refrain from similar, future posts.

Observation No. 38 – Allegation of Hyping. In March 2000, the SEC suspended trading and sued eConnect, Incorporated and the firm's CEO for fraud, alleging that he issued false news releases.

Observation No. 39 – Allegation of Cybersmear. A college student spammed a fraudulent news release about Emulex Corporation. His motivation was to recover losses from short-selling. The release indicated earnings restatements, an SEC investigation and executive resignations. The hoax resulted in a market value decline from $4.1 billion to $1.6 billion and an SEC trading halt on the day of the news release. The SEC and FBI identified and exposed the individual responsible for the false new releases within days. The Emulex stock PPS recovered in approximately two to three weeks.

Observation No. 40 – Allegation of Cybersmear. In August 2000, Fidelity Holdings, Incorporated was considering legal action against bashers. Fidelity believed that false message board posts led to the class action suit brought against the firm by shareholders purchasing the firm's stock between November 15, 1999 and April 12, 2000.

Observation No. 41 – Allegation of Hyping. FinancialWeb.com, Incorporated was included in 1 of 23 criminal complaints and indictments brought by the U.S. Justice Department (DOJ) in *Operation Uptick*. Organized crime was involved in the pump and dump scheme, bribing investment advisory services to tout the stock of this and approximately 34 other firms over a five-year period.

From June 13 through June 19, 2000, the firm's stock dropped from $8 to $1.50. By October 2000, the stock price was 6 cents.

Observation No. 42 – Allegation of Cybersmear. Fischer Imaging Corporation filed a suit against 10 aliases (e.g. *mammoman2000* and *rad1910*) posting on the YF message boards. Fischer claimed that the unflattering information caused at least one qualified job candidate to decline a position with the firm and at least one shareholder to sell their stock in the firm.

Observation No. 43 – Allegation of Cybersmear. Fonix Corporation filed a suit to identify those posting defamatory remarks on the YF message boards (e.g. *The Lost Profit* and *Fedupwithfonix*).

In a separate suit, in October 1996, Fonix sued a Salt Lake City stockbroker. The libel suit resulted in the subsequent apology by the broker. As part of the settlement he apologized and agreed to buy Fonix shares.

Observation No. 44 – Allegation of Cybersmear. In December 1999, pre-litigation discovery documents were filed to seek to identify the legal names of two YF message board posters known as *expertone 2000* and *Prognosticator Man*. Some of the posts were made in early October 1999. Comments criticized management and lobbying efforts to amend a trade bill to benefit Fruit of the Loom, Limited/Incorporated, by allowing them to import certain items duty free.

Observation No. 45 – Allegation of Cybersmear. On February 26, 2001, a federal court judge in California dismissed a case brought by Global Telemedia International, Incorporated against RB posters known as *Bdaman609* and *Electrick_Man*. The ACLU assisted posters in reaching the anti-SLAPP decision.

The court ordered the company and its officers to pay Internet posters more than $55 thousand in attorney's fees. This was the first time a court applied the mandatory attorney-fee provision in the anti-SLAPP statute.

Observation No. 46 – Allegation of Cybersmear. On September 1, 2001, the president of Golden Eagle International, Incorporated filed a suit against an unidentified stock-chat message board poster for libel.

Observation No. 47 – Allegation of Cybersmear. Great Canadian Gaming Corporation filed a John Doe suit on January 22, 2001. It was amended, once the poster had been identified. The posts were made on the Stockhouse message boards on January 17, 2001, and included allegations of wife-cheating by one of the firm's officers.

Observation No. 48 – Allegation of Cybersmear. In May 1999, the CEO of a Gyrodyne Company of America filed suit, alleging that negative YF message board posts (from November 1998 through March 1999) led to his dismissal. The suit was amended on January 12, 1999 and it was alleged that the CEOs half-brother, using the aliases *BumnStJames* and *JudgeKennethGyroStarr*, posted these negative messages.

Observation No. 49 – Allegation of Cybersmear. On August 4, 2000, H-Quotient, Incorporated announced that it filed a suit against unidentified stock-chat message board posters believed to be engaged in the short-selling and manipulation of the firm's stock.

Observation No. 50 – Allegation of Cybersmear. In July 1999, Harbor Florida Bancshares, Incorporated sued a poster (*maytricks-99*) on the YF message boards for derogatory postings, including rumors of a takeover. The suit was for $25 thousand, plus costs, interest and attorney fees.

Observation No. 51 – Allegation of Cybersmear/Disclosure of Inside Information. Healthcare Recoveries, Incorporated filed a lawsuit to stop *legal{HR1us* and *legal{HR15us* from accusing the firm of wrongdoing and offering to reveal insider information on the YF message boards. Healthcare Recoveries recovered medical expenses for insurers and employers when there was third party responsibility for the claim. The posters offered a free guide to assist attorneys involved in suits against the company, identifying key employees, describing the claims identification process, examiner training, and so on. Healthcare Recoveries claimed that this guide violated trademark, copy-right, unfair-competition and trade-secret laws. These items, offered to those outside the company, failed to protect the company's proprietary information and violated the confidentiality agreements signed by each of the form's employees.

Observation No. 52 – Allegation of Cybersmear. HealthSouth Corporation initiated a suit on October 16, 1998. This complaint alleged that defendants made anonymous posts on the YF message boards, falsely claiming that company and its CEO were engaged in fraud and that CEO's wife was having adulterous affair. One turned out to be the husband of a disgruntled employee and another was an ex-employee, a 33-year old, also known as *Dirk Diggler*.

Observation No. 53 – Allegation of Cybersmear. Price Waterhouse submitted their findings on the economic damages caused by short-sellers of Hemispherx

Biopharma, Incorporated stock during early June 2000. During June 2000, an institutional investment bank (and NASD member) specializing in corporate valuations, equity research and short-selling those firms it identifies as "grossly overvalued," was granted its request, a motion to dismiss the case brought against them by Hemispherx. The investment bank's reports led to a decline of 88% in the price of Hemispherx stock.

All six lawsuits filed against the investment bank were dismissed. According to the investment bank's *PR Newswire*, Hemispherx was a stock fraud and was controlled by an individual charged with medical and scientific fraud. According to a Hemispherx *PR Newswire*, filed on the same date, the federal court did not comment on the merits of the case, but provided Hemispherx with the option to pursue the matter in the state courts.

Observation No. 54 – Allegation of Cybersmear. Diamonds Hitts Production, Incorporated (formerly, Hitsgalore.com, Incorporated) announced its intention to file suits in May 1999. During June 1999, they announced filing a $20 million dollar lawsuit against those alleged to have posted false, defamatory, and malicious messages on RB and SI message boards about the company and certain current and former offices and directors.

Within 2 days of the allegedly defamatory articles, the first of several class action suits were brought against Hitsgalore. The firm believed that these suits were based on the false reports. On February 22, 2000, the attorneys for Hitsgalore won a dismissal of the consolidated class action suit, with prejudice. They voluntarily dismissed the suit, without prejudice, on April 4, 2000.

On April 28, 2000, the company filed a suit for libel against a news service and one of their reporters. The $500 million dollar suit claimed that defamatory articles published on May 11 and 12, 1999, were false, and resulted in a decline in the firm's stock from $20.6875 on May 10 to $9.375 per share on May 11, 1999.

Observation No. 55 – Allegation of Cybersmear. Hollis-Eden Pharmaceuticals filed a libel suit against at least 11 posters on the YF message boards. On March 9, 2001, the motion to quash had been granted for *Gpalcus* and *Dickie13_62301*. The firm's stock had declined, steadily, from a 52-week high of $19.25 in March 2000 to $5.09 in early February 2001.

Observation No. 56 – Allegation of Cybersmear. The former CEO of Hvide Marine, Incorporated resigned his position in June 1998, after 29 years of running the business started by his family. He claimed he was fired after statements were made about him on the YF message boards by *justthefactsjack* and others. Half a dozen aliases were traced to a single email address.

He went to court in September 1999, to seek the identities of his online critics. The ACLU assisted those posting messages, filing a motion to quash this effort in October 1999. However, in February 2000, YF and AOL were ordered to disclose the identities of the critics. The court decided that he had every right to face his accusers.

One of the YF critics was *The1Quiz*. On the condition that his true identity was not revealed, he consented to an interview. He was a former shareholder of Hvide Marine. He lost a significant sum of money on the firm's stock. He bought at $17 and sold, after the firm filed for Chapter 11 Bankruptcy protection (September through December 1999), at $0.17 per share.

Observation No. 57 – Allegation of Cybersmear. On May 1, 2000, a civil suit was filed by Imaging Diagnostic Systems, Incorporated. On July 12, 2000, a final judgment was entered against a stock-chat message board poster known as *docpatel*. He was identified and enjoined from continuing to post on RB (or other) message board(s), any false or defamatory statements concerning the Company, it's officers, officer's spouses, or attempting to interfere with the company's contractual or business relationships.[107]

Imaging Diagnostic Systems also filed a motion against a former employee and his current employer. This claim was discontinued on January 16, 2001, after the employer had sworn that the employee had not divulged (and would not divulge) confidential or insider information.

Observation No. 58 – Allegation of Cybersmear. A message board rumor posted on YF suggested that Impath, Incorporated was being investigated by the SEC, and sent the stock tumbling from $38 to $30.25 in less than 1 week. The firm denied the rumor.

Observation No. 59 – Allegation of Cybersmear. Imperial Sugar Company (Imperial) sought the identification of YF posters (*ducko-1999, mouthofthe-south1961, bestinthewest-95337, midwestrader, henryvii2040, shawnelson, irightuwrong,* and *buy-lower-sell-higher*). Posts alleged sexual and substance abuse at Imperial, as well as offers of insider information (e.g. forthcoming deals that only employees know about) and allegations of suspected fraud. In July 2000, the Court granted the company's request. YF was to provide registration, billing, posting and call identification records, as well as e-mail addresses for all 8 aliases.

Observation No. 60 – Allegation of Cybersmear. A subpoena was issued to YF to identify a poster from his/her alias.[108] The suit stated that its employee-confidentiality agreement had been violated. The poster allegedly leaked inside information when they stated that Informix's fiscal report would be weaker than expected. This post was made several days before Informix warned that its earnings would not meet analysts' expectations.

Observation No. 61 – Allegation of Cybersmear. In early February 2001, Infotopia, Incorporated announced its intention to file a suit against RB poster

LBJ_n_Aruba and a web site. The CEO posted his firm's intentions to respond to these negative messages on the RB board.

Observation No. 62 – Allegation of Cybersmear. In early November 2000, a spokesperson for Ingram Micro, Incorporated announced that it had filed a suit against some of those posting on the YF message boards.

Observation No. 63 – Allegation of Cybersmear. InsynQ, Incorporated announced on April 27, 2001, that they had uncovered a short-selling stock manipulation scheme and had requested FBI and SEC assistance.

Observation No. 64 – Allegation of Cybersmear. On May 23, 2000, InvestAmerica, Incorporated/Optica Communications Group, Incorporated alleged violations of the Racketeering Influenced and Corrupt Organization (RICO) Act (18 U.S. C. 1961 et seg.) in a suit filed against several John Does posting on the RB message boards. The company believed that these persons posted false statements in an effort to manipulate the price of the company's stock, so that they might profitably cover short positions taken against InvestAmerica.

Observation No. 65 – Allegation of Cybersmear. In a suit filed by ITEX Corporation and Graham Norris, 100 "John Does," including *Orangemuscat*, *Investor727*, *colojopa* and other aliases, were listed as posting on the YF stock-chat message boards. It was alleged that comments defamed the company and its president, undermining the confidence of Itex's investors, customers and barter exchange members. One comment suggested that "current management is blind, stupid and incompetent" (*Orangemuscat* in May). After identifying two of the aliases as belonging to two former employees, ITEX filed suits for $1.5 million against them.

Observation No. 66 – Allegation of Hyping. In early March 2001, the SEC halted trading for Ives Health. The firm's stock price rose from $0.06 to $0.73 on February 16, in conjunction with thousands of RB posts touting the firm's stock.

Observation No. 67 – Allegation of Cybersmear. IXL Enterprises, Incorporated attempted to identify a poster, allegedly an employee of the firm, posting negative messages about the firm on YF. Public Citizen intervened, filing a motion to Quash.

Observation No. 68 – Allegation of Cybersmear.

Kellstrom Industries, Incorporated filed a suit, during February 2000, to require YF to reveal the registration information of two persons defaming the firm.

Observation No. 69 – Allegation of Cybersmear. On June 28, 2000, an attorney for Kelly's Coffee posted a message on the RB stock-chat message board demanding that those posting negative remarks retract the false statements or be sued. Others on the board were pleased with this effort, and posted messages to support the action. One later message suggested that at three of the aliases had posted retractions.

Observation No. 70 – Allegation of Cybersmear. A firm, located in Tacoma, WA, and providing temporary manual workers issued an August 1998 press release after its stock dropped $10 in one day. Labor Ready, Incorporated claimed that the stock price declined followed a series of on-line rumors questioning the company's accounting policies.

Observation No. 71 – Allegation of Cybersmear. An investor in Milford, New Hampshire, was one of three defendants listed in a suit filed by Legacy Software. Charged with intentional infliction of emotional distress, invasion of privacy, defamation, and unfair trade practices, two others (their online aliases were *Spider Valdez* and *Rico Staris*) were included in the suit, for posts made to the SI Web site. The legal proceedings were posted on this same site, publicly, for all to see.

Observation No. 72 – Allegation of Cybersmear. Lilly Industries, Incorporated (Lilly) filed a suit against five individuals claiming to be employees, complaining about working conditions, stock performance and the actions of certain executives. The firm's stock PPS had declined by approximately $1.20 (6-7%) since the Internet messages began in mid-June 1999. Lilly notified the media of their actions on July 28, 1999.

Observation No. 73 – Allegation of Cybersmear. Liviakis Financial Communications filed a suit against 100 unnamed defendants (e.g. *ChiliBob*, *Kiddollars*, *Mr.Pink* and *Harvly*), for defamation and unfair business practices. One post called the CEO a "pedophile" and a "swindler," and accused him of "unlawful short selling of stock, unethical 'dumping' of stock and market manipulation." These messages were posted on the YF and SI sites in March and April 1999.

Observation No. 74 – Allegation of Cybersmear; poster identified.

Log On America, Incorporated filed a suit against those posting on the RB, SI and YF message boards. As a result, the settlement provided for the poster to provide an apology on the same boards containing the defamatory posts, as follows:

Re: Log On America Settlement Agreement [LOAX]
by: p_n_l_man (27/M/Your town)
4/18/00 3:00 pm
Msg: 4353 of 4390
Bashers Beware!

Subject: Log On America Settlement Agreement
As part of a settlement agreement with Log On America, Inc. ("LOA"), executed on April 17, 2000, I have agreed to make this posting to the Yahoo, Sillicon (sic) Investor and Raging Bull LOAX message boards.

From approximately December 30, 1999 until approximately April 2, 2000, I authored and posted numerous messages to the Yahoo! Log On America, Inc. (NASDAQ: LOAX) message board which were both not true and misleading. In those postings I used the following pseudonyms: "p_n_l_man" and "agressor2". I used these pseudonyms without informing anyone that I was the person using these aliases. This use of multiple pseudonyms was designed to give the impression that more than one person was posting these negative statements about LOA and it's directors and officers and to lend credibility to these remarks. I also created fictitious conversations between these multiple pseudonyms in order to lead the users of the Yahoo! LOA message board to believe that others shared my sentiments.

Contrary to statements made in my postings, I am not and have never been an LOA shareholder or short seller and I posted my messages because I was a past employee, had worked with the current CEO and was not there to participate in LOA's successful IPO. The statements I made, which were designed to discredit and embarrass management, while discouraging investors from buying LOA securities and enticing short sellers to increase their positions, were motivated by the frustration I felt over the success the CEO had accomplished since we last worked together. I apologize to the LOA management and their families. In addition, as part of the settlement agreement, I have agreed for a period of ten (10) years from the above date, to cease and desist from posting any messages or statements on the Yahoo! LOA message board, or on any other similar or internet-based message board or similar service or site, regarding, relating to, or which LOA or any of its directors, officers, employees, agents, attorneys, or representatives. In addition, I have agreed to cease and desist from making any untrue statements, material omissions or any false, misleading, inaccurate or incomplete statements about or regarding LOA or any of its directors, officers, employees, agents, attorneys or representatives. Finally, although this is not part of the agreement, it is my actual opinion that the LOA management has really accomplished something significant with the company and I applaud their perseverance and efforts.

P_n_l_man
agressor2

Observation No. 75 – Allegation of Cybersmear. In December 2000, Loislaw.com, Incorporated filed a suit against two individuals posting critical information about the firm. The suit alleged that the comments hurt the firm's stock price and revealed confidential information.

Observation No. 76 – Allegation of Cybersmear. A 43-year old posting on the YF message boards (*kauna_and_the_brain*, *hot_like_wasabe*, and *Floydian_us*) was arrested for posting false Lucent Technologies, Incorporated earnings warnings, resulting in a $7.1 billion market capitalization reduction for the firm's stock. The false release was posted on March 22, 2000. Charges were filed by the U.S. Attorney in Manhattan Federal Court (Houston, Texas) and the SEC.

Observation No. 77 – Allegation of Cybersmear/Disclosure of Inside Information. MasTec, Incorporated filed a suit to determine whether a former 35-year old senior project manager at MasTec was posting insider information on YF (beginning on February 26, 2000) and RB (beginning on June 29,

2000) message boards under the aliases *cheech951* and *formermtxbigwig*, respectively.

Observation No. 78 – Allegation of Cybersmear. Medinex Systems, Incorporated filed a suit to discover the identities of 14 John Does (e.g. *zipper-shut, awe2bad4mdnx,* and *dotcommie2000*) posting defamatory messages on the YF boards. Some were self-identified as employees of the firm. EFF intervened on May 7, 2001, in an effort to quash the firm's efforts to identify the true names of these aliases.

Observation No. 79 – Allegation of Cybersmear/Disclosure of Inside Information. MeltroniX, Incorporated discovered the identities of the anony-mous RB message board posts accused of defaming the company. In April 2001 they announced that at least one former employee and persons believed to have ties to a privately held San Diego competitor were identified.

Observation No. 80 – Allegation of Cybersmear. M. H. Meyerson & Company, Incorporated sought to identify the true identities of posters using the aliases *TheDaytrader2000, j454545j, Zzz138,* and others. They posted messages accusing the CEO of stock manipulation, insider trading and money laundering. Meyerson's suit alleged that as many as seven of the accused Internet users were short-sellers, or investors who borrowed the stock on the bet that the stock PPS would decline. These messages were posted on the YF and AOL message boards. The stock PPS decreased from a high of $21.875 to a low of $4.50 on March 5, 1999, apparently affected – in part – by these nega-tive posts.

Observation No. 81 – Allegation of Cybersmear. Medinah Energy, Incorporated (Medinah) filed a suit against anonymous stock-chat message board posters. On March 27, 2001, Medinah settled with one of the identified John Does. The settlement included a written apology.

Observation No. 82 – Allegation of Cybersmear. The California Department of Corporations (Internet Compliance and Enforcement Division), a California regulator of securities trading, won a settlement (August 2000) ordering a Manhattan Beach, California resident to post a retraction (under the new alias of *Retraction*) of earlier posts to the YF message board. Under the original alias, *frankgmancuso*, he attempted to manipulate the price of Metro-Goldwyn-Mayer, Incorporated (MGM) stock, when he posed as an insider/former executive of MGM. He was also fined $4,500.

Observation No. 83 – Allegation of Cybersmear. The SEC filed a complaint against an individual engaging in cybersmear on the YF message boards, causing market capitalization for NCO Group, Incorporated (NCO) to drop by more than $200 million. He claimed to be the CEO of the firm in a December 3, 1999, message:

Bad business relations . . .
by: <u>seanstheart</u> (23/M/Studio City, California) 12/03/99 11:33 pm
Msg: 197 of 1225

I am the president and CEO of St. Heart Productions, LLC. Today, my company has prepared
to file a 20 million dollar law suit against NCOG for their business practices.
Anyone doing business with this company has something to fear. The company uses intim-
idation and poor judgement.
Blue Angel Productions, LLC, Stamford Entertainment Ageny (sic) and ten other compa-
nies have joined us in our law suit, which we should have ready by next week.
This company has a lot to learn about people and business ethics.

The SEC complaint addressed the following facts:

(1) The poster received a telephone call about an unpaid debt owed to NCO.
(2) Several hours later, he posted false statements suggesting that he and twelve other firms filed suits for $20 million against NCO for its "business practices."
(3) The effect of these messages was a NCO stock price decline from $46.5625 to $34.3125 (approximately 28%) on a nine-fold increase in trading volume.

Observation No. 84 – Allegation of Cybersmear. In November 2000, NetCurrents, Incorporated charged the firm's ex-COO and a former sales executive with posting false and defamatory messages on the YF message boards. One of the alleged posters was the president of the privately held Infolocity, Incorporated, prior to its merger to form NetCurrents in December 1999.

Observation No. 85 – Allegation of Cybersmear. New Visual Entertainment, Incorporated (New Visual) filed a complaint in San Diego, California in December 2000. The suit sought to identify 50 John Does posting "defamatory and derogatory" messages on the RB stock-chat boards. A May 2001 settlement with one of the posters, *wbe*, involved a statement of retraction for all prior posts about New Visual.

Observation No. 86 – Allegation of Cybersmear. In August 2000, the NYSE filed suit against 10 unidentified persons for impersonating the exchange's chairman (Richard Grasso) on the RB message boards (aliases, *RichAGrasso* and *RichieGrass*). One of the messages indicated that he had shorted a stock listed on the exchange. The publisher of an online newsletter, *WallStreetJovial.com*, was identified as the poster. A 40-year-old resident of Neptune, New Jersey, he posted the messages on AOL "for the purposes of parody."

Observation No. 87 – Allegation of Cybersmear. Nutek, Incorporated (Nutek) and the firm's CEO received and accepted an apology from an individual posting on the RB message boards. He also agreed to pay Murray Conradie (Nutek CEO) an undisclosed amount in damages. Nutek also initiated a formal complaint with the SEC to establish or refute the relation of RB posts to those made on the SI message boards.

Observation No. 88 – Allegation of Cybersmear. Ocwen Financial Corporation filed a suit alleging that stock price declines were due – at least in part – to negative comments made on the Web.

Observation No. 89 – Allegation of Cybersmear. In August 2000, Original Media, Incorporated filed a complaint for libel, interference with economic relations, and intentional infliction of emotional distress. Sample posts specified in the complaint occurred on the RB message boards in February, March and May 2000.

Observation No. 90 – Allegation of Cybersmear. Osage Systems Group, Incorporated (Osage) served YF with a subpoena, dated June 16, 2000, requiring the disclosure of the identity of *wes_mooty*.

Observation No. 91 – Allegation of Cybersmear. Owens Corning filed a suit in October 1999. The subject of this action was a critical September 26, 2000 post on the YF message boards, using as an alias the name of the chairman and chairman and CEO of Owens Corning.

Observation No. 92 – Allegation of Cybersmear. In April 2001, PDC Innovative Industries, Incorporated (PDC) dismissed a suit previously filed against an individual posting on the YF and RB message boards. The posts referred to less than arms length transactions between PDC and its officers. The JDAF assisted the defendant, who was identified.

Observation No. 93 – Allegation of Cybersmear. Peak International Limited (Peak) failed to prove the identity of the party responsible for defamatory posts on the YF message boards, but continued to pursue action against his brother, the former CEO of Peak. He was terminated after disclosing confidential information. Peak was awarded $500,000 in an arbitration decision reached in August 2000.

Observation No. 94 – Allegation of Cybersmear. Philip Services Corporation (Philip), a scrap metal/industrial waste recycling company, persuaded a Canadian Court to order several ISPs (NetAccess, Weslink, AOL Canada, iSTAR, and four others) to reveal the names and addresses of users posting negative remarks about the company. Philip was granted at least 12 court orders, during July 1998, to obtain the names of critics posting on the YF message boards.

Speculation suggested that some of the posts were from former employees. One poster was identified as a former Hamilton City councilman, involved in public disputes over pollution in Hamilton's harbor. Another was a freelance journalist with a history of legal disputes with Philip.

Observation No. 95 – Allegation of Cybersmear. During July 1999, Phoenix International Limited (Phoenix) filed a suit against a former employee the Company believed responsible for a significant number of defamatory, nega-tive and false allegations posted on Internet message boards since early 1999. A settlement was reached in October 1999.

Observation No. 96 – Allegation of Cybersmear. A Florida dermatologist (*coolhl7*) and up to 49 other John Doe defendants were named in a libel suit filed by the management of PhyCor, Incorporated (PhyCor). The dermatologist was critical of PhyCor's management of his clinic and posted these criticisms on the YF message boards. At the time of the suit, PhyCor was also the target of two class-action lawsuits alleging that PhyCor grossly overstated assets, earn-ings and shareholders' equity.

PhyCor's stock dropped from the low \$30s to about \$5 per share from late 1997 through May 1999. By August 2000, the stock price had fallen to less than \$0.25 per share, when PhyCor reported a loss (i.e. asset write-down) of \$5.80 per share.

Observation No. 97 – Allegation of Cybersmear. Presstek, Incorporated filed a lawsuit accusing residents of Hampton, Virginia, Greenwood, Colorado and Hamilton Square, New Jersey of shorting Presstek stock and then spreading rumors that Presstek was the subject of a grand jury investigation, that it was losing money and that an internal auditor was about to resign. The three did not deny posting the messages or selling Presstek stock short, but claimed their Constitutional right of free speech. The complaint was settled in February 1998.

Observation No. 98 – Allegation of Cybersmear. On August 10, 2000, an alias – allegedly the co-chairman of ProNetLink.com, posted message number 38178 on the RB message board. He announced litigation against posters of false and misleading information involved in posting under multiple aliases to feign conversations with others (actually, themselves) for the purpose of misleading others on the thread.

Observation No. 99 – Allegation of Cybersmear. Quest Net Corporation was granted a permanent injunction against one of five defendants allegedly engaged in short-selling and posting false and defamatory statements about the firm and its chairman on the RB message boards. The suit was filed on February 17, 2000. The injunction was against *bcohen*, a former marketing manager at the company, fired on February 4, 2000. The other aliases named in the lawsuit were *jollyr*, *ADVISORY*, *Cats3* (later found and exposed in March 2000 to be a senior trader with J. Alexander Securities, a market maker (MM) of Quest Net Corporation common stock) and *gman007*.[109]

Observation No. 100 – Allegation of Insider Disclosures. Raytheon Corporation (a defense contractor) sued 21 John Does posting on AOL, but dropped the charges after they were identified. They included Raytheon employees. Four of these employees quit or were discharged after being identified. The remaining employees, according to Raytheon, entered corporate counseling.

Raytheon filed the suit in February 1999. The suit was dropped in May 1999, after Raytheon had obtained the real names of those posting the messages.

Observation No. 101 – Allegation of Cybersmear. Remtrak Corporation filed subpoenas during June 2000, requiring YF to disclose registered user information for a large number of aliases (*mbaandmore, callforsanity, xmaspartycommittee, dudeily, chmiss2000, mrlucky200, mild78, msbrgr, readread4, killshot1999, ipo3pfasap, recurve333, Rentmeister, bob2539, albert_meat, ads1597132, JHR0001, Pettrova, wapuff, Cowboy9983, seattleslew2u, strap68, kickhisbaldassout, iamronsbaby, kickhisbuttout, kingorpoe, watrncollet, myteemite2, muckingfess, worriedaboutrent, theyhavetogo, thirty2sixtydays, secondthemotion, clearspeak111*, and others). Several acknowledged receipt of the YF-generated subpoena notification and openly discussed it on the YF message board (e.g. *recurve333, wapuff, kdw_97203, strap68* and *Cowboy9983*). An example follows:

To my surprise . . . by: <u>recurve333</u> 07/06/00 10:00 pm Msg: 2929 of 3670
The following was in my inbox after I arrived back from the ball game last night:

"NOTICE OF SUBPOENA (from Yahoo! Legal dept.)
We are writing to inform you that Yahoo! Has been served with a
subpoena requiring disclosure of information related to your
user account at Yahoo!
The subpoena was issued in an action entitled:
Rentrak Corporation v. Kundinger, et. Al., CV00-820-HA
pending in: United States District Court, Northern District of California
The subpoena, dated 06/21/2000, requires that Yahoo!
produce documents related to your Yahoo! Account.
The attorney for the subpoenaing party, Latham & Watkins, is
Peter H. Benzian, 701 "B" Street, Suite 2100, San Diego, CA 92101
619-236-1234 (phone); 619-696-7419 (fax)
Please be advised that Yahoo! Will respond to the subpoena five days from the date of this notice, unless we have notice that a motion
to quash the subpoena has been filed, or the matter has been
otherwise resolved.
You may wish to consult an attorney to advise you about the
foregoing. Please contact the subpoenaing party to obtain a copy of the subpoena. If you wish to contact Yahoo! Regarding this matter, please direct your correspondence to . . . "

This is not an attempt at humor on my part.
What an act of desperation. I have nothing to do with Rentrak vs. Kundinger et al. I don't even know Kundinger.

Just another waste of Rentrak shareholder money. Perhaps an act of intimidation on Ron's part.

Last time I checked, we have a right in this country to free speech. Yes, I have offered some strong opinions here, but I believe that the facts are on my side. I suspect that all or many posters here have been effected (sic) in the same way. Anyone else care to share?

If anyone can, would you care to explain any of the details of Rentrak vs. Kundinger? Any ideas why I/we have now become involved in this?

As I have stated, actions of RENT management have provided significant weight to my opinions: REPLACE CURRENT MANAGEMENT. I have been a long-term shareholder and only want my investment to flourish. I want management to consider shareholders before themselves.

10Ks and 10Qs don't lie. Now I can't wait for the annual proxy notice and information regarding Ron's compensation.

Ron: I have been one of RENT's ambassadors for years, to the detriment of my pocketbook. Our company has not been successful with you and your team at the helm.

Observation No. 102 – Allegation of Hyping. Rentech, Incorporated. In October 2000, an Australian was sentenced to serve three months of a two-year jail term for posting false information in e-mails and to a variety of Internet sites (RB and YF) in May 1999. He and a co-conspirator, of Queensland, Australia, sent out more than 4 million e-mails. The SEC said these e-mails and Internet site posts triggered a doubling in Rentech's stock price and a 1,600% rise in trading volume on May 19, 1999. According to the Australian Securities and Investments Commission, the spammer sold 65,000 Rentech shares for about $8,800 (US) in profits on the first trading day after spamming the firm's stock. The co-conspirator faced similar charges in a trial scheduled for November 2000.

Observation No. 103 – Allegation of Cybersmear/Disclosure of Inside Information. Rural/Metro Corporation filed subpoenas with YF in December 2000. They wanted to identify four persons posting on the stock-chat message boards as potentially current or former employees. EFF and the Liberty Project intervened on behalf of two of the John Does, filing a motion to Quash, seeking court protection of the identities of those posting the messages.

Observation No. 104 – Allegation of Cybersmear. Sabratek Corporation filed August 1999 suits against *Pluvia* and the publisher of *Off Wall Street*, a Cambridge, Massachusetts investment advisory newsletter. Sabratek stock fell from a high of more than $30 per share to less than $0.25.

Messages were posted on both SI and RB message boards. At least one of the defendants purchased Sabratek put options in June 1999 and allegedly posted claims that Sabratek was involved in accounting fraud to personally profit from a decline in the firm's stock price.

Furthermore, at least one of the posters secretly shorted Sabratek stock on a least four separate occasions, before and during the time periods while criticizing the company. This personal financial interest was not disclosed.

The suits were dismissed in April 2000. Sabratek failed to prove that these statements influenced investors or that they were intended to represent anything other than opinions by the posters.

Observation No. 105 – Allegation of Cybersmear. In April 2000, SATX, Incorporated filed a John Doe lawsuit against RB message board posters. This suit followed an April 10, 2000, *PRNewswire* by STOVACT, Incorporated, disclosing the expiration/cessation of any business relationship with SATX.

Observation No. 106 – Allegation of Cybersmear. On June 14, 1999, SeaChange International, Incorporated filed a defamation complaint against *port_mgr, Arthur Tang, U4eek, p_dog 2000,* and *rilwiner,* Lathrop Investment Management, Incorporated and Concurrent Computer Corporation (NASDAQ NM: CCUR). An apology was posted by the single, identified individual using the aliases, *port_mgr, Arthur Tang, U4eek, p_dog 2000,* and *rilwiner* on December 30, 1998. Concurrent filed a sealed counterclaim on June 14, 2000.

Observation No. 107 – Allegation of Cybersmear. During June 2000, Seitel, Incorporated filed a petition to force disclosure of the true identities of posters on the YF message board. At least one of the aliases claimed to be a disgruntled investor, losing thousands of dollars in a Seitel spin-off.

Observation No. 108 – Allegation of Cybersmear. On July 14, 2000, Shaman Pharmaceuticals, Incorporated (Shaman) announced actions taken, in Federal Court, to identify posters allegedly engaging in stock fraud and libel against the firm since February 2000.[110]

Observation No. 109 – Allegation of Cybersmear. Inflammatory messages were posted on YF, fraudulently signed with the names of the Shoney's, Incorporated founder, CEO (*bodnar*) and chairman (*schoenbaum*). According to the suit, another alias was *truthdet* and a retired Shoney's co-founder and the company's largest shareholder. These messages claimed that the company might file for bankruptcy.

Observation No. 110 – Allegation of Cybersmear. Solv-Ex Corporation filed a suit, in December 1998, alleging an electronic conspiracy by a well-known financial institution and approximately 20 other investors. The suit charged that these individuals, first, artificially inflated the firm's stock price, then, shorted the firm's stock, followed by a cybersmear campaign, to profit from later short sale covering. News of the dismissal of the case, which was based on emailed messages/discussions between the alleged co-conspirators, was released in May 2000.[111]

Observation No. 111 – Allegation of Cybersmear. As part of a settlement agreement, on February 24, 2000, an individual using the aliases *rmpllc, bocahorses, lelysrug, grocguru* and *themagking* apologized for posting negative statements about the firm from December 1999 through February 2000. The statements made about Source Information Management Systems, Incorporated (Source) resulted in message number 1189, containing an admission of fictitious conversations between these aliases in an effort to mislead others on the YF message board into believing that others shared these negative views. These posts were in retaliation after Source had denied employment to the poster.

Observation No. 112 – Allegation of Cybersmear. On October 15, 1999, complaints were filed against Restaurant Teams International, Incorporated (Restaurant Teams; OTC BB: RTIN; see *Observation 121*), ConSyGen, Incorporated (OTC BB: CSGI) and others, by Sovereign Partners Limited Partnership and others. The suit alleged false allegations of unlawful short-selling by management, in a malicious effort to blame plaintiffs for business failures. On December 28, 1999, some of the parties involved in the action reached a settlement agreement. An apology was posted to the message board on July 20, 2000.

Observation No. 113 – Allegation of Cybersmear. Spectrum Oil Corporation announced, in a January 11, 2001 *Business Wire*, their policy on cybersmear. On March 5, 2001, a message was posted to the stock-chat board, threatening legal action against one of the aliases.

Observation No. 114 – Allegation of Cybersmear. Stampede Worldwide, Incorporated (Stampede) filed a complaint on May 15, 2000, against an identified individual, for posting defamatory messages on the RB boards, apparently, in an effort to exact revenge against a former co-worker. The director of investor relations for Stampede had resigned from Pawnamerica.com, citing problems with this same individual as one of the reasons for his resignation. Shortly after his resignation, the individual accused of making the defamatory posts was asked to resign from the board of Pawnamerica.com.

Observation No. 115 – Allegation of Cybersmear. The Star Telecommunications (Star) CEO was the target of posts, impersonating him (alias *CEO_Chris*) and falsely reporting his resignation. In a suit designed to reveal the identities of their aliases, Star served subpoenas to YF and, in July 1999 out of court settlements, three defendants agreed to issue apologies and pay small fines to charities.

At least one of the defendants worked for a San Francisco hedge fund. Both settled for an undisclosed sum. The individual attributed his behavior to an illness.

Observation No. 116 – Allegation of Cybersmear. Steroidogenesis Inhibitors International, Incorporated won a restraining order against a former, allegedly rogue, chairman. The August 2000 decision was not the results of additional allegations, that the former chairman and his agents were posting malicious statements about the firm on the stock-chat message boards.

Observation No. 117 – Allegation of Cybersmear/Disclosure of Inside Information. A Boston engineering firm, Stone & Webster, Incorporated, filed suit against 20 individuals alleged to have made false and defamatory statements about the firm on the YF stock-chat message board. It was also alleged that these posts disclosed confidential information.

Observation No. 118 – Allegation of Cybersmear. Sunbeam Corporation filed a suit alleging that stock price declines were due – at least in part – to negative comments made on the Web.

Observation No. 119 – Allegation of Cybersmear. On February 14, 2000, Talk Visual Corporation (Talk Visual) announced a lawsuit filed against *the worm*, *investordeal*, *worm06* and others. These aliases had numerous posts on the RB message boards, which began in 1998. The Talk Visual chairman won a $1 million July 2000 judgment against at least one of the posters. As part of a settlement, the chairman agreed not to enforce the judgment if an apology was posted and further defamatory messages ceased.

Observation No. 120 – Allegation of Cybersmear. Thomas & Betts Corporation filed a suit against 12 (later increased to 14) YF screen names on May 12, 2000. On May 17, 2000, the court authorized the issuance of a subpoena seeking "discovery of unnamed parties . . . " (e.g. *WatchingTNB*, *jay54_72*, *e_interested* and *thomasnbeth*). *WatchingTNB* was self-described as a salesperson for TNB's products.

YF received a third party subpoena on May 19, 2000, and notified all posters that they were about to reveal all registration information to Thomas & Betts. *WatchingTNB* secured counsel (Public Citizen), advising YF that *WatchingTNB* would be moving to prevent the subpoena in a special motion to strike under the SLAPP statue. In August 2000, Thomas & Betts voluntarily dismissed the suit.

Observation No. 121 – Allegation of Cybersmear. Thomson Kernaghan & Company Limited, a privately held Canadian investment dealer, filed suits against aliases on both YF and SI stock-chat message boards. Their objective was to identify the names of these persons, by forcing disclosure of the registration information for *Black John*, *Tech* and *Danimal2002*. The aliases were accused of making "reckless, malicious, vicious, callous, reprehensible, shocking, oppressive and high-handed" posts regarding Thomson. The libel suit also named Texas-based Restaurant Teams International, Incorporated (see *Observation No. 113*), for one of their press releases.

Observation No. 122 – Allegation of Cybersmear/Disclosure of Inside Information. A subpoena was served on YF to identify an employee of Titan International, Incorporated III, as the following post by *tomorrow_cb* suggests:

Tomorrow_cb:
YF message No. 475, June 16, 2000.

(T)he name fits
. . . I post from work. So what, you can't do anything nor can Ms. Holley. Listen, for her to catch me I would have to be accessing the net by network . . . and I'm not on a network so that leaves their ONLY option by looking at my computer files and that is not going to happen no matter what Titan's Electronic Privacy rule says. I have protected my computer and myself. I am NOT afraid of Morry or Cheri.
(Irrelevant portion removed).
Open letter to Mr. Peno or anyone else with the Union that wants information: I have access to Titan memos some of which I am reading at this moment. I assume you would find any information I can supply you with extremely helpful. I can give you current production numbers, customers, etc.
Should you want to contact me email me at Tomorrow_cb@yahoo.com that is the email I use for this message board. After I am sure you are who you say, I will give you my main email address . . . (irrelevant portion removed).

Tomorrow_cb:
YF message No. 525, June 22, 2000.
(I)t seems that Titan Corporate is scared
(H)ello again,
            (T)hought you might like to read this email I received. This proves they are scared of what information I have to release, but I have other means of distributing the information. Here is the message pasted:
Subject: Yahoo! Notice of Subpoena
NOTICE OF SUBPOENA.
We are writing to inform you that Yahoo! Has been served with a subpoena requiring disclosure of information related to your user account at Yahoo!
The subpoena was issued in an action entitled: Titan Investments v. John Doe, 4-00-CV-10303 pending in: United States District Court, Southern District of Iowa.
The subpoena, dated 06/16/2000, requires that Yahoo! Produce documents related to your Yahoo! Account.
The attorney for the subpoenaing party, Davis, Brown, et. Al., is
Gene La Suer, 666 Walnut Street, Suite 2500, Des Moines, Iowa 50309, 515-288-2500 (phone), 515-243-0654 (fax).
Please be advised that Yahoo! Will respond to the subpoena 15 days from the date of this notice, unless we have notice that a motion to quash the subpoena has been filed, or the matter has been otherwise resolved.
You may wish to consult an attorney to advise you about the foregoing. Please contact the tomorrow_ng (sic) party to obtain a copy of the tomorrow (sic). If you wish to contact Yahoo! Regarding this matter, please direct your correspondence to notice-user@yahoo-inc.com.

Observation No. 123 – Allegation of Cybersmear. Wade Cook Financial Corporation filed a slander suit against 10 YF aliases in March 1999. In January 1999, these posters suggested that Wade's Seattle investment advice firm had accepted kickbacks from companies they touted online.

Observation No. 124 – Allegation of Cybersmear. Xircom, Incorporated (Xircom) filed a suit in May 1999, to identify someone claiming to be an employee of the firm (alias, *A_View_From_Within*) and posting three messages on the YF stock-chat message boards. Xircom claimed that the information posted was false. The suit was settled in July 1999, after the poster's attorney confidentially disclosed the identity of the poster to Xircom executives. The poster was not and never had been an employee of the firm.

Observation No. 125 – Allegation of Cybersmear. ZiaSun Technologies, Incorporated (ZiaSun) settled libel suits filed in June 1999. Initially, the case was dismissed on a technicality relating to venue choice.

ZiaSun maintained that the thousands of posts made on the SI stock-chat message boards were made by eight short-sellers, including one alleged to be a money manager (MM). Under the agreement, both sides agreed to stop talking about each other and one defendant received $60,000 from ZiaSun's former president and a company's promoter/consultant, in what was characterized as a separate stock dispute.

ZiaSun had to make downward revisions to earnings measures reported for 1998, and many of the posts ridiculed the company's financial statements and accused them of fraud. ZiaSun stock was selling at about $10 at the time of the suit. It was trading at approximately $1.50 in October 2000, at the time of the settlement. Each side paid their own legal fees.

Observation No. 126 – Allegation of Cybersmear. ZixIt Corporation filed a suit against VISA USA, Incorporated (VISA), alleging that they posted more than 400 disparaging comments on the ZixIt YF message boards under at least seven different aliases. Allegations stated that the message campaign was led by a VISA vice president responsible for technology research, and that the content of these posts attacked ZixIt products, while promoting and recommending those from a rival business in which VISA had invested.

LIMITATIONS AND SUMMARY

The above cases do not represent a random sample, but were drawn from a population available on the SI web site. Still, as discussed in Chapter 9, not a single case of management intervention – in the case of hyping – was identified.

ANNOTATED BIBLIOGRAPHY

1. Akerlof, G. A. (1970). The market for "lemons": Quality, uncertainty and the market mechanism. *Quarterly Journal of Economics, 84*, 488–492.

Contribution: *Seminal* work on *asymmetric information.*

Akerlof described how asymmetric information might result in adverse selection in his "lemons market" for automobiles application. Sellers of lemons know that they are lemons while buyers do not. Therefore, the seller of a lemon receives payment in excess of the value of the relatively inferior good. Buyers come to realize that they have a greater chance of buying a lemon, so the price level of all automobiles declines. Good car owners become less likely to sell. Eventually, only lemons are sold.

2. Arbel, A. (1985). Generic stocks: An old product in a new package, *The Journal of Portfolio Management, 68*(11), 4–13.

Contribution: Bridges the gap between *managerial* and *financial* accounting sub-disciplines and research streams.

This very brief article is an excellent primer on the deficiencies of the capital asset pricing model (CAPM) and the linkage between the efficient markets hypothesis (EMH) and asymmetric information, the essential component from which agency theory evolved. Arbel's explanations are both intuitively appealing and theoretically complete. Researchers interested in the study of Enron-/Andersen-related matters should begin with this "thought piece."

3. Carvell, S., & Strebel, P. (1984). A new beta incorporating analysts' forecasts. *The Journal of Portfolio Management, 11*(1), 81–85.

Contribution: Provides insights into the incorporation of *sentiment* measures into the more traditional *beta* component of CAPM.

This novel paper provides the foundation for extensions of beta/risk measurement models to the use of stock tip newsletter, message board post metrics, whisper EPS measures, and so on. This is another "thought piece" and is likely to be useful to those seeking models leading to the improvement of predictive measures of stock returns, in light of the institutional challenges faced by financial analysts in the post-Enron period.

4. Eynon, G., & Stevens, K. (1995). The economics of taxpayer venue choice: Effects of informational asymmetries. *The Journal of the American Taxation Association, 17*(1), 71–94.

Contribution: Superior *literature review* for those researchers interested in *game theory, experimental economics* or *legal* research streams or applications of asymmetric information.

Eynon and Stevens provide a superior summary of prior research in the context of the integration of game theory and the study of asymmetric information. Their discussion of the economic modeling efforts of others, as they relate to legal dispute resolution is also excellent. This article is likely to be of greatest interest to those engaged in research involving game theory or experimental economics, and involved in the study of law.

5. Hertzel, M., & Smith, R. L. (1993). Market discounts and shareholder gains for placing equity privately. *The Journal of Finance, 48*(2), 459–485.

Contribution: Superior *literature review* and analysis of components or *decomposition* of information asymmetry.

Hertzel and Smith provide a statistical model for separate and combined evaluation of both the information hypothesis and the ownership structure hypothesis. They provide an excellent review of the literature on proxies for the valuation of information asymmetry. Their conclusions are consistent with those of Morck *et al.* (1988), that private equity placements are more representative of capital-raising events and less representative of ownership-restructuring events.

6. Krinsky, I., & Lee, J. (1996). Earnings announcements and the components of the bid-ask spread. *The Journal of Finance, 51*(4), 1523–1535.

Contribution: Superior *theory development* and *literature review* for the development of a *model* of information asymmetry.

Krinsky and Lee provide a superior information asymmetry model and theory development section in constructing their hypothesis development section of this article.

7. Le Bon, G. (1973). The crowd: A study of the popular mind. New York; The Viking Press.

Contribution: An excellent primer on *herd behavior*, though many of these positions were later disproved.

Le Bon's *The Crowd*, first published in 1895, contains many concepts now known to be misdirected, misleading, or mistaken. However, Le Bon (1973) repeatedly compares the impulsiveness, "incapacity to reason, absence of judgement, and exaggeration of the sentiments" that characterizes crowds (Introduction by Robert K. Merton).

This book is an excellent primer for what Wall Street refers to as "herd behavior," and provides thought-provoking insights into reactions to news/information releases, and the manipulation of those not privy to asymmetric information available only to those directly controlling the dissemination of information and misinformation.

8. Pratt, J. W., & Zeckhauser, R. J. (Eds) (1985). *Principals and agents: The structure of business.* Harvard Business School; Boston, MA.

Contribution: Excellent coverage of *fiduciary duties* and *insider trading*; of particular interest to *legal* scholars.

Pratt and Zeckhauser have provided a wonderful introductory chapter in their collection of edited articles. The next three chapters, contained within the first two sections on the agency relationship and institutional responses, contain materials of particular relevance to the stock market pricing mechanism (i.e. the chapters on corporate fiduciary duties and insider trading) and to this monograph.

9. Shleifer, A., & Vishny, R. W. (1997). A survey of corporate governance. *The Journal of Finance, 52*(2), 737–783.

Contribution: Excellent primer, separating *management* and *finance* issues of *corporate governance*.

This survey of corporate governance emphasizes investor legal protection issues and the international concentration of corporate governance systems. Shleifer and Vishny examine agency theory problems in contracts and incentive contracts, management discretion issues, and provide a review of the evidence on agency costs. They operationally define corporate governance, and the manner in which it deals with agency problems, as the separation of management and finance.

ACRONYMS

A	Assets (where A = L + OE)
ACLU	American Civil Liberties Union
ACP	Americans for Computer Privacy
AHCPR	Agency of Health Care Policy Research
AI	Asymmetric information
AMT	Alternative Minimum Tax
ASR	Accounting Series Release
AWW	Average weekly wage (context: unemployment insurance (UI))
AX	American Stock Exchange
B2B	Business-to-Business
BB	Bulletin Board (e.g., OTC BB)
BC	British Columbia (Canada)
BOD	Board of Directors
BV	Book value
CAPM	Capital asset pricing model
CBS	Central Broadcasting System (context: television network)
CEO	Chief executive officer
CFO	Chief financial officer
CMA	Certified Management Accountant
CNBC	Financial news cable station (context: television network)
CPA	Certified Public Accountant
CPI	Consumer Price Index
CR	Credit (where DR = CR)
DA	Dependent allowance (context: unemployment insurance (UI))
DR	Debit (where DR = CR)
E&Y	Ernst & Young
EBITDA	Earnings Before Interest, Taxes, Depreciation and Amortization
EFF	Electronic Frontier Foundation
EMH	Efficient market hypothesis
EPIC	Electronic Privacy Information Center
EPS	Earnings per share
FASB	Financial Accounting Standards Board

FBI	Federal Bureau of Investigation
FC	Fixed Cost (where TC = FC + VC)
FD	Fair Disclosure
FERC	Federal Energy Regulatory Commission
GAAP	Generally accepted accounting principles
HIPS	Health Insurance Plan Survey
I/B/E/S	Institutional Brokers Estimate System
IFEA	Internet Free Expression Alliance
IMA	Institute of Management Accountants
IR	Investor relations
IRS	Internal Revenue Service
ISP	Internet Service Provider
ITSA	Insider Trading Sanctions Act
JDAF	John Does Anonymous Foundation
L2	Level 2
L	Liabilities (where A = L + OE)
LBO	Leveraged buy-out
LLC	Limited Liability Company
LSE	London Stock Exchange
MM	Market maker
MMM	Market maker manipulation
MRQ	Most recent quarter
MSG/msg	Message
NASAA	North American Securities Administrators Association
NASD	National Association of Securities Dealers
NASDR	NASD Regulators
NASDAQ	National association of securities dealers' automated quotation system
NAZ	Slang for NASDAQ
NM	National market (e.g., NASDAQ NM)
NMES	National Medical Expenditure Survey
NYSE	New York Stock Exchange
OE	Owners' Equity (aka Stockholders' Equity; where A = L + OE)
OS	Outstanding (context: number of shares)
OTC	Over-the-counter (e.g., OTC BB = over-the-counter BB)
PAL	Protective Action League
P/E	Price-Earnings ratio
PPS	Price per share
PWC	PriceWaterhouseCoopers
RB	Raging Bull

R&D	Research & Development
SC	Small cap
SEC	Securities and Exchange Commission
SI	Silicon Investor
SLAPP	Strategic Litigation Against Public Participation
SM	Stockhouse Media
TA	Technical analysis
TC	Total Cost (where TC = FC + VC)
TSE	Toronto Stock Exchange
UI	Unemployment insurance
VC	Variable Cost (where TC = FC + VC)
WBA	Weekly benefit amount (context: unemployment insurance (UI))
YF	Yahoo! Finance

GLOSSARY OF SELECTED TERMS

Adverse selection: The process by which an insurance applicant at above average risk attempts to obtain coverage at an average or standard rate or premium.

Agency theory: An economic theory referring to the variety of ways in which *agents* and *principals*, linked by formal or informal agreements or contractual arrangements, interact. Developed in the 1970s (Akerlof 1970).

Complete information: With *complete information* and symmetric trading opportunities among *agents*, many economic models predict a *Walrasian* (see *Walras*)[112] outcome.

After-hours (AH): Referring to AH trading (typically, 4 p.m. to 6:30 p.m.; 4 p.m. to 8 p.m. with some brokers) or AH news (after 4 p.m.). The explosion in the number of individual investors (and the unprecedented U.S. Bull market) has contributed to increased volume in AH trading. Generally, institutional investors and broker-dealers who provide liquidity in regular session trading have not participated in AH trading sessions. According to William Karsh of Knight Securities, L. P., AH trading is often driven by news events or used to unwind positions taken during regular session trading.

Archipelago (ARCA): An ECN. Formed in 1996 by a consortium of major Wall Street firms, Archipelago is available on a subscription basis to institutions, Nasdaq MMs, broker/dealers and to professional traders. It is not directly available to retail investors. Archipelago merged with the Pacific Exchange in an agreement that closed in July 2000. Archipelago processes trades from 8 a.m. to 8 p.m., Monday through Friday (excluding holidays).

Asymmetry: In the context of information theory, relating to the unequal or unbalanced possession of information.

ATTAIN (ATTN): An ECN. Established in February 1998, ATTAIN introduced their ECN in February 1998. Their majority owner is All-Tech Investment

Group, Inc. ATTAIN serves active retail investors as well as broker/dealers, institutions and hedge funds. ATTAIN will process trades from 8 a.m. to 6 p.m., Monday through Friday (excluding holidays).

Basher: A slang term used, on the stock-chat message boards, for an individual making negative comments about a firm, firm management or products/services, or its stock PPS and investment potential.

Beta Coefficient (β): A measure of the volatility of a stock relative to the overall market. Beta is calculated by applying linear regression to the correlating index's week-to-week percent change for a given period of time. A beta value of 1.1 indicates a 1.10% movement for a 1% move in the index, regardless of direction (e.g. absolute value).

Big-cap: See *Market capitalization (cap).*

Bloomberg (BTRD): An ECN. Launched by Bloomberg LP in 1996 and entering the ECN arena in 1999, Bloomberg is an agency only broker. It is available to institutional equity traders, agency brokers and MMs. Bloomberg processes trades 24 hours a day, Monday through Friday (excluding holidays).

Brut (BRUT): An ECN. Formerly known as Brass Utility (BRUT) and established in May 1998, the majority owner is Automated Securities Clearance Ltd. (ASC). ASC operates the Brokerage Real-time Applications Support System (BRASS). ASC and Brass Utility are operating units of SunGard Data Systems, Inc. BRASS served more than 3,000 desktops, at approximately 175 brokerages, and represent more than 50% of Nasdaq volume. In February 2000, Brut merged with Strike Technologies. Brut processes trades from 8:30 a.m. to 6 p.m., Monday through Friday (excluding holidays).

Direct access brokerage: Permits traders with the ability to direct orders to a specific market, exchange or ECN.

Electronic communications networks (ECNs): Initially, ECNs were developed for use as a private trading system for institutional traders and investors. Prices posted on the ECNs were better than those on the Nasdaq, fragmenting the market and making information made available to the public less reliable. This created artificially wide bid/ask spreads. These inefficiencies led the SEC to adopt *Order Handling Rules* in January 1997. This required MMs and specialists to quote the same prices posted on the ECN, if better than that made available on the exchange to the retail customer. This resulted in a dramatic reduction in spreads, but loopholes do not require that all market participants display their ECN orders to the public. Therefore, transparency remains impaired. The SEC adopted Regulation ATS (Alternative Trading System) in an effort to restore transparency. Island and NexTrade have registered to become exchanges and Archipelago has achieved exchange status. All other ECNs are registered as broker/dealers. Today, they are available (to varying degrees) to include retail investors. Generally, all Nasdaq securities are traded on ECNs. Limited trading is also available for listed securities, however, (for example) NYSE stocks are subject to additional regulatory rules, resulting in limited volume for these securities.

Computerized systems, that automatically match orders between buyers and sellers, represent an alternative to "floor trading." A significant vehicle, facilitating extended-hours trading. According to *MidnightTrader* (March 2002), ECNs account for approximately 38% of all NASDAQ transactions and almost all extended-hours trading. According to Midnight Trader (March 2002), extended-hours volume averages 70 million shares per day and ECNs account for approximately 5% of all volume for listed securities. Trading of listed securities on ECNs is gradually increasing, as exchange-related rules are slowly being relaxed.

The names of ECNs operating as of March 2002 were: (1) *Instinet*; (2) *Island*; (3) *Bloomberg*; (4) *Archipelago*; (5) *REDIBook*; (6) *Brut*; (7) *ATTAIN*; (8) *NexTrade*; and (9) *MarketXT*.

Extended-Hours: Those trading hours outside of the regular session trading (9:30 a.m. to 4 p.m. Eastern time). Extended-Hours consist of the: (1) Pre-Market; and (2) After-Hours (AH). Almost all extended-hours trading is processed through computerized alternative trading systems (ATS), also known as ECNs. There are nine equity ECNs in operation. They are linked to the Nasdaq National Market System through SelectNet. Only limit orders may be placed in extended sessions.

Stock prices tend to be more volatile during extended-hours trading. This is due to a lack of liquidity and/or a lesser degree of market efficiency that is present during regular session trading. This can provide both opportunities and perils. Generally, a broader bid/ask spread is presumed to represent a lesser degree of market efficiency.

Financial leverage: A term used and associated with the level of debt in a firm's capital structure and used to finance assets on the firm's balance sheet. Higher (Lower) financial leverage is associated with higher (lower) risk. (Also see *Operating leverage*).

Firm quote rule: Generally, this rule requires a MM to execute any order to buy or sell a security, other than an odd-lot order, presented by another broker/dealer, etc. The price should reflect the dealer's published bid or offer.

Generally accepted accounting principles (GAAP): GAAP refers to a (primarily) historical cost-based financial statement methods and techniques that have been standardized and are required for use in conveying periodic releases of financial information about a firm's operations and financial position. Both the IRS and GAAP require the use of *absorption costing* or *full costing* techniques.

Good-till-cancelled (GTC): An order placed with a broker to fill all or part of the order until the remainder of the order is cancelled. Most brokers, as a matter of policy, will cancel this order after some time (e.g. 30 days or 60 days).

Hidden information: (see *Private information*).

Hyper: A slang term used, on the stock-chat message boards, for an individual making positive comments about a firm, firm management or products/services, or its stock PPS and investment potential.

Insider trading: Trading by insiders or illegal trading by insiders who trade based on insider information.

Instinet (INCA): Operates as an ECN in the Nasdaq market. Considered the father (oldest and largest) of the modern ECN, Instinet began providing extended-hours trading to institutions and professional traders in the 1970s. They do not currently serve retail investors directly, but held a 16.4% interest in *Archipelago* as of late 2000. The company completed an IPO in 2001, but Reuters PLC remains a major shareholder. They are expanding, rapidly, in Europe, and (as of late 2000) intend to expand into Asia, where they've been granted membership to the Tokyo stock exchange. Instinet processes trades 24 hours a day, Monday through Friday (excluding holidays).

Intermarket trading system (ITS): An electronic order routing system that facilitates intermarket trading of exchange-listed securities by providing the means for a broker/dealer in one market to send an order to another market center trading the same security at a better price. Provides for the elimination or arbitrage of market inefficiencies present between exchanges.

Island (ISLD): An ECN. Founded in 1996, Island is a leader in ECN volume. It is accessible to both institutional and retail investors. Island processes trades from 7 a.m. to 8 p.m., Monday through Friday (excluding holidays).

Market capitalization (cap): Refers to the cost for a purchase of all shares of common stock, issued and outstanding (OS), at any given point in time (e.g. 1 million shares at a closing price of $1 per share equals a market cap of $1 million). This number reflects the total dollar value of company's outstanding shares. Generally, a *large-* or *big*-cap stock is one over $10 billion in market cap, a *mid*-cap stock is one over $1 billion in market cap, a *small*-cap (SC) stock is one over $100 million, and a *micro*-cap stock is one with a market cap below $100 million.

Market maker (MM): Independent dealers/firms who actively compete for investor orders by displaying quotes representing customer buy and sell interests in NASDAQ-listed stocks. There are more than 500 of these firms.

MarketXT (MKXT): An ECN. Founded in 1997, MarketXT was acquired by Tradescape.com, Inc. in February 2000. Retail investors may access through subscribing online and traditional brokerage firms. MarketXT processes trades from 7:30 a.m. to 8 p.m., Monday through Friday (excluding holidays).

Micro-cap: See *Market capitalization (cap)*.

Mid-cap: See *Market capitalization (cap)*.

MidnightTrader: A news service provider, focusing exclusively on real-time, ECN-specific regular session and extended-hours coverage.

Moral hazard: Circumstances which increase the risk of loss.

Naked short: Shorting a stock without the need to borrow shares from a long investor. The stock-chat message boards are filled with claims that *penny* stocks have declined in value because MMs have naked shorted these stocks to destroy their value, effectively increasing the AS and OS and the "float." There is some evidence and reason to believe that this does, in fact, occur (e.g. articles and administrative proceedings against broker-dealers (MMs)). However, it probably does not occur to the extent of these claims.

National Association of Securities Dealer Automated Quotations system (NASDAQ): A computerized system established by the NASD and designed to provide broker/dealers with current bid and ask prices quotes to facilitate OTC stock trading.

National Association of Securities Dealers Regulation Inc. (NASDR): A subsidiary of the NASD that regulates most securities firms and brokers.

NexTrade (NTRD): An ECN. The first ECN to offer 24-hour trading to retail investors through participating broker/dealers, NexTrade is owned by Professional Investment Management, Inc. In 1999, NexTrade applied with the SEC to become a registered, fully-electronic, 24-hour securities exchange and has a pending application to become a fully-electronic futures exchange. NexTrade processes trades 24-hours a day, including holidays.

Operating leverage: A term used and associated with the level of fixed costs, relative to a firm's overall costs or expense. Higher (Lower) operating leverage is associated with higher (lower) risk. (Also see *Financial leverage*).

Order book: Each ECN has an order book. It represents the bid/ask transactions that are pending execution for each stock. This information is updated as brokers enter buy and sell orders. In the absence of market maker manipulation (MMM) or error, a review of this order book provides the trader or investor with the information necessary to determine the "breadth" and "direction" of the market for a particular security.

Order handling rules: Requires MMs and specialists to reflect in published quotes the price or orders they place in an ECN if better than their own publicly published quote.

Other OTC: Also known as the *Grey Market*, the trading of a security that is not listed on any stock exchange or quoted on the Pink Sheets or the OTC BB. Other OTC trades are reported to the NASD so investors can track price and volume, however, bids and offers are not collected in a central spot so *best execution* of orders is difficult.

Over-the-Counter (OTC): OTC securities are those issued by companies that either choose not, or are unable, to meet the standards for listing on the NASDAQ or a stock exchange. OTC equities can be quoted on the Pink

Sheets(r) Electronic Quotation Service, or, if a SEC reporting company, on the NASD OTC BB Service.

Over-the-counter Bulletin Board (OTC BB): An electronic quotation medium for unlisted, non-Nasdaq, OTC securities. Established for stocks meeting minimal requirements for listing on the OTC exchange, they are often referred to as *penny stocks*, though some may trade in the dollars per share.

Pink Sheets(r): The Pink Sheets is a centralized *quotation service* that collects and publishes market maker quotes for OTC securities in real time. Pink Sheets is a nexus of OTC dealer markets that enhances price transparency in the OTC markets so investors can more efficiently buy and sell OTC securities.

The origins of Pink Sheets go back to 1904 and the establishment of the National Quotation Bureau. In the summer of 1999, NASD began the process of de-listing over 3,000 companies from the OTC BB. In September 1999, Pink Sheets introduced their Electronic Quotation Service (EQS) for the Internet. The EQS is available at no cost to issuers. In June 2000, pinksheets.com was introduced.

Pink Sheets LLC is a privately owned company headquartered in New York City. Pink Sheets is not a stock exchange or a regulated entity. Quotations are provided by MMs. Company information is self-reported by the companies. Pink Sheets has no minimum requirements or qualitative standards for the security to be quoted. Companies do not have to be SEC reporting to be quoted in the Pink Sheets.

To become quoted in the Pink Sheets, a SEC-registered broker/dealer (MM) must sponsor a security for the Pink Sheets. The MM must then file a Form 211 with the NASD OTC Compliance Unit, along with 2 copies of required information. Pink Sheets will be quoted after a successful review. NASD rules prohibit MMs from accepting remuneration from sponsorship.

Pre-market: Pre-market trading (7 a.m. to 9:30 a.m.) or pre-market news (before 9:30 a.m.).

Principal-Agent theory: See *agency theory.*

Private information: (also see *Hidden information*). That information not immediately available to all investors (or potential investors).

Public information: That information available to all investors or potential investors.

REDIBook (REDI): An ECN. Developed by a consortium of major Wall Street firms, REDIBook is available to both institutional and retail investors (through brokers). Island processes trades from 7 a.m. to 8 p.m., Monday through Friday (excluding holidays).

Regular session trading: The regular session is defined as 9:30 a.m. to 4 p.m. for normal trading days and 9:30 a.m. to 1 p.m. for shortened trading days.

Regulation ATS: SEC-established framework for alternative trading systems (ATS). An ATS may choose to be a market participant and register as a broker-dealer, or be a separate market and register as an exchange.

Regulation FD: Adopted by the SEC in 2000, Regulation FD eliminated the practice of selected disclosure. Information must now be released, at the same time, to individuals, institutional investors, and analysts.

Semi-strong form (or *level*) *of market efficiency:* See *Efficient markets hypothesis (EMH)*.

Short squeeze: As the term suggests, pressure on those holding open short positions in equities. For example, assume that you are short 100 shares of IBM. You sold at a PPS of $110, believing that the price would fall in the next few trading days. Instead, some good news results in a rally in IBM stock and the PPS has already risen to $115 and appears to be heading higher. You feel pressured or squeezed and consider covering at $115 for a $500 loss (e.g. $115 less $110 equals $5 per share multiplied by 100 shares). Furthermore, if you purchased this IBM stock, using margin, you may be anticipating a margin call from your broker. This could require that you cover or close the position before they are forced to select and sell some stock from your portfolio (in accordance with the terms you agreed to in your margin agreement with your broker). If there are many others in this same position, the short covering (e.g. buying) pressure will cause the price of IBM to spike up (in the short term). This would be referred to as a short squeeze (e.g. a price rise in the PPS of IBM stock, caused by shorts being squeezed to buy stock (cover) or close their positions).

Small-cap (SC): See *market capitalization (cap)*.

Spoofing: Stock market manipulation, in which a trader with a long position in a stock places an anonymous buy order for a large number of shares, through an ECN, and cancels it seconds later. The price of the stock will immediately jump, giving the impression of high demand, which draws others into buying the stock, allowing the manipulator to sell at a higher price. Some market analysts believe this is one cause of increased volatility in the markets (from *Investorwords.com*).

Spread: The difference between the highest bid and the lowest ask price for a security.

Stock symbol: Refers to the *call letters* or *ticker* used to represent a firm. Symbols with up to three letters are used for stocks that are listed and trade on an exchange. Symbols with four letters are used for NASDAQ and OTC stocks. Symbols with five letters are used for NASDAQ and OTC stocks other than single issues of common stock. Symbols with five letters ending in X are used for mutual funds.

Strong form (or *level*) *of market efficiency:* See *Efficient markets hypothesis (EMH)*.

Symmetry: In the context of information theory, relating to the unequal or unbalanced possession of information.

Technical analysis (TA): A trading strategy based on the charting (e.g. chartists) of historical price and volume (e.g. supply and demand) behavior. Terms common to TA include: support, resistance, moving average (MA), exponential MA, down/up trend line, money flow, on balance volume, relative strength index, MA convergence/divergence (MACD), key reversal, etc.

Uniform Securities Act: The Act approved by the National Conference of Commissioners on Uniform State Laws in 1956, relating to the registration of broker/dealers, agents, advisors and securities.

Weak form (or *level*) *of market efficiency:* See *Efficient markets hypothesis (EMH)*.

Window dressing: Attempts by financial and money managers to manipulate stock prices and, therefore, the value of the funds they manage at the end of reporting periods.

Yellow sheets: A quotation service for OTC taxable bonds.

NOTES

1. This contemporary controversy differs from that which came to the public's attention during July 2000, when it was disclosed that Vice-President Dick Cheney, as chief executive of the firm, sold stock options valued at more than $40 million ($54.02 per share) when he left in 2000. As of July 2002, the stock was worth approximately $13 per share.

2. Related topics include theory of the growth of the firm, theory of the firm, organizational theory, managerial theories of the firm and theory of bureaucracy.

3. Throughout this monograph, the terms *information asymmetry* and *asymmetric information* are used interchangeably.

4. Some individuals may be risk averse while others may be risk-seeking (Fischhoff et al., 1981; Bazerman, 1994). Furthermore, individuals' risk preferences may be situation specific (Slovic, 1972; MacCrimmon & Wehrung, 1986).

5. For surveys of the literature on adverse selection and health insurance markets, see Morrisey (1992) and Pauly (1986).

6. Similarly, public accounting firms have entered into consulting for sales tax and property tax appeals (moral hazard) and cost minimization for firms.

7. The audit failures relating to Enron and WorldCom may prove to represent some of the more highly publicized contemporary examples of false signaling.

8. This typically applies in the context of public policy (e.g. voters who do not research candidates).

9. This does not preclude the pursuit of altruistic or social goals (e.g. volunteering for charitable works).

10. However, see Huddart (1995), where it is suggested that a reputation effect may cause an adviser to use private information too aggressively.

11. This is a testable hypothesis. This area is likely to enjoy increased academic researcher attention in the years following the failures characterized by Enron and WorldCom.

12. He also found geographical distance to be an important factor, suggesting that the oversight of local firms was less costly.

13. This section benefited from references made to the literature review section of Shapeero (1994).

14. This study was updated, with comparable results, by Alderman and Deitrick (1982).

15. See "SEC unable to confirm report of major probe into analysts."

16. See CBS MarketWatch.com, dated April 26, 2002.

17. Window dressing, as a possible explanation for a seasonal anomaly referred to as the January effect, is introduced in Chapter 2 and more fully developed in Chapter 7 of Cataldo and Savage (2000), where a summary of the literature on window dressing is provided (pp. 107–108). Therefore, though some coverage is necessary, the literature review contained in this earlier work is not reproduced for the present monograph.

18. Window dressing is one of the possible explanations suggested in the literature to explain month-end, turn-of-the-month, and January effects.

19. Background information (Reuters Company News 2002): Dynegy agreed to the acquisition of Enron (NYSE: ENE) on November 9, but backed out of the deal on November 28, 2001. Enron filed for Chapter 11 bankruptcy and filed suit against Dynegy for $10 billion for breach of contract (December 2, 2001) and dropped Andersen as their auditor (March 19, 2002).

20. A theory of risk aversion exists. It is known as prospect theory, but is beyond the scope of this monograph.

21. Stewart noted that Mester (1993, 1991) and Cebenoyan et al. (1992) found, similarly, that mutual S&Ls experienced greater agency problems that did stock S&Ls, prior to deregulation.

22. See De Bondt and Thaler (1985). In revising their beliefs, individuals tend to overweight recent information and underweight prior data (793).

23. As recently as March 2003, CNBC reported that there were approximately 30,000 day-traders.

24. Foster (1977) provides an examination of the predictive ability of quarterly accounting data in a statistical/methodological article.

25. Their relative importance, in descending order, were employment, Producer Price Index (PPI), CPI, durable goods orders, industrial production-capacity utilization, construction spending-National Association of Purchasing Managers (NAPM) survey results, and the federal budget for T-bond futures prices. Employment was also the most important variable for comparable analyses for Eurodollar and U.S. dollar-deutsche mark rates.

26. Unless otherwise indicated, all times are Eastern Standard time (EST).

27. In 1972 the "Big 8" CPA firms were: (1) Arthur Andersen & Co.; (2) Ernst & Ernst; (3) Haskins & Sells; (4) Coopers & Lybrand; (5) Peat, Marwick, Mitchell & Co.; (6) Price Waterhouse & Co.; (7) Touche Ross & Co.; and (8) Arthur Young & Co. Due to mergers, since 1972, a listing of the "Big 5" follows: (1) Arthur Andersen Consulting, (2) & (8) Ernst & Young, (3) & (7) Deloitte Touche, (4) & (6) PricewaterhouseCoopers and (5) KPMG Peat Marwick.

At this writing, Arthur Anderson was still in the news with respect to the Enron scandal and a new scandal, involving Ernst & Young, had emerged, having gained SEC attention, with respect to business relations between Ernst & Young and PeopleSoft, Inc. (NASDAQ NM: PSFT) during May 2002.

28. This section drew heavily from McCarthy (2001).

29. Moody's ratings, from best to worst, are Aaa, Aa, A, Baa, Ba, B, Caa, Ca, C, and D. S&P ratings, from best to worst, are AAA, AA, A, BBB, BB, B, CCC, CC, C, and D.

30. This typically applies in the context of public policy (e.g. voters who do not research candidates).

31. Mark Hulbert is the founder of a financial newsletter tracking service, *Hulbert Financial Digest*, and is now part of CBS MarketWatch. Hulbert has been tracking and ranking the advice of more than 160 financial newsletters for more than 20 years (1980).

32. Knobias.com.

33. Thompsonfinancial.com.

34. Weissratings.com.

35. The development of this section benefited from the theoretical background information contained in Krinksy and Lee (1996, 1525).

36. For an excellent primer on transaction cost analysis, see Rindfleisch and Heide (1997).

37. Network theory was developed to explain complex policy-making in many modern democracies, where power is fragmented and dispersed among numerous and divergent groups.

38. The development of this section benefited from a review of Xiao et al. (1998).

39. The regular trading session is from 9:30 a.m. to 4 p.m. This excludes pre-market and after-hours trading sessions, which have some variations between ECNs and broker/dealers, but generally run from 8 a.m. to 9:30 a.m. and 4 p.m. to 6:30 p.m., respectively.

40. PurchasePro's fiscal year end coincides with the December 31 calendar year end.

41. A similar, but more highly publicized mis-matching of revenues occurred with Xerox, and was reported in the popular and business press in late June 2002.

42. It is not my position that this decline, from a high of $12.13 per share to $0.75 per share, is solely or even causally linked to the Form 144 filings made by Charles E. Johnson, Jr.

43. YF msg #112977.

44. lol = lots of luck or laughing out loud.

45. YF msg #113017.

46. YF msg #113164.

47. YF msg #113229.

48. YF msg #113257.

49. YF msg #'s 113559, 113602, 113612, and 113628, posted from 6 p.m. to 10 p.m. on August 8, 2001.

50. YF msg #113582.

51. YF msg #113559.

52. YF msg #'s 113707 and 113708 (both) at 1:56 a.m.

53. As part of my research efforts into the PurchasePro case, I engaged in both telephone and emailed communications (April 2002) with Steven Stern. As the chapter/case study suggests, a primary concern of PurchasePro executives was the significance of the short interest in PurchasePro stock.

54. RB MPTT msg #460824.

55. The actual release of the report is noted in Appendix Chapter 7.1 in an 8 a.m. *PrimeZone Media Network* release. PrimeZone is also used by PurchasePro for their corporate public relations news releases. News of this shareholder-prepared financial analysis of PurchasePro was posted on the YF message boards in message #184794 at 8:05 a.m.

56. Like many financial analysts, CNBC directs their news coverage to firms based on total market capitalization. They rarely provide coverage of firms when their stock PPS falls below one dollar.

57. Mktnews.nasdaq.com/newsv2/storyoneV5 nasd.asp?usymbol+USXP&site=nasdaq.

58. RB USXP msg #8892.

59. RB msg #8924.

60. RB msg #9272.

61. Also, see RB msg #69815.

62. For an examination of the practices at Knight Securities, L. P., see Battalio et al. (1998).

63. On an anecdotal level, this author has personally experienced this problem with trades as recently as March 2002. Using myTrack, a market maker failed to honor a

trade. The problem was corrected by myTrack, but only after two telephone calls. In the first attempt, the market maker claimed that his computer was not working and he could not make the correction. In the second attempt, the market maker simply refused to fill the order. The market maker was not Knight.

64. "Market maker" and "dealer" are equivalent terms, whereas the term "broker-dealer" is broader, encompassing all agents who trade directly on an exchange for their own account.

65. Silicon Investor (SI; www.siliconinvestor.com/stocktalk/msg.gsp?msgid=15828446 and www.cybersecuritieslaw.com/lawsuits/cases_corporate_cybersmears.htm) sites and related links were used as starting points for the development of the data analyzed in this chapter.

66. See *Business Wire v. Jeffrey S. Mitchell, William Ulrich and Janice Shell*, filed in USDC for the Northern District of CA in San Francisco.

67. Yahoo changed its policy in April 2000. It used to make little or no attempt to notify posters before revealing their identities. It now gives posters 15 days notice before revealing their personal information under subpoena.

68. Upheld by the U.S. Supreme Court, in *Zeran v. America Online Inc.* on June 22, 1998; affirming the U.S. 4th Circuit Court of Appeals decision. The decision relied on Section 230(c)(1) of the Communications Decency Act, which states that "(n)o provider or user of an interactive computer service shall be treated as the publisher or speaker of any information provided by another information content provider." This case originated from Kenneth Zeran's charge that AOL failed to act quickly to remove a false message board post, resulting in a flood of hate mail, phone calls and even death threats. The message suggested the Kenneth Zeran was selling souvenirs celebrating the Oklahoma City federal building disaster.

69. In the process of developing Table 9.1, additional references were found, but not fully investigated, for: (1) American Eco (OTC BB/Foreign; ECGO(E)&(Q).ECX); (2) Ben Ezra, Weinstein (Foreign; BNEZ); (3) Diana (NY; DNA); (4) Ubuyholdings/E-Pawn (PinkSheets; UBYH/EPWN); (5) FirstPlus Financial Group (PinkSheets; FPFX); (6) Flooring America (PinkSheets; FRAE); (7) Go Online Networks (OTC BB; GONT); (8) Harken Energy (AX; HEC; this reference differs from that associated with the July, 2002 controversy surrounding the sale of 212,400 shares by President Bush in 1990 for $848,000, two months prior to an unexpected loss. Though President Bush notified the SEC of the transaction eight months late, the SEC investigation closed their investigation without taking any action against him); (9) Image Guided Technologies (OTC BB; IGTI); (10) Kimberly-Clark (NY/Foreign; KMB/855178); (11) Luby's (NY; LUB); (12) Medinah Minerals (PinkSheets; MDMN); (13) Medphone (OTC BB: MPHO); (14) Milinix Business Group (OTC BB; MIXBX); (15) Myrient Technologies (OTC BB; MYNT/925617); (16) Nanopierce Technologies (OTC BB/Foreign; NPCT/916132); (17) PairGain Technologies (Foreign; PAIR/887714); (18) ProNetLink (OTC BB; PNLK); (19) Qualcomm (NASDAQ/Foreign; QCOM/883121); (20) Seaview Video Technologies (OTC BB; SEVU); (21) Southern Pacific Funding (PinkSheets; SFCF(Q)); (22) Starnet Communications International (PinkSheets/Foreign; SNMM/910479); and (23) Varian Medical Systems (NY/Foreign; VAR/852812). There was not a single case alluding to firm intervention in a case of hyping for any of these.

70. PurchasePro's previous auditor was Arthur Andersen. Andersen had noted design deficiencies in internal controls as the reason for their resignation (see November 29, 2001). This auditor change occurred at a time when the Enron scandal, with Arthur

Andersen as their auditor, was emerging with increasingly heavy coverage in the popular press.

71. See www.sec.gov/litigation/admin/33-7891.htm, administrative proceeding file no. 3-10291.

72. These are Figs 8.3.1 and 8.3.2 for MANC, 8.3.4 and 8.3.5 for FUSA, 8.3.6 and 8.3.7 for YESS, 8.3.9 and 8.3.10 for JUST, 8.3.12 and 8.3.13 for FTEC, 8.3.16 and 8.3.17 for MSHI, 8.3.18 and 8.3.19 for WCECE, 8.3.20 and 8.3.21 for TCGI, and 8.3.22 and 8.3.23 for HVAR.

73. These are Figs 8.3.3 for MANC, 8.3.8 for YESS, 8.3.11 for JUST and 8.3.14 and 8.3.15 for FTEC.

74. MICROS RB msg #126, August 2, 1998.

75. The actual spamming posts were removed from the message boards. This is a common practice, when multiple complaints are received from other registered users. However, the responses to the spam remained.

76. DD = due diligence or research.

77. This message was copied and posted from another poster/alias. The SEC "cease and desist" order specifically noted the YF stock chat message boards.

78. All messages prior to October 25, 1999 were deleted. Recall that the SEC "cease and desist" order, in the case of the stock price for MSHI, indicated that there was a prediction of a price of $20 "very soon."

79. It is common for investors (and speculators) on the stock chat message boards to blame market makers (MMs) for failure of a stock's price to rise.

80. The details are not listed here, just the call letters for the other boards containing these additional posts.

81. The details are not listed here, just the call letters for the other boards containing these additional posts.

82. These included (by call letter) HYPR, IATV, CNTR, IINN, IMDS, YHOO, UVGI, IVOC, ARET, AZNT, IBUI, KKRS, ATHM, SNRS, HSNS, HRCT, ADVC, VDOT, DRYD, TSIG, CYBR, MONKEY, QCOM, WAVX, PCCLF, CMGIOT, INVT, PAYV, CMGI, MVEE, ANTS, AOL, and many, many more.

83. All messages prior to January 26, 2000 were deleted.

84. From Appendix 8.1, for example, one poster's alias is *diggerdawg2001* and another's is *bjmagivlry2001dawg*. Furthermore, the following messages contained in Appendix 8.1 with *dawg* in the body of the heading or message: #112482, #112809, #112833, #112901, #112929, #112972, #112996, #113009, #113017, #113025, #113030, #113033, #113043 and #113052.

85. RB MICROS msg #126.

86. Costs range from a few hundred to several hundred dollars per news or public relations release.

87. Prior to the RS, the stock ticker was PKPG.

88. RB msg #71927, suggested that the cost for this profile was $11,500.

89. I should point out that I, too, sent an email to the CEO of Universal Express and I received a brief but timely response.

90. I telephoned the CEO of a different small cap or penny stock, as well as an officer of PurchasePro (see Chapter 7). In both cases I engaged in 10–15 minute conversations with these officers.

91. A monthly share volume report of Universal Express, available through an OTC BB Internet site, showed year-to-date volume for Knight Securities at 163 million shares

(through July 2001). This compared to the second-ranked volume by Schwab Capital Markets L. P. at approximately 41 million shares.

92. This summary has been adapted from a post that has been copied over and over again from various stock-chat message boards. This copy was located at RB message # 5562 from the USXP message board.

93. For example, see Dasgupta and Nanda (1995).

94. This summary has been adapted from a post that has been copied over and over again from various stock-chat message boards. This copy was located at RB message # 5562 from the USXP message board. Others, providing additional insight, include RB msg #74841 and #74839. The original contained a listing of thirty items, but redundant components have been eliminated or merged.

95. Trading-places.net/traderclass/mmgames.html.

96. This appears to be a reference to a "hand" or the cards that a player may hold in a game of poker. Therefore, the individual investor that is manipulated into "folding" has a "weak hand."

97. Secure.nasdr.com.

98. Nasdr.com/news/pr2001/ne_section01_003.html.

99. See Howard Mintz, 'Cybersmear' Lawsuits Raise Privacy Concern, Silicon Valley News, SV.com at Mercury Center online, Nov. 28, 1999.

100. The RB message board for 2TheMart.com contains posts through April 2002, as of June 2002. As recently as January 2001, RB message board participants were receiving RB-initiated notifications of the receipt of subpoenas requiring that RB provide registration data (e.g. the identity) of participants on the RB stock chat message boards. The deadline for RB compliance was February 16, 2001. A series of articles from a variety of sources have been posted and remain on the RB site for 2TheMart, including those relating to a merger attempt with GoToWorld.com (April 2000), its parent, Language Force, and subsequent litigation relating to the failed merger.

101. Very little information was available on this civil case, which was characterized as commercial/business tort. The stock chat message board posts, apparently alleging financial misdeeds by the firm's CEO, were removed from the board where they were posted.

102. The EFF and Public Citizen filed an October 13, 2000, brief (Motion to Quash Subpoena to AOL) to support his/her First Amendment rights and his/her right to remain anonymous.

103. In a separate development, during March 2001, the SEC filed suit against Amazon for misleading product claims and overstatement of sales revenues and other accounting fraud from at least 1997 through March 2001. The SEC suit alleged that Amazon included sales of the firm's stock as revenues, including 2 million shares issued to a company controlled by Amazon's President, Titan Investments (see *Observation #122*). The president of Amazon, countered with allegation that the SEC suit resulted from Canadian brokers and American market makers, illegally short-selling 15 million shares of Amazon stock.

104. Initial message board posts suggest that the lawsuit may have never been filed and/or these message board comments were merely designed to intimidate others on the message boards. Message board links alleged that Ashton, a software firm, was one of four companies promoted by the Mob in a "Boiler Room"-like scheme, resulting in FBI investigator arrests of twenty persons in March 2001.

105. In a separate case, a libel suit was filed against a news reporter. On March 30, 2001, the libel suit was dismissed.

106. The stock was for an Irish firm, Elan Corporation (NYSE-ADR: ELN), a specialty pharmaceutical company. The firm's stock had surged on expectations that its Alzheimer's disease drug might soon be released. The messages were posted when the Credit Suisse analyst soured on the stock, rating it only as a "hold," even as the stock price continued to climb.

107. As of September 2001, the *docpatel* alias had not been deleted from the RB message board. This alias showed a posting history ranging from February 3 through May 2, 2000. Seventy-eight of one-hundred and thirty-one posts (60%) of these posts were to the Imaging Diagnostic stock-chat board. Further review of his RB posting history revealed numerous *docpatel* posts referring to the 'past fraud' of Imaging Diagnostic Systems and a single, negative post referring to specific individuals associated with Imaging Diagnostic Systems.

108. The YF message board for Informix had been closed and was not available in September 2001, but there was a reference to message #73054.

109. This was the first time that a firm's own market maker had been identified as a basher and involved in cybersmear. Market makers are responsible for the maintenance of an orderly or liquid market in a stock, ready to buy or sell shares when no one else is willing to buy or sell. J. Alexander was the seventh-largest dealer in Quest Net stock.

110. These messages were not available, as numerous posters had already been removed (i.e. TOSsed), due to terms of service (TOS) violations.

111. This case was dismissed shortly after news of an SEC investigation, suggesting that management was involved in issuing misleading and optimistic news releases, was made public.

112. Examined in the context of the Walrasian model by R. B. Wilson (chapter on *Exchange*) in Eatwell et al. (1991, p. 241).

REFERENCES

Aboody, D., & Lev, B. (2000). Information asymmetry, R&D, and insider gains. *The Journal of Finance, 55*, 2747–2766.

Acker, D., Horton, J., & Tonks, I. (1998). Accounting standards and analysts' forecasts: The impact of FRS 3 on analysts' ability to forecast EPS. Unpublished Working Paper (August 6).

Admati, A. R., & Pfleiderer, P. (1988). A theory of intraday patterns: Volume and price variability. *The Review of Financial Studies, 1*, 3–40.

Aggarwal, R., & Rao, R. (1990). Institutional ownership and distribution of equity returns. *Financial Review, 25*, 211–230.

Ajinkya, B. B., & Gift, M. J. (1984). Corporate managers' earnings forecasts and symmetrical adjustments of market expectations. *Journal of Accounting Research, 22*, 425–444.

Akerlof, G. A. (1970). The market for "lemons": Quality uncertainty and the market mechanisms. *Quarterly Journal of Economics, 84*, 3–15.

Alangar, S., Bathala, C. T., & Rao, R. P. (1999). The effect of institutional interest on the information content of dividend-change announcements. *The Journal of Financial Research, 22*, 429–448.

Al-Suhaibani, M., & Kryzanowski, L. (2000). The information content of orders on the Saudi stock market. *The Journal of Financial Research, 23*, 145–156.

Alderman, C. W., & Dietrick, J. W. (1982). Auditors' perceptions of time budget pressures and premature audit sign-offs: A replication and extension. *Auditing: A Journal of Practice and Theory, 1*, 54–68.

Ali, A., Klein, A., & Rosenfeld, J. (1992). Analysts' use of information about permanent and transitory earnings components in forecasting annual EPS. *The Accounting Review*, 183–198.

Anderson, D., Francis, J., & Stokes, D. (1990). Auditing, directorships and the demand for corporate based governance. Unpublished Working Paper, University of Queensland.

Anderson, S. E., & Cuccia, A. D. (2000). A closer examination of the economic incentives created by tax return preparer penalties. *The Journal of the American Taxation Association, 22*, 56–77.

Arbel, A. (1985). Generic stocks: An old product in a new package. *The Journal of Portfolio Management, 68*, 4–13.

Arbel, A., Carvell, S., & Strebel, P. (1983). Giraffes, institutions and neglected firms. *Financial Analysts Journal, 39*, 57–63.

Arbel, A., & Strebel, P. (1983). Pay attention to neglected firms! *The Journal of Portfolio Management, 9*, 37–42.

Arbel, A., & Strebel, P. (1982). The neglected and small firm effects. *The Financial Review*, 201–218.

Arino, A., de la Torre, J., & Ring, P. S. (2001). Relational quality: Managing trust in corporate alliances. *California Management Review, 44*, 109–131.

Arneson, G. S. (1981a). Nonmarketability discounts should exceed fifty percent. *Taxes*, *59*, 25–31.

Arneson, G. S. (1981b). Minority discounts beyond fifty percent can be supported. *Taxes*, *59*, 97–102.

Arrow, K. J. (1985). The economics of agency. In: J. W. Pratt & R. J. Zeckhauser (Eds), *Principals and Agents: The Structure of Business* (pp. 37–51). Boston: Harvard Business School Press.

Athanassakos, G. (1992). Portfolio rebalancing and the January effect in Canada. *Financial Analysts Journal*, 67–78.

Ball, R. (1978). Anomalies in relationships between securities' yields and yield-surrogates. *Journal of Financial Economics*, *6*, 103–126.

Ball, R., & Brown, P. (1968). An empirical evaluation of accounting numbers. *Journal of Accounting Research*, 159–178.

Bajaj, M., & Vijh, A. M. (1995). Trading behavior and the unbiasedness of the market reaction to dividend announcements. *The Journal of Finance*, *50*, 255–279.

Balvers, R. J., McDonald, B., & Miller, R. (1988). Underpricing of new issues and choice of new auditor as a signal of investment banking reputation. *The Accounting Review*, *63*, 605–622.

Bamber, L. S. (1986). The information content of annual earnings releases: A trading volume approach. *Journal of Accounting Research*, *24*, 40–56.

Barclay, M. J., & Smith, C. W. (1995a). The maturity structure of corporate debt. *The Journal of Finance*, *50*(2), 609–631.

Barclay, M. J., & Smith, C. W. (1995b). The priority structure of corporate liabilities. *The Journal of Finance*, *50*, 899–917.

Battalio, R., Jennings, R., & Selway, J. P. (1999). Payment for order flow, trading costs, and dealer revenues for market orders at Knight Securities. L.P. NASD Working Paper 98-03.

Bazerman, M. H. (1994). *Judgment in managerial decision making*. New York: John Wiley & Sons, Inc.

Beaver, W. H. (1968). The information content of annual earnings announcements. *Empirical Research in Accounting: Selected Studies*, 67–100.

Bergen, M., Dutta, S., & Walker, O. C. (1992). Agency relationships in marketing: A review of the implications and applications of agency and related theories. *Journal of Marketing*, *54*, 1–24.

Berlin, M., & Loeys, J. (1988). Bond covenants and delegated monitoring. *The Journal of Finance*, *43*, 397–412.

Bessler, W., & Nohel, T. (2000). Asymmetric information, dividend reductions, and contagion effects in bank stock returns. *Journal of Banking and Finance*, *24*, 1831–1848.

Best, R., & Zhang, H. (1993). Alternative information sources and the information content of bank loans. *The Journal of Finance*, *48*, 1507–1522.

Bildersee, J., & Kahn, N. (1987). A preliminary test of the presence of window dressing: Evidence from institutional stock trading. *Journal of Accounting Auditing and Finance*, *2*, 239–265.

Billett, M. T., Flannery, M. J., & Garfinkel, J. A. (1995). The effect of lender identity on a borrowing firm's equity return. *The Journal of Finance*, *50*, 699–718.

Black, B. S. (1997). Information asymmetry, the Internet, and securities offerings. *The Journal of Small and Emerging Business Law*, *2*, 91–99.

Black, F. (1973). Yes, Virginia, there is hope: Tests of the value line ranking system. *Financial Analysts Journal*, *29*, 10–14.

Bloomfield, R. (1996). Quotes, prices, and estimates in a laboratory market. *The Journal of Finance*, *51*, 1791–1808.

Bothamley, J. (1993). *Dictionary of theories*. Gale Research International Ltd., London.

Boyd, J. H., & Prescott, E. C. (1986). Financial intermediary coalitions. *Journal of Economic Theory, 38*, 211–232.

Bradbury, M. E. (1990). The incentives for voluntary audit committee formation. *Journal of Accounting and Public Policy, 9*, 19–36.

Brauer, G. A., & Chang, E. C. (1990). Return seasonality in stocks and their underlying assets: Tax-loss selling vs. information explanations. *The Review of Financial Studies, 3*, 255–280.

British Columbia (BC) Securities Commission (2002). Man who misled markets agrees to five-year trading ban. *Canadian News Wire* (February 8).

Bromwich, M. (1992). *Financial reporting, information and capital markets.* Pitman: London.

Brown, P., Foster, G., & Noreen, E. (1985). Security analyst multi-year earnings forecasts and the capital market. *American Accounting Association Studies in Accounting Research, 21.* Sarasota, FL: American Accounting Association.

Brown, P., & Kennelly, J. W. (1972). The informational content of quarterly earnings: An extension and some further evidence. *The Journal of Business, 45*, 403–415.

Brown, P., & Niederhoffer, V. (1968). The predictive content of quarterly earnings. *The Journal of Business, 41*, 488–497.

Butler, K. C., & Lang, L. H. (1991). The forecast accuracy of individual analysts: Evidence of systematic optimism and pessimism. *Journal of Accounting Research, 29*, 150–156.

Campbell, T. S., Chan, Y.-S., & Marino, A. M. (1990). An incentive based theory of bank regulation. Unpublished Working Paper, University of Southern California.

Cardon, J. H., & Hendel, I. (2001). Asymmetric information in health insurance: Evidence from the National Medical Expenditure Survey. *RAND Journal of Economics, 32*, 408–427.

Carnes, G. A., & Englebrecht, T. D. (1995). An investigation of the effect of detection risk perceptions, penalty sanctions, and income visibility on tax compliance. *The Journal of the American Taxation Association, 17*, 26–41.

Carrel, L. (2002). One-day wonder: A knight in tarnished armor. Smartmoney.com (June 4).

Carter, R. B., Dark, F. H., & Singh, A. K. (1998). Underwriter reputation, initial returns, and the long-run performance of IPO stocks. *The Journal of Finance, 53*, 285–311.

Carvell, S., & Strebel, P. (1984). A new beta incorporating analysts' forecasts. *The Journal of Portfolio Management, 11*, 81–85.

Cataldo, A. J., & Killough, L. N. (2003). Is your firm safe from Cybersmear? *Strategic Finance, 84*(7), 34–38.

Cataldo, A. J., & Killough, L. N. (2002). The "pump and dump" and "cybersmear:" An investigation of two cases of Internet-based stock price manipulation. *Journal of Forensic Accounting, 3*, 225–244.

Cebenoyan, A. C., Cooperman, E. S., Register, C., & Hudgins, S. (1993). The relative efficiency of stock vs. mutual S&Ls: A stochastic cost frontier approach. *Journal of Financial Services Research*, 151–170.

Chaffin, J. (2002). Notes on the bursting of Henry's bubble. FT.com (May 7).

Chan, L. K., Jegadesh, N., & Lakonishok, J. (1996). Momentum strategies. *The Journal of Finance, 51*, 1681–1713.

Chan, Y-S., Greenbaum, S. I., & Thakor, A. V. (1992). Is fairly priced deposit insurance possible? *The Journal of Finance, 47*, 227–245.

Chang, E. C., Pinegar, J. M., & Ravichandran, R. (1998). U.S. day-of-the-week effects and asymmetric responses to macroeconomic news. *Journal of Banking and Finance, 22*, 513–534.

Chemmanur, T., & Fulghiere, P. (1995). Information production, private equity financing, and the going public decision. Unpublished Working Paper, Columbia University.

Chen, C. R., Lin, J. W., & Sauer, D. A. (1997). Earnings announcements, quality and quantity of information, and stock price changes. *The Journal of Financial Research*, 20, 483–502.

Chow, C. W. (1982). Demand for external auditing: Size, debt and ownership influences. *The Accounting Review*, 57, 272–291.

Christie, W. G., Harris, J. H., & Schultz, P. H. (1994). Why did NASDAQ market makers stop avoiding odd-eighth quotes? *The Journal of Finance*, 49, 1841–1860.

Christie, W. G., & Schultz, P. H. (1994). Why do NASDAQ market makers avoid odd-eighth quotes? *The Journal of Finance*, 49, 1813–1840.

Christie, W. G., & Nanda, V. (1994). Free cash flow, shareholder value, and the undistributed profits tax of 1936 and 1937. *The Journal of Finance*, 49, 1727–1754.

Clark, R. C. (1985). Agency costs vs. fiduciary duties. In: J. W. Pratt & R. J. Zeckhauser (Eds), *Principals and Agents: The Structure of Business* (pp. 55–79). Boston: Harvard Business School Press.

CMS Energy Corporation (2002). CMS energy issues clarification statement on energy trades with Dynegy. *PRNewswire Press Release* (May 9).

Coller, M., & Yohn, T. L. (1997). Management forecasts and information asymmetry: An examination of bid-ask spreads. *Journal of Accounting Research*, 35, 181–191.

Copeland, T., & Galai, D. (1983). Information effects on the bid-ask spread. *The Journal of Finance*, 38, 1457–1469.

Copeland, T., & Mayers, D. (1982). The value line enigma (1965-1978): A case study of performance evaluation issues. *Journal of Financial Economics*, 10, 289–321.

Cook, E., & Kelley, T. (1988). Auditor stress and time-budgets. *The CPA Journal*, 58, 83–86.

Cooter, R. D., & Rubenfeld, D. L. (1989). Economic analysis of legal disputes and their resolution. *Journal of Economic Literature*, 27, 1067–1097.

Cramer, J. J. (2002). It's time to bring Knight into the light. Commentary, TheStreet.com (June 5).

Dasgupta, S., & Nanda, V. (1995). Tender offers, proxy contests and large shareholder activism. Working Paper 95-13, The University of Michigan; Mitsui Financial Research Center.

Davies, P. L., & Canes, M. (1978). Stock prices and the publication of second-hand information. *The Journal of Business*, 51, 43–56.

De Angelo, H., De Angelo, L., & Skinner, D. J. (1992). Dividends and losses. *The Journal of Finance*, 47, 1837–1863.

DeBondt, W. F. M., & Thaler, R. (1985). Does the stock market overreact? *The Journal of Finance*, 40, 793–808.

DeGeorge, F., & Zeckhauser, R. (1993). The reverse LBO decision and firm performance: Theory and evidence. *The Journal of Finance*, 48, 1323–1348.

DeMeza, D., & Webb, D. (1987). Too much Investment: A problem of asymmetric information. *Quarterly Journal of Economics*, 102, 282–292.

Dhaliwal, D., & Wang, S. (1992). The effect of the book income adjustment in 1986 alternative minimum tax on corporate financial reporting. *Journal of Accounting and Economics*, 15, 7–26.

Diamond, D. W. (1985). Optimal release of information by firms. *The Journal of Finance*, 40, 1071–1094.

Doherty, N. A., & Posey, L. L. (1998). On the value of a checkup: Adverse Selection, moral hazard and the value of information. *The Journal of Risk and Insurance*, 65, 189–211.

Dontah, A., & Ronen, J. (1993). Information content of accounting announcements. *The Accounting Review*, 68, 857–869.

Dow Jones (2002). Mirant affirms the integrity of its trading practices. *Dow Jones* (May 10).

Downs, D. H., & Güner, Z. N. (2000). Investment analysis, price formation and neglected firms: Does real estate make a difference? *Real Estate Economics, 28*, 549–579.

Dunne, P. G. (1994). Market making when the order-arrival process is the result of positive feedback trading. *The Manchester School Supplement*, 79–92.

Dun's Business Month (1983). 'Window dressing': Why it works. *Technical Publishing Company, 122*(July), 19.

Eakins, S., & Sewell, S. (1994). Do institutions window dress? An empirical investigation. *Quarterly Journal of Business and Economics, 33*, 69–78.

Easley, D., Kiefer, N. M., & O'Hara, M. (1996a). Cream-skimming or profit-sharing? The curious role of purchased order flow. *The Journal of Finance, 51*, 811–833.

Easley, D., Keifer, N. M., O'Hara, M., & Paperman, J. B. (1996b). Liquidity, information, and infrequently traded stocks. *The Journal of Finance, 50*, 1405–1436.

Easley, D., & O'Hara, M. (1992). Time and the process of security price adjustment. *The Journal of Finance, 47*, 577–605.

Easterbrook, F. H. (1985). Insider trading as an agency problem. In: J. W. Pratt & R. J. Zeckhauser (Eds), *Principals and Agents: The Structure of Business* (pp. 81–100). Boston: Harvard Business School Press.

Easton, S. (1991). Earnings and dividends: Is there an interaction effect? *The Journal of Business Finance and Accounting, 18*, 255–266.

Eatwell, J., Milgate, M., & Newman, P. (1991). *The new Palgrave: The world of economics*. Hong Kong: The Macmillan Press Ltd.

Ederington, L. H., & Lee, J. H. (1993). How markets process information: News releases and volatility. *The Journal of Finance, 48*, 1161–1191.

Elstein, A. (2000). VerticalNet chairman logs on to keep tabs on online attacks. WSJ.com (November 22).

Eynon, G., & Stevens, K. (1995). The economics of taxpayer venue choice: Effects of informational asymmetries. *The Journal of the American Taxation Association, 17*, 71–94.

Errand, B. (1990). The impact of tax practitioners on tax compliance: A research summary. Unpublished Working Paper, University of Toronto, Toronto, Canada.

Ettredge, M., Simon, D., Smith, D., & Stone, M. (1994). Why do companies purchase timely quarterly reviews? *The Journal of Accounting and Economics, 18*, 131–156.

Financial Accounting Standards Board (FASB) (1978-1985). Statement of Financial Accounting Concepts (SFAC). *Financial Accounting Standards Board* (Stamford, CT).

Finnerty, J. E. (1976). Insiders' activity and inside information: A multivariate analysis. *Journal of Financial and Quantitative Analysis, 11*, 205–215.

Fischhoff, B., Slovic, P., & Lichtenstein, S. (1981). Lay foibles and experts fables in judgments about risk. In: T. O'Riordan & R. K. Turner (Eds), *Progress in Resource Management and Environmental Planning*. Chichester: John Wiley & Sons, Inc.

Foster, F. D., & Viswanathan, S. (1996). Strategic trading when agents forecast the forecasts of others. *The Journal of Finance, 51*, 1437–1478.

Foster, F. D., & Vishwanathan, S. (1990). A theory of the interday variations in volume, variance and trading costs in securities markets. *Review of Financial Studies, 3*, 593–624.

Foster, G. (1977). Quarterly accounting data: Time-series properties and predictive ability. *The Accounting Review, 52*, 1–21.

Francis, J. R., & Wilson, E. R. (1988). Auditor changes: A joint test of theories relating to agency costs and auditor differentiation. *Accounting Review, 63*(4), 663–682.

French, K. R., & Roll, R. (1986). Stock return variances: The arrival of information and the reaction of traders. *Journal of Financial Economics, 17*, 5–26.

Freidlob, G. T. (1983). What are the effects of differing types of restrictions on closely held stocks? *The Journal of Taxation, 58*, 240–243.

Froot, K. A., Scharfstein, D. S., & Stein, J. C. (1992). Herd on the street: Informational inefficiencies in a market with short-term speculation. *The Journal of Finance, 47*, 1461–1484.

Fulghiere, P., & Lukin, D. (2001). Information production, dilution costs, and optimal security design. *Journal of Financial Economics, 61*, 3–42.

Giammarino, R. M., Lewis, T. R., & Sappington, D. E. M. (1993). An incentive approach to banking regulation. *The Journal of Finance, 48*, 1523–1542.

Glosten, L. R., & Milgrom, P. R. (1985). Bid, ask, and transaction prices in specialist market with heterogeneously informed traders. *Journal of Financial Economics, 14*, 71–100.

Goetzmann, W. N., & Jorion, P. (1993). Testing the predictive power of dividend yields. *The Journal of Finance, 48*, 663–679.

Goh, J. C., & Ederington, L. H. (1993). Is a bond rating downgrade bad news, good news, or no news for stockholders? *The Journal of Finance, 48*, 2001–2008.

Gompers, P. A. (1995). Optimal investment, monitoring, and the staging of venture capital. *The Journal of Finance, 50*, 1461–1489.

Gordon, M. J. (1964). Postulates, principles, and research in accounting. *The Accounting Review, 34*, 251–263.

Gorton, G., & Rosen, R. (1995). Corporate control, portfolio choice, and the decline of banking. *The Journal of Finance, 50*, 1377–1420.

Goswami, G. (2000). Asset maturity, debt covenants, and debt maturity choice. *The Financial Review, 35*, 51–68.

Goswami, G., Noe, T., & Rebello, M. (1995). Debt financing under asymmetric information. *The Journal of Finance, 50*, 633–659.

Gramlich, J. D. (1991). The effect of the alternative tax book income adjustment on accrual decisions. *Journal of the American Taxation Association, 13*, 36–56.

Graves, J. A., Davis, L. R., & Mendenhall, R. R. (1990). Forecasts of earnings per share: Possible sources of analyst superiority and bias. *Contemporary Accounting Research, 6*, 501–517.

Greig, A. C. (1992). Fundamental analysis and subsequent stock returns. *Journal of Accounting and Economics, 15*, 413–442.

Grinblatt, M., Titman, S., & Wermers, R. (1995). Momentum investment strategies, portfolio performance, and herding: A study of mutual fund behavior. *The American Economic Review, 85*, 1088–1105.

Grossman, S. J., & Hart, O. (1989). Corporate financial structure and managerial incentives. In: J. McCall (Ed.), *The Economics of Information and Uncertainty*. Chicago, IL: University of Chicago Press.

Gruber, M. J. (1996). Another puzzle: The growth in actively managed mutual funds. *The Journal of Finance, 51*, 783–810.

Harris, M., & Raviv, A. (1991a). Differences of opinion make a horse race. Unpublished Manuscript. University of Chicago and Northwestern University (August 26).

Harris, M., & Raviv, A. (1991b). The theory of capital structure. *The Journal of Finance, 46*(1), 297–356.

Hasbrouck, J. (1995). One security, many markets: Determining the contributions to price discovery. *The Journal of Finance, 50*, 1175–1199.

Hasbrouck, J., & Sofianos, G. (1993). The trades of market makers: An empirical analysis of NYSE specialists. *The Journal of Finance, 48*, 1565–1593.

Hellman, T., & Stiglitz, J. (2000). Credit and equity rationing in markets with adverse selection. *European Economic Review, 44*, 291–304.

Helou, A., & Park, J. (2001). Is there a signaling effect of underwriter reputation? *The Journal of Financial Research, 24*, 27–43.

Hertzel, M., & Smith, R. L. (1993). Market discounts and shareholder gains for placing equity privately. *The Journal of Finance, 48*, 459–485.

Holloway, C. (1981). A note on testing an aggressive investment strategy using value line ranks. *The Journal of Finance, 36*, 711–719.

Holthausen, R. W., & Larcker, D. F. (1992). The prediction of stock returns using financial statement information. *Journal of Accounting and Economics, 15*, 373–411.

Huberman, G., & Halka, D. (2001). Systematic liquidity. *The Journal of Financial Research, 24*, 161–178.

Huddart, S. (1995). Reputation and performance fee effects on portfolio choice by investment advisors. Working Paper 95-9, University of Michigan; Mitsui Life Financial Research Center.

Hulbert, M. (2002). Newsletters Gaining Respect in Markets. CBSMarketWatch.com (April 23).

Huth, W. L., & Maris, B. A. (1992). Large and small firm stock price response to "heard on the street" recommendations. *Journal of Accounting Auditing and Finance, 7*, 27–47.

Hyman, D. N. (1999). *Public finance: A contemporary application of theory to policy* (6th ed.). Orlando, FL: Harcourt Brace & Company.

Ippolito, R. A. (1989). Efficiency with costly information: A study of mutual fund performance, 1965–1984. *The Quarterly Journal of Economics, 54*, 1–23.

Jang, H., & Lee, J. H. (1995). Window dressing of daily closing bid-ask spreads: Evidence from NYSE stocks. *Financial Analysts Journal, 51*, 61–67.

Jain, P. C. (1988). Response of hourly stock prices and trading volume to economic news. *The Journal of Business, 16*, 219–230.

Jansson, S. (1983). The fine art of window dressing. *Institutional Investor, 47*, 139–140.

Jensen, M. C. (1993). The modern industrial revolution, exit, and the failure of internal control systems. *The Journal of Finance, 48*, 831–880.

Jensen, M. C. (1986). The agency costs of free cash flow: Corporate finance and takeovers. *American Economic Review, 76*, 323–329.

Jensen, M. C. (1978). Some anomalous evidence regarding market efficiency. *Journal of Financial Economics, 6*, 95–101.

Jensen, M. C., & Meckling, W. H. (1976). Theory of the firm: Managerial behavior, agency costs and ownership structure. *Journal of Financial Economics, 3*, 305–360.

John, T. A., & John, K. (1993). Top-management compensation and capital structure. *The Journal of Finance, 48*, 949–974.

Johnson, R. D., & Racette, G. A. (1981). Discounts on letter stock do not appear to be a good base on which to estimate discounts for lack of marketability on closely held stocks. *Taxes, 59*, 574–588.

Kalay, A., & Loewenstein, U. (1985). Predictable events and excess returns: The case of dividend announcements. *Journal of Financial Economics, 14*, 423–450.

Kane, A., Lee, Y. K., & Marcus, A. (1984). Earnings and dividend announcements: Is there a corroboration effect? *The Journal of Finance, 39*, 1091–1099.

Keim, D., & Madhaven, A. (1992). The upstairs market for large-block transactions: Analysis and measurement of price effects. Unpublished Working Paper, Wharton School, University of Pennsylvania.

Kelly, A. (2002). Reliant admits bogus trades puffed up revenue. *Reuters Company News* (May 13).

Kelley, T., & Margheim, L. (1990). The impact of time budget pressure, personality, and leader-ship variables on dysfunctional auditor behavior. *Auditing: A Journal of Practice and Theory*, *9*, 21–42.

Kelley, T., & Seiler, R. E. (1982). Auditor stress and time budgets. *The CPA Journal*, *52*, 24–34.

Kim, J.-B., Krinsky, I., & Lee, J. (1997). Institutional holdings and trading volume reactions to quarterly earnings announcements. *Journal of Accounting, Auditing and Finance*, *12*, 1–14.

Kim, O. (1993). Disagreements among shareholders over a firm's disclosure policy. *The Journal of Finance*, *58*, 747–760.

Kim, O., & Verracchia, R. E. (1994). Market liquidity and volume around earnings announcements. *Journal of Accounting and Economics*, *17*, 41–67.

King, M. A., & Wadhwani, S. (1990). Transmission of volatility between stock markets. *Review of Financial Studies*, *3*, 5–33.

Kirilenko, A. A. (2001). Valuation and control in venture finance. *The Journal of Finance*, *41*, 565–587.

Kirmani, A., & Rao, A. R. (2000). No pain, no gain: A critical review of the literature on signaling unobservable product quality. *Journal of Marketing*, *64*, 66–79.

Klepper, S., & Nagin, D. (1989). The role of tax practitioners in tax compliance. *Policy Sciences*, *22*, 167–194.

Klepper, S., Mazur, M., & Nagin, D. (1988). Expert intermediaries and legal compliance: The case of tax preparers. Unpublished Working Paper, Carnegie Mellon University, Pittsburgh, PA.

Kliger, D., & Sarig, O. (2000). The information value of bond ratings. *The Journal of Finance*, *55*, 2879–2902.

Krinsky, I., & Lee, J. (1996). Earnings announcements and the components of the bid-ask spread. *The Journal of Finance*, *51*, 1523–1535.

Kyle, A. (1985). Continuous auctions and insider trading. *Econometrica*, *53*, 1315–1335.

La Porta, R. (1996). Expectations and the cross-section of stock returns. *The Journal of Finance*, *51*, 1715–1742.

Lakonishok, J., & Maberly, E. (1990). The weekend effect: Trading patterns of individual and insti-tutional investors. *The Journal of Finance*, *45*, 231–243.

Lakonishok, J., Shleifer, A., Thaler, R., & Vishny, R. (1991). Window dressing by pension fund managers. *The American Economic Review*, *81*, 227–231.

Lang, M. H., & Lundholm, D. G. (2000). Voluntary disclosure and equity offerings: Reducing information asymmetry or hyping the stock? *Contemporary Accounting Research*, *17*, 623–662.

Le Bon, G. (1973). *The crowd: A study of the popular mind.* New York: The Viking Press.

Lee, C. M. C., Mucklow, B., & Ready, M. J. (1993). Spreads, depths and the impact of earnings information: An intraday analysis. *Review of Financial Studies*, *6*, 345–374.

Lee, C., Porter, D. C., & Weaver, D. G. (1998). Indirect tests of the Haugen-Lakonishok, small-firm/January effect hypothesis: Window dressing vs. performance hedging. *The Financial Review*, *33*, 177–194.

Lee, C. M. C. (1992). Earnings news and small traders: An intraday analysis. *Journal of Accounting and Economics*, *15*, 265–302.

Leland, H. E., & Pyle, D. H. (1977). Informational asymmetries, financial structure, and financial intermediation. *The Journal of Finance*, *32*, 371–387.

Lerner, J. (1995). Venture capitalists and the oversight of private firms. *The Journal of Finance*, *50*, 301–318.

Lev, B., & Thiagarajan, S. R. (1993). Fundamental information analysis. *Journal of Accounting Research*, *31*, 190–215.

Lewis, C. M., Rogalski, R. J., & Seward, J. K. (1997). The information content of value line convertible bond rankings. *The Journal of Portfolio Management, 24,* 42–52.

Lightner, S. M., Leisenring, J. J., & Winters, J. A. (1983). Underreporting chargeable time. *Journal of Accountancy, 156,* 52–57.

Ligon, J. A. (1997). A simultaneous test of competing theories regarding the January effect. *The Journal of Financial Research, 20,* 13–32.

Lintner, J. (1956). Distribution of incomes of corporations among dividends, retained earnings and taxes. *American Economic Review, 46,* 97–113.

Litzenberger, R. H., & McEnally, R. W. (1977). The adjustment of stock prices to announcements of unanticipated changes in quarterly earnings. *Journal of Accounting Research, 15,* 207–225.

Loeb, T. F. (1983). Trading cost: The critical link between investment information and results. *Financial Analysts Journal, 39,* 39–44.

Lonie, A. A., Abeyratna, G., Power, D. M., & Sinclair, C. D. (1996). The stock market reaction to dividend announcements: A U.K. study of complex market signals. *Journal of Economic Studies, 23,* 32–52.

Lorie, J. M., & Niederhoffer, V. (1968). Predictive and statistical properties of insider trading. *The Journal of Law and Economics, 11,* 35–54.

Lummer, S. L., & McConnell, J. J. (1989). Further evidence on the bank lending process and the capital-market response to bank loan agreements. *Journal of Financial Economics, 25,* 99–122.

Lustig, I. L., & Leinbach, P. A. (1983). The small firm effect. *Financial Analysts Journal, 39,* 46–49.

MacCrimmon, K., & Wehrung, D. (1986). *Taking risks: The management of uncertainty.* New York: The Free Press.

Madhaven, A., & Smidt, S. (1993). An analysis of changes in specialist inventories and quotations. *The Journal of Finance, 48,* 1595–1628.

Madhaven, A., & Smidt, S. (1991). A Bayesian model of intraday specialist pricing. *Journal of Financial Economics, 30,* 99–134.

Maestri, N. (2002). Merrill apologizes to shareholders. CBSMarketWatch.com (April 26).

Manzon, G. B. (1992). Earnings management of firms subject to the alternative minimum tax. *The Journal of the American Taxation Association, 14,* 88–111.

Marquis, M. S., & Phelps, C. E. (1987). Price elasticity and adverse selection in the demand for supplementary health insurance. *Economic Inquiry, 25,* 299–313.

Martin, R. (2002). How to Avoid the IRS' Expanded Audit Efforts. CBSMarketWatch.com (April 4).

Maug, E. (1998). Large shareholders as monitors: Is there a trade-off between liquidity and control? *The Journal of Finance, 53,* 65–98.

May, R. G. (1971). The influence of quarterly earnings announcements on investor decisions as reflected in common stock price change. *Empirical Research in Accounting: Selected Studies,* 119–171.

McCarthy, E. (2001). After regulation FD: Talking to your constituents. *Journal of Accountancy, 191,* 28–33.

Mester, L. J. (1993). Efficiency in the savings and loan industry. *Journal of Banking and Finance, 17,* 267–286.

Mester, L. J. (1991). Agency costs among savings and loans. *Journal of Financial Intermediaries, 3,* 257–278.

Michaely, R., Thaler, R. H. & Womack, K. L. (1995). Price reactions to dividend initiations and omissions: Overreaction or drift? *The Journal of Finance, 50,* 573–608.

Mishra, D. P., Heide, J. B., & Cort, S. G. (1998). Information asymmetry and levels of agency relationships. *Journal of Marketing Research, 35*, 277–295.

Morck, R., Shleifer, A., & Vishny, R. (1988). Management ownership and market valuation: An empirical analysis. *Journal of Financial Economics, 20*, 293–315.

Morrisey, M. (1992). *Price sensitivity in health care: Implications for health care policy.* Washington, D.C.: The National Federation of Independent Business Foundation.

Myers, S. C., & Majluf, N. S. (1984). Corporate financing and investment decisions when the firm has information that investors do not have. *Journal of Financial Economics, 13*, 187–221.

Niederhoffer, V., & Osborne, M. F. M. (1966). Market making and reversal on the stock exchange. *Journal of the American Statistical Association, 61*, 897–916.

Nichols, N. B. (1998). Earnings management: The interdependence of accounting choices and the adoption of SFAS 109 and 96. Unpublished Working Paper.

Nunn, K. P., Madden, G. P., & Gombola, M. J. (1983). Are some insiders more "inside" than others? *The Journal of Portfolio Management, 68*, 18–22.

O'Brien, P. C. (1988). Analysts' forecasts as earnings expectations. *Journal of Accounting and Economics, 10*, 53–83.

Osborne, E. (1999). Who should be worried about asymmetric information in litigation. *International Review of Law and Economics, 19*, 399–409.

Ou, J. A., & Penman, S. H. (1993). Financial statement analysis and the evaluation of market-to-book ratios. Unpublished Working Paper.

Ou, J. A., & Penman, S. H. (1989). Financial statement analysis and the prediction of stock returns. *Journal of Accounting and Economics, 11*, 295–330.

Pauly, M. V. (1986). Taxation, health insurance, and market failure in the medical economy. *Journal of Economic Literature, 24*, 629–675.

Pearce, D. K., & Roley, V. V. (1985). Stock prices and economic news. *The Journal of Business, 58*, 49–68.

Penman, S. H. (1987). The distribution of earnings news over time and seasonalities in aggregate stock returns. *Journal of Financial Economics, 18*, 199–228.

Penman, S. H. (1982). Insider trading and the dissemination of firms' forecast information. *Journal of Business, 55*, 479–503.

Peterson, D. R. (1995). The information role of the value line investment survey: Evidence from stock highlights. *Journal of Financial and Quantitative Analysis, 30*, 607–618.

Peterson, D. R. (1987). Security price reactions to initial reviews of common stock by the value line investment survey. *Journal of Financial and Quantitative Analysis, 22*, 483–494.

Pettit, R. R., & Singer, R. F. (1985). Small business finance: A research agenda. *Financial Management, 14*, 47–60.

Phelps, C. (1976). The demand for reimbursement insurance. In: R. N. Rossett (Ed.), *The Role of Health Insurance in Health Services Sector.* New York: National Bureau of Economic Research.

Philbrick, D. R., & Ricks, W. E. (1991). Using value line and IBES analyst forecasts in accounting research. *Journal of Accounting Research, 29*, 397–417.

Pincus, K., Rusbarsky, M., & Wong, J. (1989). Voluntary formation of corporate audit committees among NASDAQ firms. *Journal of Accounting and Public Policy, 8*, 239–265.

Pratt, J. W., & Zeckhauser, R. J. (Eds) (1985). Principals and agents: An overview. *Principals and Agents: The Structure of Business* (pp. 1–35). Boston: Harvard Business School Press.

Raghunathan, B. (1991). Premature signing-off of audit procedures: An analysis. *Accounting Horizons, 5*, 71–79.

Rajan, R., & Winton, A. (1995). Covenants and collateral as incentives to monitor. *The Journal of Finance, 50,* 1113–1146.

Reuters (2002). CHRONOLOGY: Recent key events for Dynegy. *Reuters Company News* (May 8).

Rhode, J. G. (1977). *The commission on auditors' responsibilities: Report of tentative conclusions.* New York, NY: AICPA.

Rindfleisch, A., & Heide, J. B. (1997). Transaction cost analysis: Past, present, and future applications. *Journal of Marketing, 61,* 30–54.

Rozeff, M. S., & Zaman, M. A. (1988). Market efficiency and insider trading: New evidence. *The Journal of Business, 61,* 25–44.

Scherr, F. C., & Hulburt, H. M. (2001). The debt maturity structure of small firms. *Financial Management, 30,* 85–111.

Schisler, D. L. (1994). An experimental examination of factors affecting tax preparers' aggressiveness – a prospect theory approach. *The Journal of the American Taxation Association, 16,* 124–142.

Schleifer, A., & Vishny, R. W. (1986). Large shareholders and corporate control. *Journal of Political Economy, 94,* 461–488.

Schwert, G. W., & Seguin, P. J. (1993). Securities transaction taxes: An overview of costs, benefits and unresolved questions. Mitsui Life Financial Research Center Working Paper No. 93-8.

Securities and Exchange Commission (SEC) (1975). Accounting series release (ASR) No. 177. SEC Docket 7, No. 17 (September 23), 816–825.

Securities and Exchange Commission (SEC) (1971). *Institutional investor study report.* Washington, D.C.: U.S. Government Printing Office.

Seetharaman, A., & Swanson, Z. L. (1998). The impact of taxes on the trade-off between debt and managerial ownership. Unpublished Working Paper (January).

Seppi, D. (1990). Equilibrium block trading and asymmetric information. *The Journal of Finance, 45,* 73–94.

Seyhun, H. N. (1986). Insiders' profits, costs of trading, and market efficiency. *Journal of Financial Economics, 16,* 189–212.

Shapeero, M. P. (1994). Premature audit sign-offs and the underreporting of chargeable time in public accounting: Examination of an ethical decision making model. Unpublished Working Paper (February).

Shields, M., Solomon, I., & Jackson, D. (1995). Experimental research on tax professionals' judgment and decision making. *Behavioral Tax Research: Prospects and Judgement Calls.* J. Davis (Ed.). Sarasota, FL: American Taxation Association.

Simunic, D. A., & Stein, M. (1987). *Product differentiation in auditing: Auditor choice in the market for unseasoned new issues.* The Canadian Certified General Accountants Research Foundation.

Skinner, D. J. (1992). Bid-ask spreads around earnings announcements: Evidence From the NASDAQ national market system. Unpublished Working Paper No. 92-26, Mitsui Life Financial Research Center.

Slovic, P. (1972). Information processing, situation specificity, and the generality of risk taking behavior. *Journal of Personality and Social Psychology?* 128–134.

Smith, K. W., & Kinsey, K. A. (1987). *The showdown at the 1040 corral: Confrontations between the IRS and tax practitioners.* Presented at the Annual Meeting of the American Bar Association.

Stober, T. (1992). Summary of financial statement measures and analysts' forecasts of earnings. *Journal of Accounting and Economics, 15,* 347–372.

Stewart, Y. H. (1995). Who receives the benefit of credit unions tax exemption? An examination of net interest margins and agency costs. Unpublished Working Paper.

Stickel, S. (1985). The effect of value line investment survey rank changes on common stock prices. *Journal of Financial Economics*, *14*, 121–143.

Stiglitz, J. E. (1989). Using tax policy to curb speculative short-term trading. *Journal of Financial Services Research*, *3*, 101–115.

Strebel, P. (1983). Analysts' forecasts in the capital asset pricing model. *Economic Letters*, *13*, 223–229.

Subrahmanyam, A. (1991). Risk aversion, market liquidity, and price efficiency. *Review of Financial Studies*, *4*, 417–441.

Typpo, E. W. (1996). Insider trading prior to management earnings forecasts. Unpublished Working Paper (July).

Watts, R. (1978). Systematic 'abnormal' returns after quarterly earnings announcements. *Journal of Financial Economics*, *6*, 127–150.

Watts, R. (1973). The information content of dividends. *The Journal of Business*, *46*, 191–211.

Watts, R., & Zimmerman, J. (1986). *Positive accounting theory*. Englewood Cliffs, NJ: Prentice-Hall, Inc.

Wedig, G. J., Hassan, M., & Morrisey, M. A. (1996). Tax-exempt debt and the capital structure of nonprofit organizations: An application to hospitals. *The Journal of Finance*, *50*(4), 1247–1283.

Weiss Ratings News (2002). Prudential securities, Ameritrade and U.S. Bancorp Piper Jaffray have worst record of investor abuses over last 5 years. *Weiss Ratings, Inc.* (May 14).

Williams, P. A. (1998). The relation between management forecast precision and individual analyst forecast accuracy. Unpublished Working Paper.

Wilson, C. (1988). The nature of equilibrium in markets with adverse selection. *Bell Journal of Economics*, *11*, 108–130.

Wruck, K. H. (1989). Equity ownership concentration and firm value: Evidence from private equity financings. *Journal of Financial Economics*, *23*, 3–28.

Wolfe, J. R., & Goddeeris, J. H. (1991). Adverse selection, moral hazard, and wealth effects in the Medigap insurance market. *Journal of Health Economics*, *10*, 433–459.

Xiao, Z., Powell, P. L., & Dodgson, J. H. (1998). The impact of information technology on information asymmetry. *European Journal of Information Systems*, *7*, 77–89.

Young, J. C. (1994). Factors associated with noncompliance: Evidence from the Michigan tax amnesty program. *The Journal of the American Taxation Association*, *16*, 82–105.

INDEX

Set up a Continuation Order Today!

Did you know you can set up a continuation order on all JAI series and have each new volume sent directly to you upon publication. For details on how to set up a continuation order contact your nearest regional sales office listed below.

To view related **Business, Management and Accounting** series visit

www.socscinet.com/bam

30% Discount for Authors on all Books!

A 30% discount is available to Elsevier book and journal contributors **ON ALL BOOKS** plus standalone **CD-ROMS** except multi-volume reference works. To claim your discount, full payment is required with your order, which must be sent directly to the publisher at the nearest regional sales office listed below.

ELSEVIER REGIONAL SALES OFFICES

For customers in the Americas:

Elsevier Science
Customer Support Department
Regional Sales Office
P.O. Box 945 New York
N.Y. 10159-0945, USA
Tel: (+1) 212 633 3730
Toll Free number for North-America
1-888-4ES-INFO (4636)
Fax: (+1) 212 633 3680
Email: usinfo-f@elsevier.com

For customers in all other locations:

Elsevier Science
Customer Support Department
Regional Sales Office
P.O. Box 211
1000 AE Amsterdam
The Netherlands
Tel: (+31) 20 485 3757
Fax: (+31) 20 485 3432
Email: nlinfo-f@elsevier.nl

For customers in the Far East & Australasia:

Elsevier Science
Customer Support Department
3 Killiney Road, #08-01/09
Winsland House I,
Singapore 239519
Tel: +(65) 63490200
Fax: + (65) 67331817/67331276
Email: asiainfo@elsevier.com.sg